Group Relations, Management, and Organization

Group Relations, Management, and Organization

Edited by

ROBERT FRENCH

and

RUSS VINCE

OXFORD

UNIVERSITY PRESS

OXFORD

UNIVERSITY PRESS

Great Clarendon Street, Oxford OX2 6DP

Oxford University Press is a department of the University of Oxford.
It furthers the University's objective of excellence in research, scholarship,
and education by publishing worldwide in

Oxford New York

Athens Auckland Bangkok Bogotá Buenos Aires Calcutta
Cape Town Chennai Dar es Salaam Delhi Florence Hong Kong Istanbul
Karachi Kuala Lumpur Madrid Melbourne Mexico City Mumbai
Nairobi Paris São Paulo Singapore Taipei Tokyo Toronto Warsaw

with associated companies in Berlin Ibadan

Oxford is a registered trade mark of Oxford University Press
in the UK and in certain other countries

Published in the United States
by Oxford University Press Inc., New York

British Library Cataloguing in Publication Data

Data available

Library of Congress Cataloging in Publication Data

Data available

ISBN 0–19–829367–4 (Hbk)
ISBN 0–19–829366–6 (Pbk)

1 3 5 7 9 10 8 6 4 2

Typeset in Utopia
by Hope Services (Abingdon) Ltd.
Printed in Great Britain by
Biddles Ltd.,
Guildford and King's Lynn

CONTENTS

FIGURES

ABOUT THE AUTHORS

David Armstrong is a Principal at the Tavistock Consultancy Service, the Tavistock Centre, London, UK.

Alastair Bain is Director of the Australian Institute of Socio-Analysis, Victoria, Australia.

Siv Boalt Boëthius is Director of the Erica Foundation in Stockholm, Psychoanalyst, and Professor in the Department of Education, Stockholm University, Sweden.

Francesca Cardona is an independent organizational consultant and a Visiting Tutor at the Tavistock Clinic, London, UK.

Gouranga P. Chattopadhyay is a Visiting Professor of Organization Behaviour with the Graduate School of Management, Swinburne University of Technology, Australia, and Emeritus Professor, Academy of Human Resources Development, India.

H. Shmuel Erlich is Sigmund Freud Professor of Psychoanalysis and Director of the Sigmund Freud Center for Psychoanalytic Study and Research, The Hebrew University of Jerusalem, Israel, and a member of the Executive Board of OFEK (the Israel Association for the Study of Group and Organizational Processes). He is a Training Analyst with the Israel Psychoanalytic Society and Institute.

Mira Erlich-Ginor is Chairwoman of OFEK, Faculty for the Program in Organizational Consultation and Development at the Sigmund Freud Center, The Hebrew University of Jerusalem, Israel. She is a Training Analyst with the Israel Psychoanalytic Society and Institute.

Robert French is Senior Lecturer in Organizational Behaviour at Bristol Business School, the University of the West of England, Bristol, UK.

Laurence J. Gould is Professor of Psychology in the Clinical Psychology Doctoral Program at the City University of New York, and Co-director of the Program in Organizational Consultation and Development at the Sigmund Freud Center, The Hebrew University of Jerusalem, Israel.

David Gutmann is Executive Chairman of Praxis International (Advisers in Leadership), Maître de recherche, École Normale Supérieure, Cachan, France, and Executive Vice-President, International Forum for Social Innovation, Paris, France.

W. Gordon Lawrence is Managing Partner of Symbiont Technologies, LLC, New York, USA and Visiting Professor of Organizational Behaviour in the School of Management, Cranfield University, UK.

Eric Miller is a senior member of the professional staff and consultant to the Group Relations Programme at the Tavistock Institute, London, UK.

Jean E. Neumann has worked since 1987 as Senior Consulting Social Scientist at the Tavistock Institute, London, UK.

Anton Obholzer is Chief Executive of the Tavistock and Portman NHS Trust and consultant Psychiatrist and Psychoanalyst at the Tavistock Clinic, London, UK.

Barry Palmer (1934–98) was an independent consultant, a Professional Associate of the Grubb Institute, London, UK, and a member of OPUS (an Organization for Promoting Understanding of Society). Barry Palmer died on 30 October 1998. We would like to acknowledge his contribution to the field of group relations over more than thirty years. As his chapter in this volume demonstrates, Barry was always particularly concerned to remain open to new thoughts, to work with his own reservations as well as his convictions, and to avoid closed systems of thinking. He also strove to ensure that group relations thinking stayed in touch with management and organizational realities, always working beyond general solutions to, as he put it, 'meet the challenge of the case'.

Sheila Ramsay is a manager in a large voluntary childcare organization. She is a member of the Scottish Institute of Human Relations, Glasgow, UK.

Vega Zagier Roberts is an independent consultant, and Senior Organizational Consultant at the Cassel Hospital, Richmond, London, UK.

Jacqueline Ternier-David is Managing Director of Praxis International, Paris, France, and a Member of the International Forum for Social Innovation, Paris, France.

Joseph Triest is a clinical psychologist and consultant, Manager of the Triest-Sarig Clinic, and Lecturer in the Department of Psychology, Tel Aviv University, Israel.

Christophe Verrier is a medical doctor, an Adviser in Leadership with Praxis International, Paris, France, and a member of the International Forum for Social Innovation, Paris, France.

Russ Vince is Professor of Organizational Learning at the Business School, the University of Glamorgan, Wales, UK, and a Member of the Board of the International Forum for Social Innovation, Paris, France.

INTRODUCTION

1

Learning, Managing, and Organizing: The continuing contribution of group relations to management and organization

Robert French and Russ Vince

GROUP RELATIONS, MANAGEMENT, AND ORGANIZATION

The importance of this book about group relations is in the collective contribution that the chapters make to the concepts of learning, managing, and organizing. The book represents a continuation of the fifty-year history of group relations, but it is also published at a turning-point, a period when the field is itself broadening and transforming. As group relations as an approach is transformed, the possibility of the impact that it can make in management education, in influencing the practice of consultation and organization development, and in providing institutions and organizations with strategies for sustainable organizational learning is also enhanced.

Our introductory chapter is written both from our reading and analysis of the book as a whole and from our reflections on the past, present, and future relationship between group relations, management, and organization. Our aim in this first chapter is to introduce the contributions to this volume and to draw some conclusions from our work—both as editors and as group relations practitioners—about what it is that makes group relations important to managers and within organizations. Taking the chapters collectively, we have identified a framework for learning, managing, and organizing which emerges from the experiences of the authors as a group of practitioners working from a group relations perspective. The framework we have proposed, which draws attention to some of the key themes in the field of group relations, is one way of conceptualizing the contribution that group relations can make to organizational learning.

In this chapter—and in the book as a whole—we are attempting to demonstrate to the reader the considerable impact that current theory and practice in the field of group relations can have on how managers and organizations understand and engage with both individual and organizational learning and change. The importance of the group relations approach to learning is that it addresses itself particularly to the emotional, relational, and political dimensions of organizational experience which often remain unconscious or are considered unnecessary or undesirable.

In addition, group relations can be utilized to assist organizations in moving beyond their current focus on individual learning, since it offers access to another level of insight that includes the impact of the projections that the role of manager attracts and evokes. Group relations provides a means to explore the ways in which such apparently individual and personal projections—and the resulting enactment or denial of them in an organizational context—link to organizational roles. Projection and denial create a powerful paradox at an organizational level. Organizations espouse and want learning and change at the same time as they prevent themselves from embracing them. The defensiveness of individual managers is a reflection and a re-creation of the defences of the organization, and the defences that are characteristic of an organization are enacted, perpetuated, and refined by individual managers. It is the exploration of this link between the emotional dynamics created within and between individuals and groups, and the impact of existing and emerging systemic dynamics, that is fundamental to group relations both as a method of learning from experience and as a focus of organizational enquiry into processes of change.

Extending the notion of learning in organizations away from the individual manager places a greater emphasis—both individually and organizationally—on critical reflection on the dynamics of systems. Group relations makes the underlying emotional and unconscious processes created within and between systems visible and available as an aspect of organizational learning and change. Group relations aims, therefore, for institutional transformation. This includes: the need for transformations of systems and roles, not just individuals; the need for an awareness of emotional and relational dynamics and for the transformation of the resistances and defences that are evoked; the need to recognize the institutional aspect of collective experience and action as the place where the links between the individual and the organization can be revealed. The notion of transformation also emphasizes the temporary and provisional nature of all learning and change. These ideas are further developed both in the conclusion to this chapter and—in some depth—by the contributors to this book.

Group relations past and present

Group relations is in particular an approach to learning from experience, and it is as an approach to learning that it makes its most significant contribution to and impact on management and organization. Group relations particularly emphasizes the unconscious and conscious emotional, relational, and political (as well as the rational) processes and dynamics involved in organizing. The method used to engage with these complex organizational processes and dynamics is one which creates a temporary *container* for learning from experience. The nature of this temporary container can vary, from the many well-established international group relations conferences that take place over several days, to consultancy interventions, or explicit sessions within management and organizational development programmes which combine a group relations approach with other methods for learning. In whatever way this container is constructed, participants learn in the *here and now*, which involves an exploration of what is happening in the moment within and between systems, sub-systems, and the context in which they are situated. Such exploration stimulates perception and interpretation by all involved of the feelings they have, the projections that are in play, and the issues that are at stake. The learning from the dynamics of this container, and the ways in which this connects to the dynamics of a wider organizational and/or social context, can be applied within the organizations that participants have come from, often through reaching a different understanding of their roles and relations.

Group relations initially emerged as a part of what has been referred to as 'the Tavistock paradigm' (Palmer 1998). The foundations of this paradigm include the experimental work on 'leaderless groups' initiated by Bion (1946) and developed, among others, by Bridger (1990); Bion's studies of 'basic assumption' and 'work' mentality within groups (Bion 1961); the action-research undertaken within organizations that identified both sociopsychological and socio-technical processes (Trist and Bamforth 1951; Rice 1958; Menzies 1960, Rice 1965, E. J. Miller and Rice 1967); and the Tavistock Institute of Human Relations' annual group relations conferences at Leicester University, England (E. J. Miller 1989). Since these foundations were laid, group relations institutions have emerged throughout the world, offering their own further developments of the original approach.

The variety of theories and approaches that have recently impacted on group relations have created what Gillette and McCollom (1990) call 'a new experiential tradition' within the field. The emergent forms of group relations rely not only on theories from psychoanalysis and group therapy but also on theories and methods which help to develop the sociopolitical, philosophical, and spiritual dimensions of the approach. These include: Bion's later work, Buber (1965), Bateson (1973), and Lacan (1979). At the same time, group relations conferences and other approaches to working in and with organizations have introduced new events and themes such as social dreaming (Lawrence 1998), role analysis, art materials, diversity, yoga, praxis, dialogue, and transformation.

The focus of group relations is the system, rather than the group. A systems view emphasizes that the whole and the parts are dynamically interrelated in complex and important ways; that individuality is both real and illusory, as Bion put it, 'that the human individual is a political animal and cannot find fulfilment outside a group and cannot satisfy any emotional drive without expression of its social component' (Bion 1962: 118). Group relations practitioners address the interactions between the individual, the group, and the broader systems in which these are embedded: organizations, communities, and societies, local, national, and international. Group relations offers a framework both for understanding and for intervening in systems whether from 'inside' or from 'outside', whether through interaction with individuals or with groups or at a broader systemic level, and from a wide variety of roles, such as member, manager, leader, practitioner, supervisor, researcher, teacher, trainer, coach, consultant, counsellor, or writer.

Reflexivity and relatedness as aspects of managing and organizing

In planning this volume we invited authors to produce their chapters with two things in mind, both of which are concepts that we perceive to be fundamental to an understanding of group relations in the context of management and organization. These are: reflexivity—the continual interplay between theory and practice—and relatedness.

Reflexivity signifies a process of creation and re-creation in terms of thinking and action, it suggests the impermanence of knowledge and the need not only to focus on understanding the dynamics of groups and organizations but also to engage continuously with the changing dynamics revealed in the very processes of grouping and of organizing. A focus on reflexivity therefore also raises the possibility of analysing how group relations thinks about and refers to itself.

Our view is that learning in the field of group relations—as in the field of management learning—is perpetuated through the ability of those involved simultaneously to theorize practice and to practise theory (Burgoyne 1994). We asked all the contributors to include the interplay of both theory and practice in what they wrote. All of the chapters therefore, whether they start from the desire to develop the theory of group relations and link this to examples of practice, or start from the author's practice in order to illuminate aspects of theory, support and illustrate the reflexive nature of the field. In addition, we have structured the book as a whole into two main sections, which reflect the different emphasis authors have placed on theorizing practice or practising theory.

We also asked the authors to bear in mind the notion of 'relatedness'. Relatedness can be understood as conscious and unconscious emotional levels of connection that exist between and shape selves and others, people and systems. Hinshelwood's statement (quoted in Vega Zagier Roberts, this volume) that we are all 'creatures of each other', suggests that (for example) processes of projection between people are a continuous resource, an integral aspect of everyday organizational life. The exploration of relatedness offers a way to understand what is happening in the here and now, therefore making it possible to engage with unconscious as well as conscious aspects of what is present.

Group relations explores relatedness through its attempts constantly to get behind the surface appearance of things in order to look for discrepancies, to make connections, to compare what is actually happening with what is expected, and what is reported, and with the stated aim/s of the system or group. This involves asking, for example, what is being done, said, seen, noticed, talked about, rewarded, and ignored, by whom and at what levels or from what roles (formal and informal); also what is *not* being done, said, seen, noticed, talked about, rewarded, and taken on, by whom and at what levels or from what roles. It means trying to understand what is preventing development, change, learning, communication, action, and thought—in other words, what are the defences against, and therefore also the possibilities for transformation, change, learning, communication, action, and thought in this particular context.

A FRAMEWORK FOR LEARNING, MANAGING, AND ORGANIZING

There are inevitably many ways to make sense of all the ideas and examples that collectively constitute the chapters in this book. Our reading and engagement with these chapters has led us to identify a framework containing six themes which illustrate the impact that group relations can have on management and organization. The themes are:

- anxiety, defensiveness, and the struggle to learn from experience;
- management and containment;
- reflexivity and the role of the manager;
- reflexivity and learning;
- power and politics;
- institutional transformation.

In the rest of this chapter, we explore each of these themes, linking them also to summaries of the individual chapters. At the same time, two other major subjects are highlighted by the contributions to the book. They stand, as it were, as two screens on to which the individual themes can be projected, to see what light they throw on each screen. First, there is the *role of manager* itself. Differences and tensions between the 'person', the 'person in role', and the 'person in role in group' provide a bridge between the personal (rational and emotional) world of the individual and the systemic dynamics that both create and are created by an organization. Secondly, in light of the increasing number of alliances, networks, and relations that exist within and between modern organizations, it has become less practical to talk about an organization as a coherent entity and more meaningful to think in terms of *processes of organizing*. To act effectively in role, organizational members therefore need to experience and perceive the impact of processes of organizing, including the ways in which they are influenced by unconscious as well as conscious personal and systemic dynamics. The application of group relations theory and practice points to the importance of working with these processes at an institutional level, in addition to addressing the changing of relations within and between groups.

Anxiety, defensiveness, and the struggle to learn from experience

The dominant contemporary notion of 'managing' as the thoughtful application of problem-solving abilities or as strategic decision making has both given rise to and been perpetuated by forms of management education that focus almost exclusively on an identifiable range of competencies, skills, and knowledge (French and Grey 1996). These forms of management education, the Master of Business Administration (MBA), for example, rarely choose to acknowledge and work with the impact of such emotions as anxiety, either as an experience in managing or as a structuring process within organizations, despite a wealth of literature which maintains that management and change are always accompanied by anxiety (Argyris 1994; Fineman 1993; Hochschild 1983; Menzies Lyth 1990; Schein 1993; Vince 1996; Vince and Martin 1993). The reluctance to acknowledge and include an emotional and relational perspective on managing and organizing, together with the actual fears generated by emotions in the workplace, have made it difficult for managers to be aware of the extent and effects of their own and others' anxiety, difficult to bear the experience of not knowing, and difficult to acknowledge the impact of destructive behaviour and defensiveness.

In its own way, each of the chapters in this volume highlights the impact of anxiety within a system, particularly on managers, and illustrates the nature and effects of the resulting defensiveness and avoidance. They demonstrate how such defences can be necessary at one level, just in order to cope, but when ignored or denied can become an organizational way of life and, as a result, a serious blockage to learning and change. The chapters also make clear that anxiety can arise in any part of the system and can have many origins, such as the personal history of individuals, the demands of the task, the demands that exist within a client group or the wider system of society, or the history and dynamic of the particular group or organization. Group relations can provide a space where managers have the opportunity to see the links between anxiety and learning and change, to learn to stand the experience of not knowing, and to resist settling for an understanding that is based on defensiveness.

In contrast to dominant modes of organizing and models of management, a group relations approach in practice therefore aims to create spaces for managers to experience and understand that managing is an emotional as well as a rational process, that, in addition to competence, skill, and knowledge, managing and organizing also involve confusion, uncertainty, and paradox, as well as difficult emotions such as fear, hate, envy, and anxiety. Various chapters in the book look particularly at anxiety, including those by Obholzer, Boalt Boëthius, Cardona, Erlich-Ginor and Erlich, Miller, Neumann, and Roberts.

The pervasive fear of emotions—the idea that they will be overwhelmingly destructive of the individual and/or the organization—needs to be explored in a way that both allows the acknowledgment of emotions and provides sufficient containment to ensure that they do not overwhelm or destroy. Considerable emphasis in this volume, and more generally within group relations, has therefore come to be placed on the containing, as opposed to the controlling, function of the role of manager.

Management and containment

One key theory which the group relations approach brings to the practice of management and organizing, and which appears regularly in the chapters of this volume, is Bion's 'container-contained' model (see Bion 1970). Bion developed his model to identify and describe a basic dimension of human experience, that is, the relationship between emotion and its 'containment'—the ways in which it is experienced or avoided, managed or denied, kept in or passed on so that its effects are either mitigated or amplified. He sought to trace and explore the relationship between container and contained at every level from the individual to society, from the mother–infant or analyst–patient dyad to the systemic, the impact, for example, of a new idea or a new person on the established system or organization. In these different contexts, the container can absorb, filter, or manage difficult or threatening emotions or ideas—the contained—so that they can be worked with, or it can become a rigid frame or shell that restricts and blocks. The contained, whether emotion, idea, or person, can therefore be experienced as an overwhelming threat or as the welcome messiah.

In a group or organizational context, Bion describes how the container can become an 'establishment' that necessarily creates rules which contain the complexity of an idea and its impact on reality: 'the recurrent configuration is of an explosive force within a restraining framework' (Bion 1985: 131). It is a configuration which can apply equally within the person, creating an 'internal establishment' (Hoggett 1992) where self-limiting behaviours set a pattern which restricts experience and perception. It can also act as an organizing process, as described in Francesca Cardona's chapter, where teams in organizations that work with issues such as drug abuse, child abuse, or mental illness 'are expected to protect and purify society from the negative and disruptive dynamics that these client groups inevitably bring with them'. The difficulty for managers in such settings is to provide containment and support while tolerating negative projections from both staff and clients. Jean Neumann's chapter also emphasises containment as an aspect of the role of manager, especially in terms of the need to recognize and take time to work through managers' emotional reactions to change, alongside its technical and political aspects. The role of manager, therefore, often implies experiencing and acting from very uncertain and uncomfortable feelings that are projected on to the role and into the person both from outside and within.

As a result of the leadership function that is a central aspect of the role, managers are subject to and the subject of projections and introjections, of fantasies, hopes, wishes, and expectations. The difficulty that managers have is in standing the pressure of these forces and allowing themselves to be the focal point of different and conflicting interpretations, and holding on to the internal and external worlds created through the experience of interaction with the self and others. As Siv Boalt Boëthius discusses in her chapter, the manager as a leader is often used as a container for the shared needs that arise in an organization. The projections on to the manager and leader differ from those experienced by other organizational members as a result of the power dynamics that are characteristic of the system in which they are created, enacted, and reinforced.

Eric Miller explores the changing relatedness of the individual to the enterprise and the pressure on managers to view themselves differently within a changing organizational context. He argues that organizations are no longer containers for our internal contradictions, and therefore can no longer provide a complete sense of belonging. Conceptualizations of the self involve managing multiple identities in relation to multiple others; the individual is separate at the same time as attached and belonging. As the workplace becomes a less secure setting, psychological investment is reduced and the individual's relation to it is more instrumental, more guarded, more calculated, often cynical and calculating. The challenge for organizational members and for managers is to find ways of becoming what he terms 'citizens of the enterprise', choice-making individuals who can engage collaboratively with others. This notion involves changed interpersonal relations with others, both within and outside their immediate subsystem of work roles, and suggests a need for an increase in the dependability of the organization, rather than dependency on it. The move from dependency to dependability implies increasing emphasis on partnership and containment.

Gordon Lawrence also addresses the changed and changing nature of social and work relations, proposing a new relationship between container and contained in the context of work and organization. He suggests that in the emerging 'information society' the accepted relationship between organization as the container and work as the contained is being turned on its head. Where once, in a more stable and predictable organizational environment, the organization was experienced as the container for the work, with all that work implies as a social as well as technical enterprise, now the work has become the container for the organization. He explores some of the implications for established ways of thinking about the nature of management and containment.

Reflexivity and the role of the manager

Group relations in the context of management and organization is informed by an underlying commitment to reflexivity which—as we have stated above—involves the continuous interaction between practising theory and theorizing practice. Such an interaction, especially when it engages with unconscious as well as conscious processes, creates possibilities for learning and change that are transformational rather than orientated towards maintenance and growth. A reflexive stance offers managers opportunities to discover ways of doubting what they 'know', to learn to be suspicious of their own suppositions, to be aware of the influence of projection and countertransference, and to connect the internal world of individuals and groups with societal processes of knowledge and power as they are enacted through processes of organizing.

The notion of reflexivity is explored in a variety of ways in this volume. Siv Boalt Boëthius describes a self-reflexive process linking her personal dissatisfaction with a working situation where she felt 'tied down by too many demands and too little space for thinking' to reflecting on and revitalizing her experience in her own role as a manager and leader. She utilizes the distinction between herself 'the person' and herself 'in my role as leader' as a way of creating a process through which both she and her organization could analyse and reformulate her leadership as well as instigating the possibility of organizational transformation. Although the whole process took some months, it happened 'in the nick of time' in terms of enabling creative change and fresh engagement at all levels of the organization and, as a result, with clients.

Sheila Ramsay identifies the impact of the experience of group relations conferences on her role both as a manager of and as a consultant to teams. A manager returning from a group relations conference has had a powerful experience of a temporary organizational environment which, unlike most work settings, addresses itself explicitly towards an understanding of the unconscious meanings and impact of behaviour. This exploration of unconscious dynamics offers a wealth of opportunities for a radically different slant on managers' 'theories-in-use' (Argyris 1982) as well as the relationship between these theories and their application in the everyday experience of managing.

The fundamental importance of this learning to managers is that it can create opportunities for reflexive engagement with a very defended notion of organization, one which Sheila Ramsay characterizes as 'a culture of measurable performance, predetermined outcomes, and management by technique [which] will not provide the necessary containing environment for the continuation of the individual's learning and its subsequent import into the system'.

'Organizational Role Analysis' (ORA) has emerged from the theory and practice of group relations as an important way of working, a containing environment for the interaction between individual and systemic learning. It is a method for exploring 'the internal objects that have been patterned by the client to form his or her "organization-in-the-mind" ' (Hutton, Bazelgette, and Reed 1997: 120). This can then be examined, through a process of hypothesis building and testing, in relation to external phenomena in the workplace. ORA has tended to focus on one-to-one interaction with managers, but there is increasing interest in its development as an action-research method, as a working method between managers, and as a way of working within a group setting. In his chapter, Joseph Triest explores 'the drama of taking a role' that became apparent in a role analysis group. This drama is a consequence of the tensions created between several factors: the formal role of managers linked to their organization's primary task; managers' informal role, designed to reduce anxieties and gratify emotional needs; internalized relations with significant past roles and figures; and an ability to maintain a differentiation between the needs of the self and those of the role. In a detailed presentation and analysis of his work with one group of managers, he demonstrates the qualities and capacities required—including the use of his own counter-transference to them from his role as consultant to the group—to identify those events, metaphors, and images which link participants' respective inner dramas with their present and past outer roles.

Reflexivity and learning

The group relations approach enables practitioners—managers, organizational members, consultants, researchers—to bring to the surface everyday organizational processes which generally remain hidden, concerning the impact of behaviour within and on systems as well as of systems on and within behaviour. The intention is to create a learning environment where the uncertainties and complexities of human interaction and 'structuration' (Giddens 1984), that are generated around processes of organizing, can be explored. Despite the apparent predictability offered by the structure of a group relations conference, for example, the actual experience is not predictable. Such events do not conform to expected patterns of development, rather they are environments which make emotional and relational dynamics of organizing visible, and through this offer many possibilities for learning. The group relations approach attempts to meet the desire to learn from experience by offering a setting where it is possible to explore the defences, such as splitting and projection, that reduce opportunities for learning from experience.

David Armstrong argues in his chapter that the importance of the practice of group relations is that it offers a method for providing insights into the dilemmas, challenges, paradoxes, and discontents of organizations and their managers and leaders that may elude other methods of enquiry and development. Group relations achieves this through a focus on mental acts of attending to, formulating, and seeking to interpret emotional experience within a bounded setting. Through an example of a meeting of staff within the counselling department of a university he explores one such area of insight, the move from 'this is what I feel' to 'this is the feeling I am aware of in myself'—a move which creates a space in which the location of the feeling and its possible organizational meaning can be opened up for exploration. This space, and the creativity that might be generated within organizations, can depend on a capacity to entertain 'shadows'—areas of darkness in the manager's relation to the organization or the organization's relation to its context. This is illustrated with a second example, of a consultancy intervention over four years with the principal of a large college of further education. The reflexive exploration of emotions, and the capacity to entertain shadows, are central to his notion of how organizations can move beyond survival and towards learning and development. He also reminds us that what makes it difficult to sustain the desire to learn is that when we venture into the territory of the meaning of an experience, we cannot predict what the outcome will be.

Barry Palmer's chapter offers both a critique of the idea of coherent stages or phases of development within groups and insights into the nature of 'grouping' as a reflexive process. He invites us to rethink our ideas about the boundaries constituting 'group' or 'organization', in part using Lacan's (1991) notion that groups and masses are animated as they locate the cause and object of their desire. Team members, for example, unconsciously identify the work of the team with the object of their desire, which is impossible to attain. The challenge in terms of organizational design therefore is not only to define requisite boundaries, but also to prevent people becoming addicted to them. In other words, to be able to produce teams that are flexible enough to allow themselves to regroup. As a demonstration of its own reflexive nature, his chapter provides an ending without an end as he invites the reader to continue to reflect on and critique the foundations for the development of new theory he is laying.

At the centre of Barry Palmer's exploration of 'grouping' is also the awareness that the key theories and practices of group relations need to be revisited in the light of the current complexities surrounding organizing within, for example, increasingly globalized and diverse social and technical contexts. Alastair Bain continues this theme. By looking at the 'establishment' of group relations itself, he provides a rich example of the dangers of institutionalizing processes—becoming 'frozen in time'—through addiction to an established tradition and set of methods. He bases his reflections on his experience of the three international group relations symposiums that took place in 1988 (Oxford, UK), 1990 (Spa, Belgium), and 1993 (Lorne, Australia).

Power and politics

Central concerns of the field of application of group relations are, on the one hand, the socially constituted basis of organizational life and, on the other, the emotions evoked by, and involved in, organizing. Authority, power, and politics are, therefore, fundamental themes, both in the context of group relations conferences, where they are ever-present themes, and in terms of application in organizational and social contexts. Group relations practitioners attempt to keep these themes in mind at several levels: the issues of authority that arise in the act of 'taking up a role'; the ways in which defensive routines give rise to structures and designs which are themselves then taken to constitute legitimate or authorized behaviour; the nature of leadership and management—and of challenges to these.

Jean Neumann's chapter introduces the notion that identifiable political and psychological forces, or 'systems psychodynamics', are evoked with particular force during periods of comprehensive change. She describes various contexts where uncertainty of direction combines with participative methods of change to create at the same time both anxiety and mechanisms for political activity. She demonstrates through her case examples that overt political goals provide a baseline from which confusion begins; that overt co-operation is not always the chosen political tactic; that projection, overt and hidden, plays an essential role on all sides of a political issue; and that there can be considerable tension between two necessary tasks—containment and political decision making: 'Containment is not the same as resolving political concerns, although containment can be a result of doing so. However, political concerns that require decisions cannot be addressed through containment alone.'

Gouranga Chattopadhyay takes a new look at authority and organization by enquiring into three key terms: boundaries, process, and hierarchy. His starting-point is the idea that all boundaries are illusions. It is necessary to work with the illusion of boundaries, but if we relate to them as if they were real they become problematic and 'take on a life of their own'. Hierarchy is seen as a particularly powerful illusory boundary, which maintains its impact on organizing because of its roots in the dynamics of both the family and religion. Hierarchy has a high emotional content, and yet an overt denial of its underlying emotional impact within organizations makes it difficult to explore politically. The continuation of hierarchical forms of organizing is explained in terms of the inability of organizations to manage difference, which therefore remains an unmanageable experience in the unconscious. He also argues that the survival of hierarchy in modern work organizations depends on religion as a societal feature that strongly underpins the transference phenomena in organizations, providing an enduring structural model. Hierarchy needs to be replaced by a different system of levels of authority that will eliminate its built-in destructiveness, for example through an exploration of the nature of possible upward delegations made by subordinate role holders.

Larry Gould also adapts literature—and history—by using the story of Oliver Cromwell as a metaphor to address the nature of authority. He explores, from a hitherto ignored angle, the continuing tensions between individual power in organizations and the possibilities and problems of a developing political vision on the part of an organizational leader. The questions he raises concern the impact on leaders of the changing perspective and aspirations that come with age. He identifies the fact that in organizations 'powerful developmental processes in the individual leader collide with powerful group, institutional, and social processes and are subverted by them'. The dilemma both for the individual and for the organization is the difficulty of role change, refusal, or abdication. His conclusion is that leaders, to the extent to which they find themselves 'role bound', must attempt to transform the system in which their role is embedded, if their own development potential and that of the organization is to be fully realized.

Vega Zagier Roberts argues that an 'essential dilemma of our times' is the difficulty of taking authority, or managing the boundaries between our inner and outer worlds. On the one hand, managers seem to want to submerge the self in the system and its leader without any personal boundaries and, on the other hand, there is a counter-impulse, where managers hold back from joining with others through a denial of interdependence. She suggests that withdrawal from membership into isolation or autonomy is an increasing issue for managers. It emphasizes the importance for them of reflecting more on their own emotional responses, using their emotional experience as data, and working together to conceptualize their relatedness to others within a system as well as to the system itself.

In a detailed and moving account of an intervention in a 'wounded' system, Mira Erlich-Ginor and Shmuel Erlich show how group relations traditions and practices can provide many levels of insight in work with organizations and in the wider societal context. An important theme in their chapter is that 'Organizational work . . . is also political action, in that it always aims to alter and change the existing balance of power'. They describe an intervention in a mental health organization where four members of staff were murdered by a patient-client. The interventions were made at two levels. The first was in helping the organization involved as a 'wounded system' where staff had lost faith in themselves and in their ability to understand and cope with what they encountered. Secondly, it transpired that the staff had also lost faith in the larger society on behalf of which they worked. Thus the emphasis of this second level of intervention was on the 'wounding of the entire system'.

Reflecting on their interventions revealed three important areas of exploration. First, the meaning and implications of group trauma, linked to the fact that 'the mental health system contains . . . the murderous, violent, and mad fantasies and impulses that exist in everybody's unconscious, regardless of external circumstances'. Secondly, the holding environment and its breakdown. They picture a well-functioning management and organization as an 'oxidation basin', a place where toxic waste matter can be contained, detoxified, and turned into useful materials. Thirdly, the extent to which transference and counter-transference relationships are used as a resource. Transference and counter-transference are seen as inherent in all relationships and in relatedness.

Institutional transformation

Over the past thirty years a central feature of the drive for organizational development has been the awareness of different 'levels' of organizational learning and change. This has been described in a number of ways: as first and second order change (see Siv Boalt Boëthius, this volume); as single-loop or double-loop learning (Argyris 1982); as adaptive versus generative learning (Senge 1990); and as the difference between the maintenance or growth of organizations and organizational transformation (Schein 1993). This is an important point at which group relations can combine with organization theory to have an impact on management practice. The meeting can occur because of the emphasis in group relations on learning (Palmer 1979; E. J. Miller 1989), on maintaining a systemic perspective—keeping the parts and the whole and their interrelatedness constantly in mind—and on taking account not only of overt behaviour and demands but also of the ways in which hidden or unconscious dynamics may affect publicly stated objectives.

The chapter by David Gutmann, Jacqueline Ternier-David, and Christophe Verrier explores a case example of leadership and institutional transformation. Managers in a company learned to transform their role as managers through a process of preparing to become staff in an in-company group relations conference. The authors outline this process of personal and institutional transformation through a discussion of the workings of two major affects—envy and desire. Their hypothesis is that the fundamental task of managers consists of moving from envy to desire through a specific process of transformation. They argue that envy emerges from the anger that managers feel (within and as a result of institutional systems) at falling short of perfection, irrespective of past successes and satisfactions. The inability to attain perfection causes managers to adopt a posture of omnipotence, in which they seek refuge, and which the rest of the organization accepts. They argue that desire is not only present in institutions but fundamental to their construction, development, and transformation. The role of managers is to reveal and bring into interaction the desire that exists in an organization. They highlight a process of transformation which occurs in three stages: first, an awareness of how managers become paralysed by the idealized object of their envy (inviting mimicry, uniformity, cloning); secondly, an awareness both of the possibility of differentiation and of one's own diversity; and finally, a recognition of how one's own specific desire emerges and is enacted.

The theme of transformational change is also explored in Gordon Lawrence's chapter. He describes and analyses the problems that are created when the social realities that are emerging in an information society continue to be understood using a framework of thinking relevant to the industrial era. He discusses the 'new work' of management that necessarily emerges in organizational environments of increasing uncertainty. This new work involves managers immersing themselves as directly as possible in the flow of events, in order to become 'participating instruments for experiencing their experience'. The requirement for managers to develop a reflexive capability represents the broader need for a new 'mind for business': a new mind which includes the capacity to acknowledge the impact of the unconscious in group and organizational experience and which is bound up with the expanded notion of organizing referred to above, the shift from the experience of the organization as the container and work the contained, to work being the container for the organization.

CONCLUSION

In recent years there has been a growing recognition in the field of management education and also in organizations themselves that the capacity for learning is a crucial factor in the ability of individuals, teams, or whole organizations to generate lasting change. The framework we have proposed is one way of conceptualizing the contribution of group relations to learning in management and in organizations. The impact of the group relations approach to learning comes from its concerns with an in-depth understanding of the 'here and now' of managing and organizing, in terms of both behaviour and politics. Group relations is an approach which promotes organizational learning because it attempts to engage with the psychological and political dynamics that are mobilized by processes of managing and organizing. The very process of organizing creates boundaries that impose limits to learning; group relations calls into question the continuing value of such boundaries. Group relations, therefore, addresses itself particularly to the emotional, relational, and political dimensions of organizational experience which often remain unconscious or are considered unnecessary or undesirable. If managers are going to become more competent in relation to these emotional, relational, and political dynamics in the workplace, they will inevitably also have to become more familiar with—and accepting of—processes of experiential learning which provide contained spaces for the exploration of precisely these aspects of organizing.

Organizational approaches to development are currently dominated by programmes designed to perpetuate individual learning, such as performance appraisal schemes (often linked to skills training programmes) and initiatives that support self-managed learning. This focus on individual learning undermines the ways in which the organization can also be included in what is learned and changed. The relationship between the individual and the organization—and the way that these combine to create and re-create each other—is often underplayed. Because of its perspective on learning, group relations makes it possible to address both individual and organizational learning. The individual manager is offered access to another level of insight that includes the impact of the projections that the role of manager attracts and evokes. In addition, group relations provides a means to explore the ways in which such apparently individual and personal projections link to organizational roles as well as how the enactment of these roles both shapes and is shaped by the organizational context.

Both for the individual manager and in organizational terms there is a continuing need for critical reflection on taken-for-granted assumptions. The increasing emphasis on new forms of communication within the context of new forms of organizing (see, for example, Senge 1990; Isaacs 1993 on dialogue), has allowed some organizations to address what has long been a fundamental aspect of group relations, the underlying emotional and unconscious processes (or relatedness) created within and between systems and the impact of these processes on behaviour. One 'taken-for-granted assumption' that might need to be questioned is the very idea that 'management' is itself anything more than an illusion made possible mainly by the self-policing of the managed. Similarly, at an organizational level, it is increasingly important to break through the illusion of the boundaries of hierarchy, power, and design which quickly come to assume a life of their own. It seems unlikely to us that organizational learning and change can occur without considerable impulse towards reflexivity, both in terms of the ways in which individual managers enact and learn from their roles, and in the ways in which an organization brings learning to bear on itself.

The connection between defensive routines, particularly projection and denial, and their enactment within organizations as resistance and avoidance create a powerful paradox at an organizational level (Vince 1998). This paradox is that organizations espouse and want learning and change at the same time as they prevent themselves from embracing them. The paradox is sustained through the impulses that organizations demonstrate towards learning and change mixed with the considerable resistances that they can also mobilize against them. Questions of authority, power, and politics are central to this paradox—as they are to group relations. All attempts at organizing are forms of political action and are bound up with possible changes to the existing balance of power. The defensiveness of individual managers is a reflection and a re-creation of the defences of the organization, and the defences that are characteristic of an organization are enacted, perpetuated, and refined by individual managers.

In terms of its own dynamics and development, the field of group relations also faces the paradoxes and tensions evoked by issues of learning and change (see Alastair Bain, this volume). This is reflected, for example, by the range of terms, all represented in this volume, that exist alongside 'group relations', such as 'socio-analysis', 'systems psychodynamics', and 'institutional transformation'. In different ways, the approaches represented by these terms emphasize not only different aspects of the traditions which have characterized group relations, but also broader perspectives, such as the sociopolitical, philosophical, and spiritual dimensions of organizing.

The concept of institutional transformation emphasizes: the need for transformations of systems and roles, not just individuals; the need for the mobilization of thoughts, feelings, and desires, and, as a result, also for transformation of the resistances and defences that are evoked; the need to recognize the institutional aspect of collective experience and action as the place where the relatedness of roles and systems is revealed, because this is where the political, emotional, and spiritual dimensions of experience emerge as products of the psyche and the system. Finally, the notion of transformation emphasizes the need to hold in mind an awareness of the temporary and provisional nature of all learning and all institutions. Institutional transformation aims not only at analysis and understanding in depth, but also is reflexive in the sense of being committed to continuous action.

Whatever the outcome of both current and future debates about institutional transformation and group relations, the compilation of this book has reinforced for us, as editors, a sense of the importance of extending and transforming the established traditions of group relations, and embracing new ways of thinking and acting within organizations and institutions as leaders, managers, and consultants. The chapters in this volume have been written by men and women from a wide variety of different cultures, roles, and institutional backgrounds, as well as with a variety of perspectives on the past, present, and future of group relations and its impact on management, organizations, institutions, and societies. The chapters demonstrate that, as a field of thought, enquiry, and application, group relations is already very broad. Our feeling is that the contributions to this book also offer a varied and insightful starting-point from which the theory and practice of group relations in the context of management and organization can continue to evolve and transform.

THEORIZING PRACTICE IN GROUP RELATIONS

2

Grouping

Barry Palmer

According to the *Shorter Oxford English Dictionary*, there are two roots for the word 'group' . . . The more ancient Germanic origin of the word 'group' is derived from the word for 'crop'; that is, the gizzard of a bird. For within the crop of an animal is to be found an agglomeration of substances . . . which have lost their discrete nature and are now clumped together to form a fibrous mass.

The other origin of the word 'group' comes from the Latin, and is connected with a concept of 'grouping' as an active process. (Pines 1994: 53–4.)

The most obvious error to be got out of the way at the beginning is organismic idealism, in terms of which the group is seen as a hyper-organism. (Laing and Cooper 1964: 129.)

INTRODUCTION

My intention in this chapter is to lay a foundation for a reflexive theory of group behaviour. I shall suggest that such a theory requires three levels of articulation: a descriptive account of the behaviour of groups; an interpretative account of the grouping process; and a deconstructive account of the language and context in which these theories are formulated, and the interests they serve.

I shall also put forward an account of the grouping process, in which groups are constituted within the domains of the Imaginary, the Symbolic, and the Real as defined by Lacan.[1]

Some clearing of the ground will be necessary before this foundation can be laid. One of my difficulties is that there is considerable confusion in the literature, or perhaps amongst readers of the literature, between theories of the behaviour of groups, and theories of social behaviour which use interpretative work in face-to-face groups as a method of studying it.

There are also considerable variations in the meaning of the word 'group'. For example, in group relations conferences (e.g. E. J. Miller 1989) and in the work of the Institute of Group Analysis (e.g. de Maré *et al.* 1991) a large group consists of, say, thirty to one hundred people; whereas in the writings of the nineteenth-century sociologist Georg Simmel, a large group is a group of over two thousand people (Simmel 1950). Historically, various sizes of group have been deemed to be too large. Under the *ancien régime* in France, twenty noblemen were not allowed to assemble together without special permission from the king. More cautiously, the Conventicle Act under Charles II included punishments for religious home assemblies of more than five persons (Simmel 1950: 174 ff.).

There is also a tendency to overgeneralize from studies conducted under very particular conditions, and a lack of reflexivity about what I shall refer to as the discursive practices by which theories are framed.

In addressing these problems I shall propose that it may often be useful to think of 'grouping' as something which people do, rather than of groups as objects. Charles Handy illustrates what I mean:

Put random collections of people into groups—for instance on a management training course—and they will, if they wish to be a group . . . , start to find a name, or a private territorial sign, or a ritual, which will give them an independent identity. If they do not do this, it often means that membership of such a group is not important to them, that they are happy to remain a random collection of individuals. (Handy 1981: 146.)

Handy might have omitted 'to be' and simply said: 'if they wish to group'. He uses the word 'group' in two senses: people may be put into groups, but they do not necessarily wish to be a group.

This chapter is in two parts. The first clears the ground and puts down some markers; the second uses texts by Yvonne Agazarian and by Lyman Ketchum and Eric Trist to illustrate the three levels of theorizing I have proposed. Several of the key concepts I shall use are the outcome of many conversations with Philip Boxer, the influence of whose intellectual clarity and audacity I acknowledge gratefully.[2]

CLEARING THE GROUND

What is a group?

There is an extensive literature in which groups are objects in a real world, whose properties can be described; the behaviour of their members can be in part understood in relation to theories of group formation and development, the influence of group size, intergroup relations and other factors. For example, Handy writes: 'Groups mature and develop. Like individuals they have a fairly clearly defined growth cycle. This has been categorised as having four successive stages' (Handy 1981: 160). He goes on to describe Tuckman's (1965) stages of 'forming', 'storming', 'norming', and 'performing'.

In the first chapter of a book on group relations, in a section entitled 'Clearing the ground', it would be nice to feel that this body of knowledge provided something solid under our feet. Unfortunately it does not, for at least two reasons. The first is that groups are not objects in a world existing independently of our perceptions. With a hint of the discourse of Zen, K. K. Smith and Berg (1987: 151) call them 'organisations of emptiness'. This is not a serious difficulty: nobody supposes that groups are fundamental constituents of the universe. A group is a useful construct—an object in the social world of the same status as organizations, communities, associations, tribes, and nations. Thus Brown (R. Brown 1988: 2) proposes this definition: 'a group exists when two or more people define themselves as members of it, and when its existence is recognised by at least one other'. I am not adopting this definition, but I am agreeing with Brown's assumption that the existence of groups is of a kind that comes about through human activities like defining and recognizing.

There is a second, linguistic difficulty which is more serious. This is that the word 'group' is used to refer to several different collectives:

1. *A cluster of people.* This might not conform to Brown's definition: although I might say, 'Look at that group outside the pub', they might not see themselves as members of a group.
2. *A series.* This is a term used by Sartre (1960)[3] to refer to a number of people who are related by virtue of being linked to the same object, but who have no relationship to each other, like people standing in a bus queue. For Sartre, grouping was the process by which a series becomes a group.
3. *A face-to-face meeting.* In the handbook that goes with the training video *Meetings, Bloody Meetings*, Anthony Jay writes: 'In the world of management, a meeting is very often the only occasion where the team or group actually exists and works as a group' (Jay 1976: 5). Handy (1981: 145) says senior managers can spend 80 per cent of their working day in 'one sort of group or another'.
4. *A session* of a therapeutic or experiential learning event; as when a member says: 'We had a good group this morning'.
5. *A social grouping* of which people define themselves as members, both when they are meeting and when they are apart. So the members of a family living apart and meeting for festivals and funerals, or of a branch of a political party meeting together and then going out canvassing, constitute groups according to this usage.
6. *A social system.* I use this term to refer to a whole range of collectives up to the large and complex associations and communities discussed by nineteenth-century sociologists, and by Freud in his *Group Psychology and the Analysis of the Ego* (1921). These early studies of large social systems were uneasily preoccupied with their potentiality for breaking down into undifferentiated masses. Hopper (1997) has interpreted the behaviour of simple

and complex social systems in terms of processes of aggregation, massifi-
cation, and cohesion.

7. *A category.* Groupings like 'men', 'women', 'black people', 'white people',
'cyclists', 'diabetics', and 'the unemployed' are classificatory categories
which imply no necessary sense of relationship between the persons concerned. (However, under some circumstances, people in all these categories may have a sense of affinity when they meet each other. Two black
people may be glad to see each other in a predominantly white gathering;
cyclists often greet each other on lonely roads.)

With what kinds of group is group relations concerned?

The question posed in the subsection heading is not a simple one, for several
reasons. Wilfred Bion's early work on groups, described in *Experiences in
Groups* (1961), has become a normative model for group relations practitioners.
The title of his book, and the theories set out in it, imply that his object of study
was the periodic meetings of patients or trainees he describes. On the other
hand, he says on more than one occasion that the phenomena he seeks to elucidate are ubiquitous:

The only point about collecting a group of people is that it enables us to see just how the
'political' characteristics of the human body operate . . . I do not consider it necessary for
a number of people to be brought together—the individual cannot help being a member
of a group . . . The individual is a group animal at war, not simply with the group, but with
himself for being a group animal and with those aspects of his personality that constitute
his 'groupishness'. (Bion 1961: 131.)

In Isabel Menzies Lyth's phrase (1990), Bion is concerned with 'the dynamics
of the social'—perhaps we should add 'and political'—rather than solely with
the dynamics of meetings of five to eight people. This is I think the best way to
define the focus of contemporary group relations conferences. There has been
a shift in the discourse of some conferences, from talk of groups to talk of systems. Participants meet in groups (meaning 3 or 4), but the focus of study is
whatever social systems (meanings 5, 6, and 7) can be distinguished, within and
across the boundaries of these meetings and of the conference (e.g. Grubb
Institute 1997).

What is group theory about?

There is now a considerable sociological, psychological, and psychoanalytic literature on group processes. Much of the psychoanalytic literature is based on
work with meetings of small therapeutic groups, a smaller part on work with
larger meetings and in educational study groups and group relations confer-

ences. From time to time it is asserted that the phenomena described can also be observed in everyday committees and working groups, if not overtly then below the surface. Thus Bion invites his reader to test the theories he is putting forward by recalling to himself (or herself) 'the memory of some committee or other gathering in which he has participated, and consider[ing] to what extent he can recall evidence that could point to the existence of what I call work-group function, not forgetting the actual administrative structure, chairman and so forth, as material to be included in his review' (Bion 1961: 146).

Yvonne Agazarian makes a similar claim (1994: 48), to which I refer later. These assertions have been insufficiently examined. Although even the most cynical person might expect to see some evidence of work group function in a committee meeting, the meetings and task group activities which make up the day-to-day life of organizations are in many respects very different from the meetings of therapy groups and study groups. For many years I have conducted a course on chairing meetings for middle managers in the Civil Service. It is based on a series of simulated meetings, which are videotaped and played back, with each manager chairing in turn. In debriefing these meetings, I have seldom found myself calling upon psychoanalytic or group analytic concepts, either in my comments or in making sense of them for myself, except on the rare occasions when a meeting has seriously fallen apart.

I suggest therefore that the existing body of psychoanalytic group theory:

(a) is essential for work with therapeutic and experiential learning groups;
(b) is sometimes useful but in itself is insufficient for understanding and participating in the working meetings of 'ordinary' organizations like businesses, educational institutions, and welfare agencies;
(c) provides a valuable perspective upon the 'dynamics of the social', that is, on the processes which shape our micro- and macro-social reality.

Specification for a reflexive theory of group behaviour

We have established that groups are constructs, and that the term 'group' embraces a range of human collectives. So theories of groups as objects with properties will prove inadequate at the point where the processes by which they are constructed are in question. I wish therefore to propose a framework for constructing theories of groups and of the social which are reflexive, in the sense that their own presuppositions can be called into question.[4] Such a theory will have first, second, and third orders of articulation:

1. *Descriptive* (first order): accounts of the behaviour and properties of groups as social or organizational objects, how they evolve, the effects of size, and so on.
2. *Interpretative* (second order): accounts of the processes by which men and women construct, and act in relation to, groups as objects. These

'grouping' processes may be self-conscious or unreflective. Psycho-analytic theories are generally of this second order, since they offer inter-pretations of the mental processes of group members: they are theories about the (tacit) theories of those who group.

3. *Deconstructive* (third order): analyses of the terms (or more accurately the discursive practices) within which these accounts are framed. The term 'discursive practice' was introduced by Michel Foucault (1972). Among the practices of different professions and disciplines he included their 'discur-sive practices', that is, their practices of speaking and listening. These include the distinctive language they employ, and in particular the objects and concepts which furnish the 'reality' they construct; the tacit rules gov-erning who speaks with authority, and under what circumstances; and the latent intentions or ideologies which determine the thrust or bias of the discursive practice. To stop short of this third order of theorizing is to ignore the fact that Simmel, Freud, Lewin, Foulkes, Bion, and this writer speak and write in a historical context, creating and drawing upon ways of speaking which construct reality in a particular way, which support par-ticular interests and intentions, and which maintain their distinctive silences.

ILLUSTRATIVE EXAMPLES

In the second part of this chapter I shall develop these propositions by means of two illustrative texts. They differ in many respects and it is not my intention to set them up in opposition to one another. The first text, by the American group analyst, Yvonne Agazarian, is a description of unconscious processes in group development, drawing upon concepts from psychoanalysis, group dynamics, and systems theory. The second, by an American management con-sultant, Lyman Ketchum, and the late Eric Trist, who was English and one of the founders of the Tavistock Institute, describes what is entailed in building self-regulating production teams in industry. As well as introducing a number of concepts of groups and grouping, these texts illustrate two particular issues:

1. The second text, unlike the first, makes no reference to unconscious processes, although it is clearly informed by psychoanalytic and systemic understanding. This highlights the question of the usefulness of theories evolved in group relations events and therapeutic groups outside these specialized contexts.
2. In spite of their different contexts, purposes, and readerships, both texts are descriptive (first order) and interpretative (second order), and both are susceptible to a deconstructive (third order) reading which questions the terms in which these accounts are framed.

First illustrative text: Group development

The group dynamics literature contains several accounts of the development or evolution of groups over time (see, for example, Ashbach and Schermer 1987; Bennis and Shepard 1956; Sartre 1960; Schutz 1958; Tuckman 1965). I have chosen for discussion a more recent paper by Yvonne Agazarian, 'The phases of group development and the systems-centred group' (1994). This paper draws upon general systems theory and develops Bion's group theory. It therefore shares its theoretical underpinning with writing from the Tavistock tradition.

Agazarian identifies a series of phases and subphases through which groups develop. She makes clear that groups do not pass through these phases in a tidy way: they regress to earlier phases and progress forward again many times. Her scheme is an elaboration of that of Bennis and Shepard, which explicitly drew upon the work of Bion. She identifies these phases:

1. A *leader-oriented phase*, which centres on the group members' expectations of the leader, and their responses to the frustration of these expectations. There are explicit parallels with Bion's account of groups dominated by the dependency and fight/flight basic assumptions. Members expect the leader to solve their problems for them, and are disappointed by her responses. There is a first, flight subphase, in which members avoid facing their frustration. They offer the leader patients or problems on which to display her power. This is followed by a second, fight subphase, in which the failed leader is denigrated, attacked, and disowned. This leads up to what Agazarian, following Bennis and Shepard, calls a 'barometric event'. It is a moment of transformation, in which the group symbolically kill off the leader and in so doing are released from the constraint of their identification with her.

2. A *group-oriented phase*, which centres on the relatedness of members to the group itself. There is a first subphase of enchantment, in which the group and its members become idealized objects to each other. The mood of expectancy is reminiscent of Bion's pairing basic assumption. This leads into a second, disenchantment subphase, characterized by disillusionment with the group and jealousy of each other: the parallels with Bion are less clear. This concludes with a second turning-point, which Agazarian characterizes as a transition from intimacy to maturity. So the first phase leads to the end of the fantasy of the omnipotent leader, the second to the end of the fantasy of the omnipotent group; it entails, as Agazarian says, 'risking that, in spite of one's inner convictions, one has been mistaken' (Agazarian 1994: 73).

3. A *goal-oriented phase*, in which the group is able to work on the purposes for which its members came together. It is the stage at which there can be 'transactions across the boundaries', and at which 'the first step in any difficult work is to establish a containing reality (of time, place, and person),

within which regression to other levels of experience can take place' (ibid.: 75–6). It corresponds to Tuckman's 'performing' stage. In Bion's terms, the work group is now able to control the powerful emotional drives of the basic assumption group. It is the stage of what Agazarian calls 'transformation—and the many splendoured phoenix' (ibid.: 37). Agazarian compares the difference between the developing group (Phases 1 and 2) and the developed group (Phase 3) to 'the difference between the patient in individual therapy who is helplessly tossed on the sea of transference, and the patient who is familiar enough already with the experience to be able to navigate through its shoals' (ibid.: 74 f.).

Group as organism and process

What kind of a text is this? It contains descriptive (first-order) material, including samples of the kinds of conversation that take place between members and with the therapist. But it is primarily an interpretative (second-order) account of the way people 'group', offering explanations of the mental processes which give rise to this behaviour. It is also shaped by her systems orientation; the introduction to her paper begins:

Systems-centred theory approaches all living things, as small as a cell and as large or larger than society, by defining them as systems that are similar in structure, function and dynamics . . . The advantage of describing all living human systems isomorphically in this way is that what one learns about the dynamics of any one system says something about the dynamics of all the other systems in its hierarchy. (ibid.: 37.)

This makes groups feel more solid: they develop the way living organisms develop. But we might also choose to say that there is no group apart from a grouping process, any more than a dance has any existence apart from the dancing. Adapting what Gianfranco Cecchin says of social systems: 'the group is simply doing what it does, and this doing is the it that does it' (Cecchin 1987: 408). When we introduce this complementary mode of description, we call into question the 'reality' which is the object of group theory.[5]

The systemic fallacy

How useful is Agazarian's scheme as a general theory of grouping? She claims that this pattern is followed by all groups: 'Underlying system dynamics are no different whether the "groups" observed are therapy groups, training groups or groups of people working on a board or in committee; no different in organizations or even in nations!' (Agazarian 1994: 48).

I believe this statement illustrates what we might call the systemic fallacy. Armed with general systems theory, we may be able to perceive an isomorphism between single cell organisms, birds and mammals, and between small face-to-face groups, organizations and nations; this is true. However, this does not mean that someone who knows all about amoebas understands human beings, or that someone with knowledge of small groups is able to run an organization or govern a country. The systemic fallacy arises from a disregard for complexity.

Agazarian's claim discounts the influence of context upon the phenomena she observes. Differences of context explain some of the similarities and differences between theories. For example, Bennis and Shepard based their account on a study of groups of university students over a five-year period. Like Agazarian, therefore, they were working with small groups of people in a relationship of dependence upon their institutions. In contrast, Sartre based his theory on a historical analysis of the emergence of the revolutionary masses during the French Revolution. Not surprisingly, the phases he identifies are different (see Laing and Cooper 1964; Rosenfeld 1988).

The process Agazarian describes reflects the distinctive organization of the therapy group. This is one in which a task is not, or cannot, be defined in a way which enables people readily to identify with it, as their unconscious object of desire. Without this anchor, relations between members, and between members and leader, are flooded by primitive drives. Unable to sustain a stable transference upon a task, the participants transfer their idealizing expectations in turn to the therapist and then to the group, with the consequences Agazarian describes. They are 'helplessly tossed on the sea of transference'. Only after much emotional work does the group reach her third, goal-oriented phase, and not always, for she says: 'Unfortunately, it is not unusual for the therapy group to remain in the first phase throughout its entire life' (Agazarian 1994: 46). This emotional work is the stuff of therapy, but in most contexts task groups are not organized in this way.

The myth of development

The focal object of the discursive practice which shapes Agazarian's scheme is the group conceived of as an organism which ideally develops from infancy to maturity. I stress the word 'ideally', to draw attention to the fit between the metaphor of an organism, which develops, and a therapeutic ideal of maturation. Many group therapists, with the exception of those following Sartre, read the life of the groups they lead in the light of a myth of human psychic development—whether or not they draw upon systems theory. The resulting theories are not just descriptive, but also normative: they are accounts of how groups should develop, and of the kind of development the therapist is seeking to promote. As Agazarian says, 'unfortunately' groups do not always develop in this way.

Such is the power of the developmental myth that Bion's theory of work group and basic assumption group activity is frequently recast as a developmental theory. For example, Ashbach and Schermer's group analytic grid represents the group as developing from fight, through fight/flight and dependency, 'higher level competition', and pairing, to work (Ashbach and Schermer 1987: 284). Agazarian's paper includes a perceptive deconstructive reading of Bion's later, Kleinian theory,[6] in which she describes him as a pioneer 'who lived at a time when either/or thinking was the norm'. She goes on: 'He also observed consistent defensive responses to group conflicts that did not appear to be the property of individual members but rather to be the property of the group-as-a-whole. He failed to observe that these conflicts tended to occur in a sequence' (Agazarian 1994: 43).

Maybe he did, but I think Agazarian fails to observe the influence of the theorists' desires and ideals upon their theories.

Second illustrative text: Teambuilding

My second illustrative text is taken from *All Teams Are Not Created Equal: How Employee Empowerment Really Works*, by Lyman Ketchum and Eric Trist (1992). Ketchum trained at the National Training Laboratories in Bethel, Maine. Trist contributed to the development of the concept of socio-technical systems. I shall focus upon the chapter entitled 'Designing the new plant' (Ketchum and Trist 1992: 140–66), which sets out principles for constructing core production teams in an industrial unit, of which I shall select six.

Design principles for a core production team

1. *Motivation.* The writers suggest that the first step in building an effective team is to decide what is to be the principal source of motivation for its members. Is it to be the intrinsic satisfactions of task performance, or extrinsic rewards and sanctions? They advocate the former, on the grounds that the root cause of bad work is lack of intrinsic commitment to a task. The designer's goal is 'to get everyone to do what needs to be done because they want to do it'. The work process is then designed in a way which removes obstacles to intrinsic motivation. This is a key feature of a 'new paradigm' for work organization.

2. *Technical analysis.* Teambuilding is not just a matter of designing the social system, but of studying the technical system and the stages in the work process at which quality and productivity may be liable to vary significantly. The essential groundwork also includes a technical analysis of the task. Working together on this analysis is also important in building the team: 'As one busy manager noted, "It gets people together for two days to talk about the technical system when they otherwise would not find the time to do so."' (Ketchum and Trist 1992: 147)

3. *Boundaries.* It is necessary to determine the boundaries of the team's work. 'Making good use of the completed technical analysis, designers fix the extent of the technical system over which the team will have

jurisdiction' (ibid.: 147). Preferably, the limits of this jurisdiction coincide with discontinuities in the work process, so that the team has the satisfaction of carrying out a complete task.

4. *Mission statement.* The team produces a mission statement, defining the 'purpose or reason for the team's being'. This 'is another of the forces that both brings them together and makes them a distinctive group apart. Thus the mission is another form of boundary' (ibid.: 148).

5. *Team leader.* There is a team leader, who is external to, and managerially responsible for, the team. His or her task is to act as 'the custodian of the design; the anatomy of self-regulation must be made right and kept right' (ibid.: 159). He or she receives 17½ days' training, which includes boundary management and behaviour analysis (ibid.: 270).

6. *Team meeting.* The team is a self-regulating, learning system. Integral to this system is a regular team meeting. In this meeting they step out of the frame of their work on the shop-floor, into another, from which they helicopter over themselves at work and assess how they are working. Then periodically they step into a third frame of reference, from which they can assess the way they are assessing their work in normal team meeting time. 'Essentially the final step of the meeting is a self-critique and employs well-known techniques of group dynamics' (ibid.: 153). Tantalizingly, we are not told what these techniques are.

Creating the conditions for goal-directed work

What kind of a text is this? The style is primarily first order and prescriptive, setting out what must be done to create a self-regulating production team, although it also includes descriptive case studies. So what we are reading is what the writers believe practising managers need to know in order to be able to act. In this respect it appears to be different from the Agazarian text, but perhaps is not entirely so. Agazarian is also concerned with what therapists need to know in order to act. But the kind of action she is concerned with is interpretative intervention; she is not talking about designing the setting for an effective therapy group.

We should note that Ketchum and Trist make no reference to stages through which a team develops, though later they say it is 'like a living organism . . . which must grow and develop from an initial, embryonic state' (Ketchum and Trist 1992: 174); neither do they discuss unconscious processes which may disturb its work. At first glance they seem to imply that teams can attain goal-oriented functioning if the right conditions are created, and to agree with Elliott Jaques's statement, that 'the reason we have bad or dysfunctional organizations is not a reflection of pathological forces to be understood and resolved by the application of psychoanalytical concepts and methods. Far from it . . . We have simply not yet learned how to construct adequate organizations' (Jaques 1995: 343).

However, this impression is not altogether accurate. First, it is evident from the whole book that the writers are only too aware that the work of self-regulating teams can be undermined by ways of thinking which are, from their point of view, destructive. These are rooted in what they call the 'old paradigm' of organization (Ketchum and Trist 1992: 40), characterized by external motivation and hierarchical control. They thus interpret destructive processes in cultural rather than psychological terms.

Secondly, the design of the new paradigm plant includes a number of devices which are necessary to support the team and senior managers in holding to the mission and ethos they have adopted. The team meeting institutionalizes occasions for assessing how the team is functioning. The team has access to outside facilitation, and may call in a senior manager to arbitrate when team members have been unable to reach a decision. The team leader acts as custodian of the design.

So for these writers, understanding of processes in teams is a significant but secondary element in an account of teambuilding for managers, the content of which is left to the psychologists and trainers. Their first concern is with designing a form of organization which will support self-regulating, goal-directed work. But as I shall go on to suggest, their injunctions for the setting up of the team imply or require psychoanalytic scrutiny if they are to be adequately explained and assessed.

'Good work' and the object of desire

What then are we to make of the interpretative content of this text? On what theory of the grouping process is it based? The key proposition, as I have said, is that 'good work' is a function of the personal investment of team members in the achievement of its goals. The writers assert that there are 'certain basic needs that people . . . require from their work: to join with others in a common task; to have some latitude to make decisions; to receive recognition for one's contribution; to learn and go on learning' (Ketchum and Trist 1992: 10: from a longer list).

The writers go no further in explaining these so-called needs. Their use of the word 'need' requires examination. It tends to foreclose further enquiry: people have a need for these things, and that's it. At the same time it suggests a theory that people combine in collaborative groups as they discover in them a shared object which satisfies fundamental drives. Freud's thesis (1921) was that members of large collectives like an army or the Church become an integrated social system as each member identifies with the leader—with their general, or with Christ. They each substitute an image of this leader for their own ego ideal, and so identify themselves with one another in their egos (Freud 1991 edn.: 147). This, he says, explains why the Assyrian army scattered in panic when their general Holofernes was killed (ibid.: 127).

Lacan's version of this is that groups and masses are animated as they locate in the group the cause and object of their desire (Lacan 1991: 56). (No imaginable object can satisfy this desire: it is rooted in what Lacan calls the domain of the Real, outside language.) This formulation suggests a third order reading of Ketchum and Trist. Team members strive to do good work and overcome difficulties to the extent that they unconsciously identify the work of the team with the object of their desire. So the writers' aim is that team members should be animated, not by identifying with a leader, nor by idealizing the group, but by the desirability of the task itself—or, more precisely, by what it unconsciously stands for.

More generally, we might say that one aspect of grouping is this process of transference, upon a leader or a body of knowledge, upon the group itself, or as here upon a task. We might also distinguish between two strategies for developing goal-directed functions in working groups, exemplified by our two texts. One is that of interpreting defensive formations, what Agazarian (1994: 37) calls 'inexorable pressure on the outer shell of defences'. The other is that of evoking an object of desire which draws group members to transcend their defences in the (impossible) hope of attaining it.

Defining boundaries

How do the writers conceptualize the structure which is required to support such inwardly motivated work? As we have seen, they talk about the necessity of defining the team's technical boundary, and later about defining a mission statement which constitutes another boundary 'that both brings them together and makes them a distinctive group apart' (Ketchum and Trist 1992: 148). Emphasis on the importance of drawing clear boundaries is a key element within the group relations tradition, and reflects the context of the 1960s in which this tradition was formalized.

However, although defining boundaries is necessary for coherent functioning, the more firmly they are drawn, the more strongly the subject identifies with them, and therefore the more strongly he or she resists attempts to change them. It is a commonplace of social psychology that the process of grouping can be set in motion simply by allocating people into categories according to an arbitrary principle. For example, Sherif and Sherif describe how boys at a summer camp were divided into two lots of twelve, matched by age, education, class, and so on, by assigning them an identifying colour, red or blue, and allocating them to different bunkhouses. Within a short time they had become close-knit groups with distinctive names and cultures, and when they were brought into contact with each other they become intensely rivalrous (Sherif and Sherif 1956, cited in Handy 1981: 148 ff.).

In Lacanian terms the technical and territorial boundaries of the team are Imaginary. This does not mean that they are illusory, but that they organize an indeterminate hurly-burly of activities in a bounded, holistic image. In the turbulent environment of the 1990s, which the writers allude to in an earlier chapter, and which Trist himself identified (Emery and Trist 1965), the self-regulating team may be insufficiently flexible to respond to change, if its members are strongly identified with an Imaginary team. The challenge of organizational design is therefore not only to define requisite boundaries, but to prevent people becoming addicted to them.

One way in which, in practice, the writers' design may reduce this tendency is through the institution of the mission statement, although they obscure this by referring to it as a boundary (Ketchum and Trist 1992: 148). Within the Tavistock tradition statements of task are frequently referred to as defining a boundary (e.g. E. J. Miller 1959). This reflects the fact that this discursive practice includes no developed concept of language. A mission statement does not create a distinction between an inside and an outside. It is what it says it is—a statement, a form of words, deriving its meaning from a larger discourse. In Lacan's terms it defines the team and its intended work within the Symbolic domain—that is, the domain of law and language. It can be seen as a statement which symbolizes the object of desire which motivates the team. The object of desire is necessarily outside language, but working on the mission statement provides a vehicle by which the team can negotiate, and federate around, a formula which stands for what each member wants to achieve.

Reflection on the second text has thus suggested a theory of grouping, in which groups are constructed in three domains: in the domain of the Imaginary, through a holistic image with a boundary between inside and outside; in the domain of the Symbolic, through statements which anchor the group within a universe of language and law, and so make it an object of communication; and in the domain of what Lacan calls the Real, outside language and unmarked by Imaginary boundaries, which makes itself known as the cause which motivates group members to pursue their task (or, we might add, to subvert it for the sake of their own satisfaction).

What is missing?

What is missing from this account? First, its prescriptive style conceals how much depends on the skill with which it is operationalized—on the efficacy of the team meetings, on the way the team leader fulfils his or her custodianship of the design, on the quality of the team leader training, and on the finesse of senior managers in judging whether and when to intervene. Much depends on the competencies of consultants or managers in enabling teams and their managers to maintain, rather than close down, a number of creative tensions: between the different ways in which senior managers and production teams may define task boundaries, between explicit formulations of how things work and those implicit in what actually happens, and between adhering to the ideals enshrined in mission statements and responding creatively to unforeseen circumstances.[7]

Secondly, Ketchum and Trist regard their concept of the self-regulating team as a manifestation of a new work paradigm. They also refer to the fact that the concept has been around for forty years now, but do not seem to recognize the extent to which it may also be shaped and limited by its historical context. As they expound it, and in particular as they assert what people 'need' from work, it becomes apparent that their theory comes out of the same box as McGregor's Theory X and Theory Y, Maslow's hierarchy of needs, Elton Mayo's Hawthorne experiments, and the human relations ethos which was integral to the early work of the Tavistock Institute. That does not in itself mean it is out of date; but my conclusion is that it is theoretically and pragmatically unsound, in the tur-bulent environment of the 1990s, to base the design of a working team on assumptions about the needs of the workers. Many organizations seek to give their members maximum scope to exercise discretion and creativity, but their viability depends on their ability to be responsive—to be open to what their users want, and to be quicker to respond than the competition. So the team can only be constructed round the desire of its members, if their desire is to be responsive to user demands. A turbulent environment has a life of its own; a responsive business or agency is one which is able to rejig its organization to intervene in, or respond to, that life. Although Emery and Trist (1965) described the dynamics of turbulent environments in the 1960s, their concept of the socio-technical system was not explicitly open to an environment of this degree of complexity.

If I am right, implementation of the Ketchum–Trist design as it stands would lead to the creation of organizations which in the short term produce motivated teams and good work, but in the longer term tend to be outflanked, because they are too committed to their own ethos and structures, and hence too inflex-ible, to be able to regroup to meet new market opportunities or public service demands.[8]

CONCLUSION

By now the reader may wonder whether we are still within the domain of group relations. We are a long way from the phenomena described by Wilfred Bion and Yvonne Agazarian. As others have suggested, it is possible to see group rela-tions as comprising two distinguishable discursive practices: (a) theories of unconscious processes in groups and organizations (e.g. Agazarian 1994; Bion 1961; Foulkes 1990; Freud 1921; Menzies Lyth 1988); and (b) systems theory as applied to groups and organizations (e.g. von Bertalanffy 1950; Emery and Trist 1965; E. J. Miller and Rice 1967). My intuitive choice of case studies placed me with one foot in each domain. Writers in the group relations field tend to see (b) as outside the scope of psychoanalytic enquiry. I have sought to elucidate how both these bodies of theory are elaborated in a way which is rooted in uncon-scious desire and unconscious defences. But we need Lacan's concepts of language and of desire, and Foucault's concept of discursive practices, or something like them, to see and say this. I have been unable to see or say this, as long as I have believed that (a) represents the totality of what psychoanalysis has to say about groups and organizations.

There remains the question of the reflexivity of the ideas put forward in this chapter. The discursive practices I have called into question here, by means of a third-order analysis, are very much part of myself. They shape the way I habitually think, when under pressure to respond to the demands of client organizations. This is thus an attempt to work through my transference upon this body of theory and practice.

I can however claim no privilege for the concepts I have introduced: they are no less determined by the desire of the writer and his historical and linguistic contexts than the texts he has studied. There are limits to the extent to which a writer can deconstruct his own text if he and his editors wish him to finish it. It may be best to offer this task to the reader, and to suggest some questions which may be of assistance (questions like this also provide a way in to the third order of analysis of any text of this kind):[9]

1. In what ways does the writer's account appear to be historically, contextually, or ideologically determined, in ways of which the text has no knowledge?
2. Does the text at any point imply that there is a right approach to a deconstructive reading of the illustrative texts? If so, what is its supposed source of authority?
3. Are there gaps or disturbances in the text which suggest that the writer has been unable to face some truth, perhaps about himself?

NOTES

1 For these terms, see, for example, Evans 1996; Fink 1997: 32–41; Muller 1996.
2 I would also like to acknowledge the pertinent suggestions of the editors, which have had an important influence on the final form of this chapter.
3 See also Laing and Cooper (1964: 121 ff.); Rosenfeld (1988: 1 f.).
4 Philip Boxer has suggested to me that there is a distinction between a reflexive framework for constructing theories, and a theory which is reflexive in use. I have not worked this distinction through in what follows.
5 Cf. the way the emergence of the wave and particle theories of light raised questions about the observing system which brought these complementary accounts of reality into being.
6 Eric Miller (1998) has recently proposed that Bion's later, Kleinian reading of his experiences in groups overlays an earlier theory in which the basic assumptions were manifestations of drives rooted in bodily instincts.
7 For an account of the three dilemmas of organizations which I have paraphrased here, see Boxer (1994).

8 This seems to have happened to designs for responsive local government evolved by Roger Hadley and Ken Young (1990).
9 For similar questions directed at the critical examination of consultancy practice, see Boxer and Palmer (1994).

3

A Mind for Business

W. Gordon Lawrence

The industrial revolution raised the possibility of creating a world of plenty. But a century after the heroic period of Japanese, European and US industrialization we are no closer to realising the dream of the industrial revolution, the dream of modernism, the dream of progress. Our productive economy is riddled with the inefficient management structures in which people who know most about the work tend to have little say about how it can be improved, and are generally not permitted to talk to us directly about their experience. If they take the risk to do so, we are in no position to act on what they tell us. (Schwartz 1992: 201–2.)

Heavy industry has been in decline in Britain since the early 1970s. Throughout the 1980s and 1990s there followed a wave of redundancies through 'downsizing' that resulted in some industries ceasing to exist. This decline coincided with the growth in information technology (IT), but was not caused by it. At first management were able to integrate IT to help them keep a better control on the business. Management information systems provided them with up-to-the-minute facts on the state of the business. Now IT has spawned very much more sophisticated 'meta-technologies' that create business through the system itself, such as 'e-business'. The use of IT has brought about a 'quantum leap' in thinking about generating business. The 'information society' is upon us.

 The central working hypothesis of this chapter is that business can no longer be conducted using the conscious mind exclusively, but will have to access that which has been locked in the unconscious hitherto. This offers an opportunity for extending the scope of the mind for registering the nature of reality and for continuing to bring that reality into being. The 'mind for business' which was successful in the context of industrial society is now inadequate. At this point in history we are caught with our feet in the gutter of industrial society but increasingly are fascinated by the starry sky of the information society.

MIND AND BUSINESS

Without mind, or our capacity for thinking and thought, the sciences, technology, art, philosophy, literature, and the social, political, and spiritual processes which make for that collective cultural experience we call 'civilization', would not have existence. Without thought there would not be businesses, which are a defining feature of contemporary civilization. When people come to their business enterprise each day—be it a commercial company, a hospital, a university—they 'have to think to know what they are supposed to be doing—if they all forgot this the company would collapse and would cease to exist' (Bohm and Edwards 1991: 8).

Mind has no material reality. Although neuroscience, the science of the brain, is attempting to produce a unified theory, we 'know', as opposed to 'opine', little of the mind. What is known is what the mind is capable of achieving, even though we do not know precisely how it functions except that mind is related to the polyneural functioning of the brain. Christian de Duve has summarized the achievements of the mind:

The mind generates our thoughts, reasonings, intuitions, ponderings, inventions, designs, beliefs, doubts, imaginings, fantasies, desires, intentions, yearnings, frustrations, dreams and nightmares. It brings up evocations of our past and it shapes plans for our future; it weighs, decides and commands. It is the seat of consciousness, self-awareness, and personhood, the holder of freedom and moral responsibility, the judge of good and bad, the inventor and agent of virtue and sin. It is the focus of all our feelings, emotions and sensations, of pleasure and pain, love and hate, rapture and despair. The mind is the interface between what we are wont to call the world of matter and the world of the spirit. The mind is our window to truth, beauty, charity and love, to existential mystery, the awareness of death, the poignancy of the human condition. (de Duve 1995: 245.)

Just as it was mind that brought industrial society into being, so it is currently realizing the information society. As, however, the pace of transformation from one to the other accelerates there is always the risk that whatever social realities are emerging as a result of IT will continue to be understood and interpreted from the framework of thinking and thought which sustained the industrial era.

THE LIMITS OF COMPREHENSION HYPOTHESIS

The experiences of the information society push all its members to the limits of their comprehension. Consciousness is that ability to think about things that are not present and imagine unreal things; it has the capacity for alternative interpretations of complex and ambiguous data; it can work with the contents of several sensory modalities within a single unified experience; it disappears in deep sleep and reappears in dreaming (Calvin 1996: 30). What we are not aware of lies in the unconscious. Using their consciousness human beings come to comprehend the world in which they live.

The evidence that managers are coming to the limits of their comprehension as the information society starts to be brought into being comes from working with managers in a mail order company over a number of years. The managers' mental world was formed during the epoch of industrial society. The companies were in decline after a long history of comparative success. Among the principal reasons they identified for their predicament was the increasing competition from newly formed mail order companies that seemed to address the specific needs of customers. The real reason, however, was the recognition that the mass market to which they had been selling successfully had now become differentiated. The psychology of their customers had changed. They had learned since the post-war years of scarcity to manage themselves in the role of consumers. The companies were failing despite the fact that the technology was comparatively simple and the business had a clear 'logic'. The managers became increasingly anxious about the necessity to attain a position of financial stability; to secure the 'bottom line'. But this eluded them as they tried solution after solution.

When the managers acknowledged, albeit implicitly, that they had come to the limits of their comprehension of how the business related to its customers, they began to *think*. But this was only after they had rescued strategies for survival from memory, tried them, and found them wanting. The managers were imbued with the 'logic' of the business. It now had to be unpacked and reworked to fit the changing market.

The managers were experiencing misfortune of a public nature in that the market had changed dramatically for reasons which were not of their making. In time, I came to see this as a tragedy, though it was never expressed as such, because if the misfortune were to continue ultimately the company would cease to exist, thus making them all out of work. The company would dissipate.

The managers engaged in thinking that was centred on the state of the market as it was in reality; not as they imagined it to be or fantasized it should be. They had to work with a differentiated market when the logic of the company was directed at servicing a mass market. Whereas the managers could understand this there was enormous resistance on the part of other role holders in the company, who had been trained as managers and buyers during the time when the ethos of industrial society had been fully accepted. They all had competence in their area of expertise. They had clearly defined jobs and knew their responsibilities. Now they were being asked to rework these competencies and exercise their intuition on the basis of their direct experience of the market.

This new role meant thinking of and devising new catalogues and new ways of selling and marketing. This was a major upheaval of the hub of the business. In time they were able to do this. It was not that these managers at all levels were lacking in competence; they were competent in business but as it had been performed in the past. When they gradually reached the limits of their comprehension, they went on to discover new insights, perceptions, and intuitions which, for the most part, had their sources in the unconscious.

The recognition that one has reached the limits of comprehension is an achievement not only intellectually but also emotionally. These come together in what Bion called 'catastrophic change' (Bion 1970: 92 ff.). Although Bion was writing about the analysis of psychotic patients, he argued that all change is inevitably represented as catastrophic change because a successful analysis must include the treatment of the psychotic part of the personality. Catastrophic change and the emotional growth of the human mind are inevitably linked. I think that the attainment of the limits of comprehension is accompanied by a feeling of desperation that what one understood in the past no longer makes sense. It is non-sense. To put this more strongly, it is accompanied by a feeling that one is mad to follow the old conceptualization and that one has to make sense of the new circumstances that are being presented to one's senses.

Here I offer a contingent, working hypothesis:

> Fears and anxieties of catastrophic change shadow the acknowledgement of the limits of comprehension.

Bion's formulation of catastrophic change can readily be applied to organizations. In the example I have given, the key managers were working with an accepted conjunction of facts and concepts construed in their minds and which had illumined the nature of their business for decades. Now new facts were bombarding them that were disruptive of their taken-for-granted logic. What could be faced only with difficulty was the imagined recognition of the pain, frustration, and distress that the recognition and accommodation of new facts inevitably would produce. Bion uses the terms 'container' and 'contained' to study these disruptions. The new idea is the 'contained' and the minds of the role holders in the group, or company, or organization, or society are the 'container'. The understanding of the dynamic between these is critical for capturing the evolving life of contemporary organizations as their role holders continue to bring an extended purview of reality into being and, therefore, a developed sense of reality. What seems to be becoming almost a way of life in organizations is that catastrophic change is now the norm rather than the exception. As it is, both the limits of comprehension and the shadowed fears and anxieties of catastrophic change tend either to be avoided in a phobic manner or to result in 'acting out'. It takes time for the limits of comprehension to register in order that they can be internalized and worked through. At the same time, it has to be recognized that the managers under discussion were thinking and working within the inherited structure of industrial society as it had been known.

THINKING-TO-BE-IN-TOUCH WITH REALITY

Attaining the limits of comprehension, and freeing oneself from one's inherited conceptualizations, through internalizing the necessity for catastrophic change, comes about through thinking-to-be-in-touch with reality even though it is known, at some level, that the absolute truth can never be apprehended. Reason alone cannot capture the truth about the ultimate nature of things. Truth, which Bion signifies as **O**, is the thing in itself, the essential ineffability of things, the godhead, the absolute. It can be known about but cannot be known by any person (Bion 1970: 26–40). This thinking-to-be-in-touch with reality I am to denote as **RT+**, for ease of exposition. This, to repeat, is an emotional achievement as much as an intellectual one. **RT+** is the ability that comes from the will to entertain reality (which demands courage). Reality has both its good and bad aspects, both its tragedy and comedy, and highlights the gap between human strivings and the indifference of the universe. Tragedy is being used not in the sense of a dramatic form but more in the sense of overwhelming fate.

The tendency, however, is to evade **RT+** and whatever new meanings and versions of the truth it will yield. These evasions can be clustered, first, around thinking-not-to-be-in-touch with reality, which I will denote as **–RT**. This process of evasion begins from a fear or terror of reality that becomes a hatred of reality. The reality is both of the internal and external worlds. This is because reality is construed and felt to be a 'catastrophic chaos of utter unpredictability' (Rayner, 1995: 159). To entertain reality experientially would threaten to burst asunder the psychic limits between the conscious and the unconscious, between that which is safely held in the domain of the finite and that which remains to be 'won from the void and formless infinite', to echo Milton.

This hatred of reality invokes a hatred of the capacity to think; thus any mental process that would facilitate the attainment of **RT+** has to be denied. Emotionally, this arises from the anxiety that if **RT+** were to be engaged with, the resultant experience would overwhelm and overpower the individual. It is felt that the experience of reality would annihilate the thinker who dares to see reality in all its complexity. Furthermore, the individual would be persecuted by reality. So reality has to be destroyed or, more accurately, the human desire to make meaning of the experiences of reality has to be not only denied but also sadistically obliterated. One way in which meaning is drained from reality is through concretization and by the evacuation of any symbolic content to the experience of reality. Another way is through the simplification of reality by the process of 'splitting' into categories of good and bad objects in the environment. (Technology and the organization are good; workers are a cost and therefore bad, for example.) They become invested with qualities that make them into 'bizarre objects' (Bion 1992: 276), and so can be safely kept at a distance and construed as not worth coming to know. To be sure, this is to be in a state of illusion, to be living in the lie.

The behaviour that is driven by −**RT** occasionally will configure as basic assumption groups, which provide participants with ready-made meanings to their existence (Bion 1961; Turquet 1974). This meaning is unexamined and 'acted out'. The basic assumption of 'me-ness' (Lawrence, Bain, and Gould 1996) is particularly prevalent when the desire of individuals simply to survive in the organization takes over their capacity for managing themselves in their role.

Readers with psychoanalytic experience will recognize that in writing about −**RT** and **RT**+ I am referring to psychotic and non-psychotic thinking. I wish, however, to shift from the term 'psychotic' in the context of organization. 'Psychosis' refers to those mental illnesses that cause their victim to become *non compos mentis*. In organizations the role holders are not insane. Role holders, furthermore, do not expect to be treated as analysands or patients by organizational consultants, even though the role holders may be committed to a psychoanalytic understanding of the nature of organizations. They resent being infantilized or treated as less than adult and immature. Role holders in organizations are human beings who, for the most part, want to engage with the work of the organization if only because it is the source of their professional identity and their income.

Like all human beings, of course, they have had the experience of being fearful in infancy and have experienced the anxieties of survival, which are integral to the mother–baby relationship. At times of severe existential crisis in adult life these fears and anxieties can be reawoken to result in the adult having the same feelings as when he/she was a baby. My working hypothesis is that these fears and anxieties can be clustered together as fantasies of tragedy, which are formed during infancy and, indeed, before birth. I say 'tragedy' because the baby first experiences the tenuousness of life both before and during the process of birth. It is tenuous because life can so easily be lost.

The evidence that the baby has his/her first intimations of tragedy in the process of birth comes from Stanislav Grof. Over a period of thirty years, both in Prague and in Maryland in the United States, he worked with patients who were prepared to undergo a profound exploration of their unconscious. In the course of these explorations 'there consistently emerged a pivotal sequence of experiences of great complexity and intensity' (Tarnas 1996 edn.: 426). He found that his analysands, as they moved back through their biographical, lived experiences, were able to re-experience being in a state of undifferentiated unity with the mother. But this was replaced by a time when they experienced being in a state of separation from that primal unity. Then came a time of 'a highly charged life-and-death struggle with the contracting uterus and the birth canal, and culminating in an experience of complete annihilation' (ibid.). It is at this point that the baby experiences the possibility, even probability, of death. That experience gives rise to the fantasy that death is always a real outcome of the process of being born. When the environment is experienced as being persecuting, and is such that it evokes feelings of being overwhelmed, annihilated, being made into a non-being, we can identify the existence of fantasies of tragedy that exist in the inner world of the individual, albeit at an unconscious level.

Through infantile and subsequent maturational experiences these fantasies of tragedy are modified or put into perspective as life events are experienced and learned from. These infantile fantasies of tragedy influence how real, lived tragedy is interpreted in the adult mind. In other words, events that are potentially tragic will be understood as such depending upon the salience of the fantasies of tragedy that are held in the mind of the individual. The fantasies of tragedy, which are of a private nature, can be so salient that the chances of learning from the experience of tragedy as a public issue are diminished. The chances of growing in maturity, through struggling with the fateful events in life in order to find a sense of destiny by recognizing that the human spirit can triumph over adversity, are reduced. It cannot be gainsaid that life is tragic in fact.

The second evasion lies in the space between **RT**+ and –**RT** when there is an ambivalent state of mind that cannot bear the frustration of learning from experience, but which is not so intolerant as to deny or evacuate experience completely. This I am to call 'hubristic thinking'. In individual terms this is to be omniscient and omnipotent. In the context of an organization, or group, or social system in which individuals have roles it is hubris because this term connotes arrogance, or being in the place of the gods. So hubristic thinking, denoted as **HRT**, is evident when 'truth' is asserted without learning from experience what the truth might be.

Elsewhere I have developed ideas about the rise of the totalitarian state of mind in organizations (Lawrence 1995*a*; 1995*b*). There I argued that fears and anxieties about the unpredictable and chaotic environment could become so high in organizations that all the role incumbents, or the majority at least, colluded in excluding any thought that acknowledged uncertainty or fateful surprises. Such role holders could only make themselves available for thought and thinking which supports certainty. In such conditions the majority sanctions a form of leadership which is hubristic. Leaders are called upon to assert unequivocally what the 'truth' is, which is a lie, and to offer (and command) clear decisions that will lead to executive action. This action is fantasized as being sure and certain and, most important of all, capable of rescuing the organization from its fantasy of tragic, institutional death through failure, bankruptcy, and dissipation. Preferably these decisions have to be simple, such as downsizing or re-engineering. Arrogance in the face of death is called for in such leadership by, in fantasy, taking the place of the gods, that is, hubris.

RT+ is only possible if –**RT** has been experienced. **RT**+ is entered into through the experience of –**RT**. These are emotional states as well as intellectual ones and so have to be experienced at first hand. Human beings need to have the experience of being in –**RT** temporarily if they are to be in touch with their humanity because it is in the indulgence of –**RT** that they recapture the earlier stages of their development that provide some of the roots of creativity. To be in –**RT** is to be able to 'play'. Here, I am stating that –**RT** and **RT**+ are linked and that without the experience of the two people would be less than human. Essentially, –**RT** lies in the inner world of the individual, embedded in fantasies of tragedy, and is an attempt to control the often surprising outer world of other people and events. Furthermore, the –**RT** position is held on to because it supports good memories that are remembered in order to keep distasteful events in abeyance, which are associated with **RT**+.

This I can illustrate. Currently, I am consultant to a health system that belongs to a congregation of nuns. Because they could no longer service the work of the hospitals, due to declining numbers, they were advised to form a company for the hospitals. They did so. However, there is a small minority of sisters and a few older lay, medical consultants who were against this development. Some of them still have key roles in the hospitals as managers, or matrons, or consultants. There is much that is changed in the new company as the majority attempt to keep abreast of developments in the environment in terms of health care. The majority is very much aware of the necessity to generate income that will keep the group of hospitals in a sound financial position. This majority is sabotaged periodically by the minority referred to above. They, in the main, subscribe to –**RT**, which is based on their, now, idealized memory of what it was like in the past before the formation of the new company. In short, they hate the new reality that is being brought into being to accommodate to the changes in the environment. They wish to control in the way that they did in the past. They evince a propensity for splitting which is accompanied by a selection of evidence that supports their position and justifies their hatred of the new, emergent reality of the hospitals. At times, their behaviour has the characteristics of **HRT** causing a disruption of the +**RT** processes that are directed at continuing to bring the work of the health system into being. In reality the religious sisters are facing the ending of their congregation which they continue to deny. Thus they project on to the health system their fantasies of tragedy.

THE INHERITED MENTAL DISPOSITION OF MANAGERS

Mind is the guardian of memories that are routinely used to pre-structure experiences; not to allow experiences to be experienced at first hand; to leave them as unexamined happenings. These memories, together with desires and associated mental attitudes, can be clustered together to constitute a 'mental disposition'. The mental disposition is as much about ideas 'held in the mind' about management as it is about management as it is practised. The mental disposition is a cluster of habits of the mind which make sense to the individual. These habits of the mind are founded on their value for the intelligibility of the individual rather than their intelligibility in the light of the external world of reality. At times in history they will coincide or match to a considerable degree, but as reality changes or evolves, there is a lack of fit between the inherited mental disposition and the emerging reality of the external world.

My contention is that the mental disposition of managers during the time of industrial society is swamping their capacity for thinking in the emergent era of the information society. Managers, if you will, are full of memories of what it was like to manage in the past and of the desire to manage in the future as they did in the past.

The thinking that gave rise to industrialization has its roots in the scientific revolution and the Enlightenment. Because of the thrust of these two major intellectual forces, Europeans came to hold a mechanistic, Cartesian view of the world. The way of arriving at an understanding of the phenomena in the world was to reduce their complexity to its basic building blocks. The external world of physical reality came to be construed as being separate from the observer, was 'out there', and so was objective. Human beings were separate from nature; mind was separate from matter. Only thinking that was unequivocally rational was accepted in public discourse. Thinking which tried to take account of the subjectivity of individuals was despised, even reviled. Those who made their living by making use of technology had to divorce their minds from any thoughts that would question the nature of reality from a subjective perspective. Their overarching preoccupation was with order, rationality, and predictability. They pursued these ideals even though, on occasion, it resulted in a rational madness in the organization.

Industrialization was possible because of the invention of machines. The machine became the pre-eminent metaphor of the times and was used to explain both natural and social phenomena. The new owners of factories brought machines and human workers together under one roof. Their problem was the co-ordination and control of this new labour force. There had to be order. They did so by adopting Adam Smith's ideas on the division of labour and constructing the social organization of their factories on this principle. Smith claimed that the division of labour increased the manual dexterity of each worker, saved time, and, by substituting machines for workers, not only reduced the amount of labour required but also enabled one worker to do the work of many. The new trades that grew up in the process of industrialization resulted in older craft categories being subdivided. All this contributed to a speeding up of the production process. Furthermore, this subdivision of work tasks increased the standardization of quality control and so reduced the risk of error. Thus the ideal, as once expressed by Josiah Wedgwood, to 'make machines of men as cannot err' (quoted in Thompson 1963: 244–5) came to be realized.

The ideal of managing human beings as if they were machines was further developed and codified by F. W. Taylor in the USA. His theory came to be known as 'scientific management' (a term coined by a prosecuting lawyer). Taylor's goal was to increase the output of workers by applying scientific methods. He analysed all the tasks and functions of workers and timed how long they took in order to be able to devise more efficient methods. By selecting the best of workers and training them it was possible to organize work on a planned basis. This model of systematic analysis was soon to be applied to every other aspect of the industrial process. For this the thought processes that informed the professional skills of engineering and accountancy became highly valued in the industrial process and formed the bases on which the emergent science of management was developed.

The ideas that Taylor formulated lasted in different guises throughout the industrial age. They were driven by an overwhelming anxiety for order in the workplace. Managers in the industrial age had to hold the belief that they could control things, events, and people. The illusion was that everyone involved in any role in the industrial process was governed by rationality and working in a rational, predictable environment. Techniques and concepts such as management supported this by objectives, appraisals, and assessments, and the redesign of jobs that justified the work of the manager. These techniques and concepts provided the delusion of purpose.

THE NEW WORLD OF INFORMATION TECHNOLOGY

One fundamental difference between industrial society and the emergent information one is that the former dealt with and manipulated 'atoms' whereas the latter processes 'bits'. Atoms belong to the familiar, physical world of our everyday business reality; raw materials are manufactured as finished products and marketed. Management has been about controlling such atom-based businesses. A bit, on the other hand, 'has no colour, size or weight, and it can travel at the speed of light . . . It is a state of being: on or off, true of false, up or down, in or out, black or white' (Negroponte 1996 edn.: 14). To be sure, there will always be the use of both atoms and bits in business for the foreseeable future.

This new information age makes use of *acoustic* space through which the information in bits travels. Industrial society was grounded in *optical* space, at least till the discovery of radio waves. In that period of history we lived, more or less exclusively, in a bounded world of three dimensions. Now acoustic space is becoming as important as optical space ever was. What was in the realm of the imagination, say a hundred years ago, is now an identifiable reality which is known to exist. It is called 'cyberspace', but I prefer 'acoustic space' because this carries the meaning of a space in which thinking and thought are available to be listened for.

In that acoustic space, digital technology enables this thought to be communicated, most spectacularly through the World Wide Web of the Internet. Users have mental associations to these communications. These mental associations arise from the inner world or mind of the user and so these mental associations come to exist in acoustic space. They bring into being new associations and meanings to the phenomena that constitute optical space.

One other difference is that whereas industrial society was grounded in the metaphor of the machine governed by cause and effect, the new information society gives rise to associations between phenomena and events. Industrial society was a specific environment understood readily in terms of Euclidean space. Acoustic space is not so readily mapped and thoughts and thinking are not subject to the principles of cause and effect, despite the efforts of logic. We recognize now that the only material bonds between particles of being are a wide range of resonating associations. So in the information society we find ourselves increasingly in a mental environment in which we identify the resonating associations between events and phenomena through exploration. Such explorations go beyond the reaches of conscious awareness, as it is presently understood. We live now in a non-specific environment that demands the use of a wider gamut of mind—an enlarged consciousness—than did industrial society.

The information society engenders complexity and turbulence because thoughts and thinking are available in acoustic space and their resonance cannot be controlled. So there is the experience of information overload; of the inadequacy of the rules of causality; of surprising new links and connections that have never before been available. Because there are increasing numbers of users of IT in the business environment, what we are experiencing is an amplification of interdependencies between events and phenomena reported through bits that have to be processed ever more quickly than in the past. This can be summarized in the experience of 'globalization'.

With this speedier-than-ever connection between events in the environment there grows the sense that the world of work is complex and feels chaotic. It is no longer possible to subscribe to absolutes because the world is experienced as becoming relative, at least in popular imagination. The result is that the world of business is experienced as being disturbing or exciting, stressful, or challenging, depending on the mental disposition of the individual.

WORK AS THE 'CONTAINER' HYPOTHESIS

The emergent information society is in the process of subverting all that we believed about organization that had its foundation in the experience of industrial society. Industrial society evolved organizations that were postulated on the assumption that people had to be motivated and managed to execute work, with all its related tasks and activities. (We have developed a substantial body of managerial and organizational concepts with their related vocabulary to effect this execution.) Our experience of organization in industrial society has left us with the legacy of the idea that authority and leadership are focused at the 'top' of the organization. There, we have come to believe, is located the responsibility for managing the whole enterprise. This has been supported through the top management setting policies, the formulation of mission statements, and the establishment of goals and objectives to be attained, together with the exercise of delegation and accountability. These are all posited on the assumption that there are those who manage and those who are managed.

It is, therefore, not surprising that organization has come to be reified and come to be experienced as the 'container', with work as the 'contained'. Organization was, first, established to execute work. Organization preceded the work in the imagination. When businesses were put under pressure from competition by other, similar businesses, and it was found that the labour costs were too high, this was construed by the management of the time as an attack upon the 'container', and so they sought a final solution in an effort to save the organization as the container by trimming costs through getting rid of workers that were the biggest cost. In such circumstances one could see the operation of –**RT**, even, on occasion, of **HRT**. The work of the enterprise, what was 'contained', was never questioned for its validity in the context of the changing environment (Lawrence and Armstrong 1998). But then the legacy of industrial society is such that it is impossible to think about the issues except in the terms I have used.

In the information society this inheritance of the organization as the container and work as the contained is being subverted. This leads to the following hypothesis:

> As the information society continues to be brought into being we shall experience the transition from the accepted assumption that the organization is the 'container' with work as the 'contained' to one where work is the 'container' and the organization is the 'contained'.

The evidence that marks the beginnings of this shift comes from the computer industry. Now the greatest growth industry is the production, processing, and selling of software information. Much of the labour content of this work is carried out in acoustic space, as well as Euclidean space. The work is being brought into being across the boundaries of the enterprise in response to changing realities in the environment. Mind engages with mind across the frontiers of the company and expands the content of work through the process of mental association. Those who do this carry the risk factors of the business. The organization of the business has to follow the moves of the risk-taking workers who are engaging with the changing realities of the environment.

Another example is in university research. Research in universities is conducted globally on the Internet as researchers engage with the minds of others in the environment. This is a far cry from when the university and the head of department were the containers for the conduct of research. Now the researchers are the containers and the department is becoming the contained.

AN EMERGING MENTAL DISPOSITION FOR MANAGERS

The transition from industrial to the information society is generating multiple and multivarious difficulties at an increasing rate. Business is now being conducted in what appears to be absolute uncertainty. James Joyce, writing in the earlier part of this century, anticipated the metaphor of living at the end of the twentieth century when he wrote in *Finnegans Wake*:

every person, place and thing in the chaosmos of Alle anyway connected with the gobblydumped turkery was moving and changing every part of the time, the travelling inkhorn (possibly pot), the hare and turtle pen and paper, the continually more and less intermisunderstanding minds of the anticollaborators, the as time went on as it will variously inflected, differently pronounced, otherwise spelled, changeably meaning vocable scriptsigns (Joyce 1992 edn.: 118.)

IT is just that: 'changeably meaning vocable scriptsigns' contained in electronic pulses, bits, communicating through thought and thinking; 'the travelling inkhorn (possibly pot)'—is that the PC?; 'the hare and turtle pen and paper' of snail mail is now e-mail. They all exist in the 'as time', which goes on 'as it will', and often are used by 'intermisunderstanding minds'!

Now IT is exploding through its own momentum to create global financial markets, global production processes, the global, cultural bazaar, and the global shopping mall. What I perceive as happening is that the taken-for-granted structures that, with modification, have sustained us since the Industrial Revolution are now dissipating. We are witnessing the demise of old structures of organization as they increasingly become redundant. Now we see that politicians are less able to direct their country's destiny in the face of fateful circumstances operating internationally. Billions of pounds can be written off a nation's reserves, for instance, as a result of a 'Black' Monday or Wednesday if a currency speculator like George Soros so organizes it. A futures trader can ruin Barings Bank in London while operating from Singapore. National economies always run the risk of meltdown, as demonstrated in the serious problems facing the so-called tiger economies of the Pacific Rim. In short, we exist in societies in the process of transforming, that are producing chaos-inducing experiences that bring about the 'abnihilisation', to use another Joycean term, of much that was cherished in the past. We live in a world in which nothing is certain but uncertainty.

The combination of interacting factors at the end of the millennium makes for a difficult life for the manager. Hospitals and health care systems have to provide medical care with ever-scarcer resources from governments and insurers. Educational institutions are under pressure to be economically viable. Commercial companies have to trade in national, international, and pan-national markets.

The patterns of experiences that these new circumstances are throwing up bypass the traditional concepts of management. We now live in a world that is non-manageable in the accepted sense. We now have to use percepts and intuitions to capture the changing reality. Interacting events create environments that have no precedents in previous experience.

What is now required of managers is that they have to be sensitive to what is going on in the environment. What is going on is not what managers planned to happen. What is going on does not belong to their inherited logic and conceptualizations. Anita Roddick, who founded Body Shop, intuited what was going on in the environment and pursued her ideals accordingly. The result was that conventional suppliers of body care products had to rethink their market position radically. She eschewed the current techniques of management and was able to use her intelligence to see what no other manager could see. She experienced her environment using her feelings, perceptions, and intelligence to bring a new market into being that had never existed before. And she continues to do so today in the way she manages her chain of shops through the values she espouses.

THE NEW WORK OF MANAGEMENT

The work of management, I have argued, is changing radically. Management is now the work of experiencing as directly as possible the business as a series of events in its environment. The corollary of this is that managers can do this if they make themselves available as 'participating' instruments for experiencing their experience, otherwise they cannot make insights or intuitions, and have new percepts. Reality has to be experienced at first hand. It cannot be left to remain 'out there'.

Essentially management in the late twentieth century, when the information society is rapidly being brought into being, is working with outdated concepts. These concepts and principles were formed in the time of industrial society. Now in the information society we are operating in a non-specific environment in which surprise is the norm rather than the exception. Modes of management are now in the process of being postulated on different assumptions than in the past. It is this kind of thinking which leads to understanding work as being the container and the institution or organization as being the contained. This reformulation will take some time to realize for there will be those who cherish the institutions of the past. What is happening is that the traditional, inherited concepts and principles of management, with all their associated paraphernalia of managerial discourse, are redundant in the light of the emerging circumstances of the information society that is demanding new ways of understanding organizations that we cannot as yet imagine, or dream of.

4

Systems Psychodynamics in the Service of Political Organizational Change

Jean E. Neumann

Comprehensive organizational changes normally touch employees' emotional and political concerns. Employees who lead and implement such changes cope with challenges to their interests by engaging in political activities. Typically, they enact psychological dynamics in the service of overt and covert aims. These dynamics, inherent in social systems change, can be both functional and dysfunctional. However, in particularly messy and confusing situations, psychological dynamics may be so severe that valid political concerns cannot be addressed effectively.

POLITICAL ORGANIZATIONAL CHANGE

Comprehensive changes evoke strong political and psychological dynamics because so many aspects of organization are implicated. Such changes involve multiple, simultaneous, and sequential initiatives. Aiming for increased performance, executives usually target alterations to work organization, asserting new norms for behaviour and thought. They anticipate or react to technological and economic changes that create requirements or possibilities for different approaches to work. The language and character of such developments follow trends particular to a period and sector.

At the time of writing, several illustrations readily can be offered. Many UK public enterprises and government offices have been carved into smaller units called 'trusts' and 'agencies', with income-generating demands and alterations in how they purchase and supply services. Deregulation of markets and the availability of sophisticated information technology motivate financial services firms to shrink their work-force, redefine 'front office' and 'back office' jobs, decrease or increase the products they offer, and 'subcontract' with brokers and agents. Globalization of shipping and privatization of railways result in 'outsourcing' maintenance jobs and replacing full-time employees with those on temporary 'contracts'.

Manufacturing research suggests that such fundamental organizational changes require several, interconnected systems to be aligned (Neumann, Holti, and Standing 1995). In moving from individual jobs to group working, for example, five aspects of organization must be altered:

- business and organizational strategy;
- work design and related training developments;
- quality, manufacturing, and engineering systems;
- business planning and accounting systems;
- industrial relations and personnel practices (ibid.: 15).

Significant changes to one organizational aspect always affect others. It is this quality of interconnection which makes comprehensive organizational change so political. Changes acceptable to those people concerned with one aspect of organization may challenge the interests of people who are concerned with another aspect.

For example, a typical change to business and organizational strategy would cancel one product and introduce another. The implicated departments might need to be restructured and the annual bonus minimized in favour of an extensive advertising campaign. Changes to work design, possibly due to computerized technology, might eliminate less-skilled jobs and lead to the promoting and training of workers for élite positions. Payment systems, including grading structures, might need to be altered to reward the new work. Indeed, changes in operational systems frequently cannot be made due to limitations from existing working practices and employee competence. Business planning and accounting systems commonly follow on from changes to strategy and operating systems, although strategic changes can be driven by new ways to measure company and sub-unit performance.

Employees (including executives and managers) view such changes through the filter of their own emotional and political concerns. They can be negatively affected by being made redundant or having their unit dissolved or they might benefit positively through promotion, more satisfying work, or higher pay. Usually, comprehensive organizational changes have an impact on different groups in different ways, thus fuelling political activity.

> Proposition One: During confusing and messy comprehensive organizational change, employees will express overt political goals related to those particular changes in an organizational system that concern them.

Organizational leaders often have goals in mind while lacking clear directions for the many detailed alterations necessary to achieve their 'vision'. State-of-the-art methods for organizational development and change involve employees in extensive planning and implementation (e.g. Bunker and Alban 1996; Bushe and Shani 1991; Mohrman and Cummings 1989). Thus, uncertainty of direction can combine with participative methods of change to create at the same time both anxiety and mechanisms for political activity.

POLITICS AS NECESSARY TO ORGANIZATIONAL CHANGE

Political activities include debating, negotiating, or taking some other action. During comprehensive organizational change, political actors attempt to achieve a set of ideas, principles, and commitments relevant to organizational structures and processes. Political changes are those that affect deeply held beliefs, especially those related to authority, status, power, and resources.

Miles defines organizational politics as: 'the processes whereby differentiated but interdependent individuals or interest groups exercise whatever power they can amass to influence goals, criteria, or processes used in organizational decision making to advance their own interests' (R. H. Miles 1980: 154). Periods of transition tend to be periods of intensive politics since so many aspects of organization are under consideration. Politically oriented employees intentionally adopt means for carrying out a plan or achieving ends.

'Political' behaviour, however, usually carries the connotation of being illegitimate, especially for people who are not in the dominant coalition. Therefore people will use tactics which tend to be unobtrusive or to be seemingly legitimate, as, for example with the selective use of objective criteria, the use of legitimate decision procedures, and secrecy (Pfeffer 1977: 241). Employees argue for decision-making criteria that reflect their interests and against criteria that do not. They use existing decision-making mechanisms to debate, negotiate, or take some other action. During comprehensive change, additional committees and task forces create more opportunities to influence outcomes. Those political actors who have access to information may withhold or selectively release information as a power tactic.

> Proposition Two: During comprehensive organizational change, employees will use conscious political tactics designed to communicate their cooperation while, simultaneously, working towards the achievement of covert goals.

Part of the purpose of using particular tactics is to create 'the impression that both the decision-making process and outcome are congruent with objective, universalistic standards' (R. H. Miles 1980: 162). Overt co-operation during changes is often supplemented with covert activities designed to achieve goals that might not be considered acceptable to the 'dominant coalition' (March 1962). Typically, covert goals have to do with retaining or increasing sub-unit differentiation and power and with retaining or increasing the status and rewards of individuals or groups (R. H. Miles 1980: 157–8).

BUILDING BLOCKS OF SYSTEMS PSYCHODYNAMICS

During political organizational changes, employees have to cope with uncomfortable situations and disturbing possibilities. They feel upset about a particular change, feel threatened by a known or possible outcome, and find participative decision-making meetings with bosses awkward and difficult. Employees often deal with their feelings and thoughts by moving closer to those people with whom they have something in common and by distancing themselves from those with whom they disagree. Also, they tend to hold certain positions and opinions related to the change programme, colluding with others to take up complementary positions and opinions.

These behaviours, less conscious than political goals and tactics, are motivated by forces usefully understood as psychological dynamics. Employees engaging in political activities during organizational change tend to do so in groups or on behalf of groups or sub-units. These motivational forces, therefore, operate in collectives, that is: pairs, groups, between groups, and at the level of the organization as whole. A term used to refer to collective psychological behaviour is 'systems psychodynamics'.

The word 'psychodynamics' is borrowed from individual psychology where it is used to describe the energizing or motivating forces resulting from the interconnection between various parts of the individual's personality or character structure. 'System', in this conceptual framework, draws attention to the connected parts of a complex organizational whole. Systems psychodynamics, therefore, provides a way of thinking about the energizing or motivating forces resulting from the interconnection between various groups and sub-units of a social system (E. J. Miller and Rice 1967; Trist and Murray 1990).

In organizations, the concept of a 'boundary' can include territorial differentiation as well as other ways of marking the inside and outside of a group or sub-unit of the larger system, such as time and task (E. J. Miller 1959). Being able to draw a metaphorical boundary around employee groups by shift, grade, or hierarchical level, gender or racial identity, and occupational identity (L. D. Brown 1983) can be important. Boundaries matter because it is across these literal and sentient lines that emotions, opinions, perceptions, and fantasies travel.

During political organizational change, employees move closer in to whichever group identity feels most relevant for the outcome they desire. From inside a particular group, they react 'backstage' to what is going on, evaluate the change initiatives that affect them collectively, plot their 'frontstage' political tactics, and assess the effectiveness of enacted tactics (Goffman 1959). They interact with other groups and sub-units politically, supported by a few basic psychological mechanisms. Three such mechanisms—projection, introjection, and dissociation—can be understood as building blocks for the dynamics described below.

Proposition Three: During comprehensive organizational change, employees will unconsciously use systems psychodynamics as a useful and powerful element of their political tactics.

In individual development, introjection and projection have been identified as 'some of the earliest activities of the ego' (Klein 1959: 8). Miller and Rice state that 'the ego is the equivalent of the boundary control region that mediates between the inner world and the environment' (1967: 16). Much research into group and intergroup behaviour demonstrates that these psychological mechanisms can operate collectively as well (see, for example, L. D. Brown 1983; Kreeger 1975; Rice 1969).

Introjection is the unconscious incorporation of external ideas and feelings into an individual's mind or the group's way of thinking. Instead of experiencing the outer world as external, the individual or group takes it into the self or group as a part of their inner life (Klein 1959: 8). During comprehensive organizational change, a group or sub-unit will enact introjection when ideas and emotions held by organizational leaders or outside reference groups are accepted mindlessly. Introjection can help minimize lengthy debates and resistance, assist employees to tolerate slow implementation, and encourage them to learn new roles. However, introjection can also create difficulties, for example when directors announce a policy from headquarters without customizing it for the local site, or when employee representatives resist plans for change based solely on inconvenience to their occupational group.

Projection is the unconscious transfer of one's own or a group's impressions and feelings to external objects or persons. This capacity to attribute certain mental contents from one person or group on to another can alter the behaviour of the person or group (Horwitz 1985: 21). Termed 'projective identification', this dynamic involves projection from Group A to Group B, to which Group B responds by undergoing introjection or 'identification or fusion with the projected content and its unconscious meanings and thus [having] the experience of being manipulated into a particular role' (ibid.: 23).

Projection and projective identification can, like introjection, be helpful dynamics. Uncomfortable, even intolerable thoughts and feelings, such as fear of redundancy or of organizational violence or destruction, can be projected on to another group, thus releasing feelings of co-operation in the unburdened group. Similarly, it is not unusual for employees to project knowledge about a clear, confident outcome on to organizational leaders, thus making actual uncertainty tolerable.

During especially difficult change programmes, however, it is the negative aspects of projection that preoccupy change managers. Some employee groups become stuck in an ineffective position, seemingly unable to move forward regardless of efforts to address their political concerns. Environmental figures, such as consultants or executives from headquarters, become figures of hate and untrustworthiness; ideas offered by them are rejected automatically.

Thus, projection can be joined with dissociation. At its mildest, a group denies the possibility of a particular outcome even though it is blatantly going to happen. Under the stress of fundamental change, employees may engage in mild dissociation by denying the connection of particular facts to themselves. Once a group or individual is caught up in a serious dissociative state, however, it can be difficult to know what to do.

In an individual, a serious dissociative state may indicate that 'a certain function of the mind becomes isolated from the remainder of an individual's experience' (Reichard, Siewers, and Rodenhauser 1992: 49). A group isolated during a change can become seriously dissociative. Czander describes this state as 'gross psychological distortion . . . a specific breakdown in perceptual and/or sensory/motor behaviour' apparent in a group that has been 'robbed of its defences' (1993: 224). Change programmes that remain stuck for a year or more often have a significant actor or powerful group dissociated from participating in the reality of a changing organization.

Roles for change managers

These three psychological mechanisms—introjection, projection, and dissociation—contribute to a group's ability to use systems psychodynamics in the service of political aims. Other individual and group defences may be used as well. These techniques seem especially powerful when combined with political action during comprehensive change. Because of their power, they frustrate even the best change managers.

> Proposition Four: During political organizational change, change managers need to take up roles that both contain uncomfortable and disturbing emotions and also address effectively the content of political disagreement.

Managers need to use mechanisms for negotiating political decisions during comprehensive change. Management team meetings and collective bargaining procedures may exist already for appropriate use. However, only a few people are authorized to participate in them. Change managers usually offer other meetings and forums for consultation and involvement. Although such mechanisms provide legitimate means for working through political disagreements, they also can play an important function in addressing emotional concerns.

The psychodynamic concept of 'containment' suggests a core task for change managers and consultants (Winnicott 1958). Containment means 'treating emotional problems by non-interference, by the provision of a holding environment in which "natural" growth processes could reassert themselves' (Phillips 1988: 98). In other words, change managers need to accept employees' emotional reactions to fundamental changes, understanding that time and space need to be provided for employees to work through these reactions. Expressing negative feelings towards executives, change managers, and consultants is often an initial stage in such a process, followed by similar reactions towards other groups.

Many change managers find it difficult to supply a 'holding environment'. They expect to take a political role in a decision-making meeting or to facilitate a change process. They feel unprepared to provide the non-anxious presence necessary for allowing employees to work through emotions. Investment in outcomes and in a particular change process makes non-interference difficult.

Indeed, change managers can exacerbate psychological dynamics by failing to establish effective mechanisms that are necessary for resolving political differences. In order to avoid strong emotional expression, they cancel collective meetings. Presenting their concerns as objective and universal, they criticize the so-called private agendas of other groups. Such actions prevent a more effective working through of controversial decisions and emotional disturbances.

Basis of case descriptions

Five cases are described below and briefly analysed according to the descriptive framework reviewed above. Those aspects of organization implicated in comprehensive change are identified, along with the overt political goals employees express. The political tactic used is noted, along with an indication of the covert goal that emerged over time. The building blocks of systems psychodynamics are identified, along with other individual and group defence mechanisms that might be operational. Finally, the role of the change managers and consultants is indicated.

Access to the sites came from working as paid consultants an average of four days each month, for a period of not less than eighteen months nor more than five years. Although the most senior manager paid the fee, explicit and written contracts made it possible and desirable for work to be undertaken with all levels of hierarchy, most sub-units, and most groups.

Data were recorded using qualitative sociological and anthropological methods (see, for example, Glaser and Strauss 1979). Notes were made on each site visit, with observations being kept separate from interpretations. Field notes from the ten organizations were scanned for incidents in which systems psychodynamics blocked resolution of political change issues. Each selected incident was studied by carefully reviewing related field notes. As the conceptual framework was developed, a descriptive analysis in the form of a case scenario was written for selected incidents (M. B. Miles and Huberman 1984). Five are offered here.

Routine irresolution

When hesitancy about taking necessary decisions becomes repeated, then the systems psychodynamic of routine irresolution is being enacted. Such inability to take a decision can be identified as a dynamic precisely because the political actors normally do not prevaricate. However, during comprehensive organizational change, one issue stands out routinely as irresolvable. Routine irresolution can help slow down some decisions until interconnected ones are addressed or until difficult issues are worked through. More often, however, this dynamic damages trust between organizational leaders and implicated employees, thus hindering progress.

The pensionless operators

A group of European paper companies emphasizes positive treatment of employees. The Group Board decide to evaluate human resources management (HRM) in all companies. A consultant advises a participative evaluation process. Early on, a problem emerges in one of the smaller companies: twenty older shop-floor employees do not have company pensions, whereas all other employees do. When the consultant raises the issue with the Board, they explain that each company is a profit centre: once the smaller company is more profitable, it can buy pensions for the twenty. The fact that the other 6,000 employees have pensions is treated as irrelevant.

During its evaluation, the smaller company lists pensions as an HRM priority. The company's director proposes that this issue could be resolved with a small grant from the Board, who are offering money for special HRM projects. The Board refuse to buy company pensions for the twenty, however, fearing that the profit centre concept would become meaningless. They convince the directors that to accept a grant would violate their autonomy.

A year later, a joint meeting between directors and the Board reviews progress and plans for ongoing HRM development. The twenty pensionless operators are discussed. The directors believe that the integrity of the HRM programme is undermined by the symbolic lack of caring demonstrated by the Board. The Board offer the same debate, now routine, and the directors give up.

Over the next two years, the consultant confronts the Board three times about the issue. They agree that the situation seems irrational, but they cannot manage to decide otherwise. However, once the Chairman retires, the others give the operators their pensions. The decision took five years.

The case of the pensionless operators illustrates how routine irresolution was used in a political debate about how to fund Group-wide projects within five companies. The Board and directors fought passively about profit centres during legitimate decision-making meetings. They argued the validity of different criteria for evaluating HRM. Concern for people was projected on to the pensionless operators who symbolized this strategic tension, as did, of course, the consultant. Both the directors and the Board dissociated themselves from direct concern for the operators—as people and not as a symbol—compartmentalizing their heads for business from their concerns with people.

Routine irresolution allowed the Board to avoid their anxiety about the uncertain outcomes of relaxing the profit centre strategy. The directors took advantage of the Board's HRM project to request funds to support extra costs. Covertly, the directors challenged the need for any common policies, symbolically HRM, in a profit centre structure. The Board insisted on retaining the right to take final decisions 'for the good of the Group'.

Intergroup split

Intergroup splits occur when two or more groups break into parts which hold complementary or necessary elements of a change-related debate. The quality of dialogue degenerates as the groups involved become increasingly hostile and/or increasingly disconnected from the other side of the debate. Typically, each group becomes convinced that it is as good as or better than the other on some dimensions; an attitude that can also turn into a belief that the other group is bad or worse in some way. Such differentiation, especially during comprehensive changes in which new boundaries are drawn around subunits, can be helpful in forming the identity and focus of a group. However, a more common result is a 'tendency . . . to split good from bad in themselves and to project their resultant feelings onto others', leading to 'major barriers to the understanding and control of the relationships between human resources and the tasks to which they contribute' (E. J. Miller and Rice 1967: 16).

The editorial versus commercial departments

Subscriptions to a small, niche market magazine grow rapidly. The magazine emphasizes high quality of life, particularly positive interpersonal relationships. The owner-editor feels upset, therefore, by an emerging tension between employees who edit the magazine and those who sell advertising. Her attempts to organize both departments for planning for growth fail, so she hires a consultant.

Diagnostic interviews with all employees indicate that tension has moved into hostility. The editorial employees are convinced that the Commercial employees do not care about editorial quality: 'Commercial care about bureaucracy and making money, they are turning into dress-for-success, business types'. The Commercial employees are equally unimpressed with developments in editing: 'They have their heads stuck in the sand' and are trying to hold the magazine back by 'appealing to hippies and drop-outs'; they are seen as refusing to accept ideas from Commercial for articles and behaving in 'arrogant and elitist ways'.

This interdepartmental hostility results in a growing disparity between the types of article published and the types of advertisement included. Initially, two inter-group meetings are held to address the breakdown in relationships, with a view to then involving everyone in thinking about the future. As a result, employees improve some interdepartmental communications and procedures.

It becomes apparent that a larger magazine means internal restructuring as well as better co-ordination across sub-unit boundaries. Each department appoints an assistant manager and divides other aspects of work. The departmental managers take on more strategic tasks along with a new managing editor and a financial con-troller. This organizational strategy allows the owner-editor to decrease her involve-ment in daily operations. A new weekly meeting schedule contributes to appropriate differentials between Editorial and Commercial while minimizing dysfunctional splits.

In this case, an intergroup split was enacting a number of unacknowledged issues related to the magazine's success. Both departments actively projected their ambivalence about rapid growth on to each other. The owner-editor dis-sociated herself from 'their conflict' by naming the problem an interpersonal issue, even though organizational strategy and operational systems were impli-cated. The main political tactic was the secrecy of 'backstage' complaining and withholding of cross-departmental information. Once disclosed, information held within each sub-unit eventually contributed to workable solutions.

Division of emotional labour

The division of emotional labour is enacted when different groups take on and/or are given different parts of the emotional and positional workload nec-essary to a change programme. The division of labour may be permanent, wherein a group, department, or other sub-unit specializes in one psychological stance, ideological opinion, and/or direction for a change initiative. Altern-atively, there may be some rotation of division of labour, wherein individuals, groups, and sub-units take on certain attitudes or roles at different stages of the change programme. Resistance *versus* co-operation and being a scapegoat *versus* being a champion are typically attitudes and roles that are divided up dur-ing comprehensive change. This psychodynamic can be helpful as some pro-portion of the organizational membership devotes itself to progress. However, many a change programme has been derailed by resistant employees whose co-operation and good will are incompatible with their given role.

The craftsmen's resistance

The UK chemicals manufacturing site of a USA multinational expands from one facility and product to two. Into the new facility, the USA headquarters introduces 'semi-autonomous work groups' for operators who are paid more for working without supervisors. The introduction, assisted by a consultant, goes so well that the UK management team decides all shop-floor workers should work in teams. Operators in the original plant express enthusiasm for learning more skills and earning more money.

The craftsmen, mechanical engineers, and electrical engineers are not pleased. They feel threatened by the potential loss of their wage differentials and specialized skills. The new operators make almost as much as the craftsmen's entry salary, and managers speak of operators doing some routine, low-skill, maintenance tasks. Craftsmen assigned to the new plant resent being given breakdown work by operators, insisting on taking instruction only from a senior engineer or a supervisor from the old plant.

Two years on, the management team establishes participative planning and implementation committees for work and payment design. The craftsmen complain that they have not agreed to work in teams. The operator-dominated trade union wants to speed things up and not wait for the craftsmen to make up their minds. The craftsmen vote to send representatives to the committees in order to protect their differential and skills.

Every time significant progress is made, the craftsmen walk out of the committee because their differentials have not been guaranteed. The managing director and personnel manager meet with the craftsmen's trade union and propose solutions which are voted down repeatedly. Engineering senior managers, who fear losing control over maintenance and the power that comes with many subordinates, stir up resistance in their employees. The operators in the new plant taunt the craftsmen and try to negotiate more money for themselves in secret.

The craftsmen's resistance continues for three years. Once all the operators are working in groups and gaining additional pay for multiple skills, the craftsmen express interest. This happens shortly after the management team comes up with a new organizational strategy that reassigns the most negative senior engineers to technical specialist positions.

The craftsmen were not the only employees at the UK site who were suspicious and scared about the US idea of 'teamwork'. The division of emotional labour, however, meant that they identified with others' projected negativity and got stuck while the operators benefited from making progress. Their resistance to changing industrial relations and personnel practices to be in line with new work designs and related training developments meant that others would dissociate from them and focus on furthering their interests. The management team, mostly manufacturing and not 'engineering men', were happy to leave the 'arrogant bastards out to dry'—something that was blatantly impossible and undesirable for successful 'teamwork'.

Change missionary

When caught up in a change missionary dynamic, organizational leaders manage and facilitate changes with evangelical zeal. Dogmatic comprehensive change is composed of principles basic to its particular school of thought related to both processes and outcomes of change. These must be adhered to rigidly. The change missionary dynamic can take different forms, such as when consultants or change managers over-identify with one group or sub-unit in the organization, thus representing their concerns as central to the change processes; alternatively, external consultants bond with executives and senior change 'champions', thus forming a formidable pair who see it as their job to convert others to their beliefs.

The 'stake-in-the-ground' consultants

A European site of a USA health care manufacturer struggles to compete with sister factories within the same corporation. European labour costs are high compared to those of Mexican and Korean sites. The director, protecting the survival of 'his site', seeks 'to get more productivity at less cost immediately'. He hires change consultants to redesign jobs and pay by working with a labour-management committee. In a few months, he suspects the change consultants of not being serious about cutting his labour costs. He hires engineering consultants.

The engineering consultants specialize in a particular school of shop-floor layout and materials handling. Secretly, they work with the director and come up with a plan. Going public together, they convene a series of 'new direction' meetings. At these meetings, the engineering consultants describe how they work: 'We put a firm stake-in-the-ground and then move the organization to it, and then put another stake-in-the-ground and move—it is very simple.' The director indicates his pleasure with this approach by stating that 'his consultants will take over' the labour-management committee and 'make change happen'. He says to the change consultants, 'Either you guarantee that I won't have a higher wage bill or you are against us'. They resign.

Resistance to the 'stake-in-the-ground' consultants is strong and persistent. However, the director gives support and authority to the engineering consultants. He routinely speaks 'backstage' to resistant managers and 'lends his presence' at meetings in which there is trouble with progress. It takes much longer than they had planned, but eighteen months later, they announce a first round of redundancies and introduce the new shop-floor layout with fewer employees.

In this case, change missionaries took over both the approach to and content of a fundamental organizational change. All three political tactics were mobilized, although secrecy and 'backstage chats' played a significant part. Almost all organizational systems were implicated. The change agent pair—the engineering consultants and the director—dissociated themselves from approaches to change without outcomes known in advance. They projected 'enemy of site survival' on to the change consultants, and on to the trade union representatives who expressed fears that the main goal was to decrease staff. All the directors and managers learned to introject some elements of the 'stake-in-the-ground' approach or lose their jobs.

Hidden or displaced agenda

A hidden or displaced agenda is one of the more difficult systems psycho-dynamics to diagnose precisely because of the often invisible link between that which is observable and its antecedent. In a displaced agenda, an issue that is being avoided within one sub-unit or group gets shifted from the place in which it needs to be addressed to another, somehow related, sub-unit or group. For example, suppressed conflict at senior management level often emerges in con-flict at lower status levels. With a hidden agenda, something is put or kept out of sight, probably as a political tactic. This hidden something bothers those groups or sub-units trying to address comprehensive change issues. This dynamic may be functional for a short period: for example, withholding information or deflecting attention until a suitable opportunity can be provided to work through reactions. However, hidden or displaced agendas tend to block progress by increasing distrust that cannot be addressed directly.

The retiring owner's share value

A construction management firm expands from three founders to 300 employees in five years. Projects necessary to finance the business get larger and more challeng-ing. Although the founders have the competence necessary to attract these lucrative contracts, they simply do not have the capacity. Some senior staff can negotiate their firm's responsibility to design and build large buildings; but they tend to be assigned for two to three years to manage these projects once awarded.

To solve this dilemma the founders try several different organizational and finan-cial structures to motivate senior staff. They pay higher than average salaries and reward top performers with promotion and status. They convene special problem-solving and strategic planning meetings with those middle and senior managers whom they have identified as 'worth developing'.

Pressures to enlarge the business mean that pressures to solve these problems increase. Nevertheless, the various structures and rewards do not seem to help. Over a two-year period, half of the more senior managers leave the company.

A consultant, brought in to address the problem, interviews thirty top managers who express serious concerns and doubts. They feel that the business is growing out of control, and that too many new employees are being hired who do not share the company ethos. Money needs to be invested in developing an organization to sup-port the business at its existing level. A few suggest that the pressure comes from a hidden agenda—one of the founders 'wants to retire wealthy'.

When asked by the consultant about this, the founders confirm its truth. The founders convene an emergency, strategic meeting with a handful of the most trusted senior managers. They agree more realistic financial targets, release money for internal investment, and decide to institute an employee share ownership scheme. These decisions are used to initiate another series of problem-solving and planning meetings more broadly.

In this case, a displaced or hidden agenda motivated rapid and continuous growth. Conflict about strategic direction, operating systems to handle growth, and related financial targets emerged through legitimate decision procedures. However, the political tactics of secrecy and debates about growth *versus* internal development were aided by psychological mechanisms. The owners projected their desire for growth on to senior managers, dissociating themselves from human resources concerns. The senior managers introjected the goal of growth for several years, but began to resent the pressures.

The founders overtly needed their 'top guys' to take over their business as they aged. However, they were ambivalent about sharing the wealth in general and, more particularly, in investing in a business that would go on without them. They enacted this ambivalence by projecting irresponsibility on to their senior employees and establishing unrealistic financial targets. For their part, the senior employees did not want yet more responsibility without greater reward. They allowed developments with which they did not agree, telling themselves that they were young and highly marketable. They were ambivalent about staying in such a demanding firm.

DISCUSSION AND CONCLUSION

Systems psychodynamics do not exist disembodied from the people in the social systems enacting them. Psychodynamics are always psychodynamics of something and someone. The people involved in these cases are in particular roles within sub-units or groups, with particular identities that contribute to their attitudes, concerns, and political interests. Their emotional and political concerns result from comprehensive changes initiated by their executives and change managers.

> During confusing and messy comprehensive organizational change, employees will express overt political goals related to those particular changes in an organizational system that concern them.

Indeed, these five cases demonstrate that overt political goals provide a baseline from which the confusion and messiness begin. Each group in the scenario could express its overt political goal. On the surface, however, the seeming incompatibility of the goals led to increased concerns and escalating difficulties. In some cases, the incompatibility was about the actual change decision itself (for example, the rate and nature of growth in the magazine and in the construction management firm), and how that decision affected aspects of organization closest to the implicated group. In other cases, the sticking points seemed to be the processes of change and the conditions—particularly money and status—under which people co-operate (job and payment design in the chemicals plant, funding for Group-wide projects in the paper companies).

> During comprehensive organization change, employees will use conscious political tactics designed to communicate their co-operation while, simultaneously, working towards the achievement of covert goals.

The cases described and briefly analysed here show that overt co-operation is not always the chosen political tactic. In four cases, some groups argued over criteria and participated in legitimate decision-making meetings to make their points (the directors in the paper company, the department managers in the magazine, the operators in the chemicals plant, and the trade union in the health care manufacturer). But other groups chose secrecy, withdrawal from legitimate meetings, or passive aggressive behaviour (the health care products director and his engineering consultants, the craftsmen in the chemicals plant, and junior staff at the magazine). Further, it appears that work is not always undertaken towards covert goals (for example, the senior staff at the construction management firm, who did not attempt to achieve greater reward for more responsibility).

> During comprehensive organizational change, employees will unconsciously use systems psychodynamics as a useful and powerful element of their political tactics.

Interestingly, it *is* possible to identify the psychodynamics being used by the main groups acting in each case. Such a detailed analysis requires more space than is available here, but it is possible to note that elements of all three building blocks appear in all cases. Projection played an essential role for everyone on all sides of a political issue even when it was not overt (the change consultants projected their frustration with participative methodologies on to the health care director, the paper companies' directors projected their need for autonomy on to the Board, senior staff in the construction management firm projected their ambivalence about taking over on to the founders). In these particular cases, introjection seems to have been enacted with dissociation to remove selected groups or issues from the change project (the craftsmen, the owner-editor, the pension-less operators, the change consultants, and the retiring founder).

> During political organizational change, change managers need to take up roles that both contain uncomfortable and disturbing emotions and also address effectively the content of political disagreement.

Most of the change managers in these cases experienced difficulty in combining the tasks of 'containment' with political decision making. They tended to run meetings as if only their political concerns were legitimate (for example, the 'new direction' meetings in the health care manufacturer, the editorial meetings at the magazine, the planning for growth meetings at the construction management firm). Consultants tended to be brought in to provide emotional containment (as with the diagnostic interviews at the magazine and the construction management firm) or to hold the concern for emotions (such as with the pension-less operators, the craftsmen, and the health care manufacturing shop-floor). In three cases resolution of disturbing emotions seemed to come only when managers' anxieties were soothed over time (the Board took five years to give the operators a pension, the craftsmen got their guarantee after all operators worked in teams, the health care products trade union's concerns were ignored until the new shop-floor layout and materials handling system was operational). In the other two cases, managers allowed organizational development methods to be used to work on emotional and political concerns sequentially (the intergroup meetings at the magazine, an emergency meeting in the construction management firm).

Understanding and accepting that employees enact systems psychodynamics in the service of overt and covert political objectives can help managers and consultants cope. Planning and implementing particularly challenging changes always evokes political actions and related systems psychodynamics. It is a mistake to treat such situations as only political or only psychodynamic. Persistent, messy, and confusing change initiatives require appropriate attention to both dimensions.

Change managers often squash political activity as a way to stop severe psychological dynamics. They intend to control messy, often conflictual behaviours through such action. By denying employees a satisfactory solution to political concerns, however, managers force dynamics underground. Such 'get tough' behaviour usually backfires in comprehensive organizational change.

Even when whole groups are 'outsourced' or whole departments dissolved, the unacceptable feelings and thoughts go underground and disrupt or minimize further developments. The resistance moves from the targeted group to another, or one change initiative goes smoothly while another, seemingly straightforward issue defies resolution. As these cases illustrate, many a change programme faces expensive delays in implementation precisely from unresolved emotional and political concerns.

Managers and consultants need to provide containment for the systems psychodynamics, while providing effective mechanisms for controversial decision making. During comprehensive organizational change, these are two related but separate concerns. Containment is not the same as resolving political concerns, although containment can be a result of doing so. However, political concerns that require decisions cannot be addressed through containment alone.

5

A Political Visionary in Mid-Life: Notes on leadership and the life cycle

Laurence J. Gould

INTRODUCTION

A substantial body of contemporary work now exists about adult development. Much of this work began in earnest with the publication of a number of books which attempted to conceptualize the adult life course from a psycho-dynamic/psychoanalytic perspective. Notably these were: Levinson and his co-workers' major study (1978), R. Gould (1978), and Valliant (1977). These volumes significantly carried forward several prominent earlier enquiries regarding the stages of life by Erikson (1959), Jung (1971), and Jaques (1965). Although this body of theory and research, together with a large body of subsequent work, has con-tributed a great deal to an understanding of the many aspects of a person's life as it unfolds, it has not specifically focused on the relationship between adult development and the nature of leadership. The purpose of this chapter, there-fore, is to provide an initial outline for the integration of adult developmental theory with psychoanalytic and open systems perspectives on leadership—drawing particularly on the works of Freud (e.g. 1921), Klein's object relations perspective (e.g. 1928, 1935, 1940, 1945, 1959), Bion's small group theory (1961), and Rice's (1969) and E. J. Miller and Rice's (1967) concept of primary task.[1]

To illustrate these ideas, I shall provide a case study of the life and leadership of an extraordinary man, and related biographical materials. He was born, as noted in the Register book of the Church of St John the Baptist, 'in the year of our Lord 1599, and named Oliver, the son of Robert Cromwell, gentleman, and of Elizabeth, his wife' (Wedgwood 1966: 15). He came to possess in the final years of his life the rather imperial title of Cromwell, Lord High Protector of England and Ireland. My enquiry focuses specifically on Cromwell's mid-life, and how the developmental forces which shaped him, at this time, profoundly influ-enced and informed the character and quality of his leadership.

Given my purposes, I believe that four brief questions are in order before beginning:

- Why study an extraordinary man, rather than an ordinary one?
- Why the emphasis on mid-life?
- Why this particular man—Cromwell the Lord High Protector? and
- Why a man?

As to the first, Gardiner, the great nineteenth-century English historian, for example, described Cromwell as 'the most typical Englishman of all time' and noted that 'he stands there, not to be implicitly followed as a model, but to hold a mirror to ourselves, wherein we may see alike our weaknesses and strengths' (quoted in Wedgwood 1966: 13). I believe that the substance of Gardiner's observation is both accurate and generalizable. The essential interest in extraordinary men lies in their resemblance to the average man, only with a greater grandeur and dramaturgy, so that to witness their leadership struggles is to see ordinary life magnified—ennobled by success and made tragic by failure. The archetypal extraordinary leader owes his power, in part at least, to the sense among his people that he is the apotheosis of each one of them. It is this quality which is shared by all such men who have acquired exceptional ascendancy over their fellows.

The life course and struggles of extraordinary leaders also illustrate, in a mode writ large, the irreconcilable conflicts and contradictions between ethics and politics, between the right and the expedient, and ultimately between both individual ideals, integrity, and gratification, on the one hand, and social responsibility, on the other. In this sense, the lives of such men are admonitory—they are morality tales which serve both as example and warning to any who assume leadership. They caution us by illustrating that ennoblement is often ephemeral and that both personal and enterprise tragedy may be the price of visionary hubris—a point to which I return later in this chapter.

As to my second question—why the emphasis on mid-life?—a simple answer will suffice. It is the time of life, when men (and increasingly women)—from either the society's or the organization's point of view—have accumulated the requisite wisdom, knowledge, and seasoning for leadership positions. They are, therefore, the generational leadership cohort, who carry the responsibility to create and manage society's institutions and have the responsibility, among others, to bring along the next generation. But entering mid-life is also a time, as a number of theorists have noted, of a major life transition, informed by the emergence of powerful psychological forces and the reactivation of conflicts and dilemmas associated with earlier stages of development. Specifically, it is during this time that a major transformation of self-in-world occurs, which includes a reassessment of values, relationships, rules, and career choices, as well as an assessment of dreams fulfilled and unfulfilled. How these developmental aspects of mid-life inform and shape the normative assumption of leadership, and the interpersonal and institutional dilemmas encountered in its exercise, is the focus of this enquiry.

My answer to the third question—why this particular leader, this man whom Milton appraised as a 'chief of men'?—must be unsatisfactory, or at least questionable. First, I take the notion of being 'typical', noted above, quite seriously, not only with regard to Cromwell's Englishness, but with regard to his leadership dilemmas as well. Further, and equally important, I can only say that his life has long been an interest of mine, and in fact stimulated my enquiry; I did not conveniently use it to illustrate my theories. Since you could well argue that this particular choice may, in fact, only illuminate aspects of my own character and personality[2]—and a poor occasion for a book chapter, you will think—I ask you to suspend such judgement until you can consider the situation of this man in light of your own experience. If there is any affinity that I feel for him, it is because I too am an everyman in a leadership position and he is an everyman's heroic leader; many others, I believe, would have sufficed.

And finally, as to the fourth question—why a man?—my answer must also be only partially satisfactory. First, the overwhelming majority of extraordinary leaders throughout history have been men. And although there have always been notable exceptions of extraordinary women leaders as well, they have been just that—exceptions. In this sense therefore, I believe the great women leaders in history are not as representative of the struggles of everywoman leaders today, as are their male counterparts. More to the point, however, at least for me, is the issue—currently much debated—of the extent to which the adult life cycles of men and women are substantially similar or different in ways that are not yet either clear or sufficiently documented. Therefore, it is at least a serious question as to whether they are directly comparable. Further, although there has been some excellent research about both women's adult development and women's leadership,[3] considerably more research on male leadership and the male life cycle has been undertaken, although the balance is rapidly being redressed. From both these perspectives, the choice of an illustrative man seemed to make sense. I would hope, however, that if the hypotheses and propositions I elaborate in this paper about the leadership transformations of men in mid-life have any value, others will take up the task of working out the necessary modifications with regard to women. This leads directly to my last apologia—namely that, as an everyman leader myself, I am necessarily able to draw upon internal experience in that role and so feel more sure-footed and grounded in the views I put forth about men who occupy it.

My approach to the life of Cromwell is biographical in the ordinary sense. I have also attempted through interior dialogue to develop a relationship with him and I have taken a participant/observer role in the various major episodes I refer to in this chapter. For example, I sat in the gallery of Parliament, both before King Charles closed it down and after Cromwell re-established it. I attended his eldest son Robert's funeral and observed his military leadership in several major battles. The imagery of these occasions, and others, is derived principally from two excellent biographies (Church 1978; Wedgwood 1966).

To begin, I would like to outline briefly some of the major current notions about male adult development in general and the mid-life transition in particular. In this summary the work of Levinson and his colleagues (D. J. Levinson *et al.* 1978) provides the central focus. My outline also draws, as does Levinson's, on the works of Jung and a paper by Jaques (1965). Following this outline I will expand the discussion through the application of other, related concepts and enumerate several propositions directly linking the dilemmas and requirements of leadership to the developmental issues and challenges that are hypothesized to emerge at mid-life. Then, to provide substance to these propositions, by way of illustration, I will attempt to apply them to the situation Cromwell finds himself in as he approaches his fortieth birthday and assess what happens to him subsequently. I will comment on his earlier development only in so far as it is necessary to understand what he is about at the point in his life where I will introduce him to you. I will also briefly describe the sociopolitical context of Parliamentary England, so you may better appreciate his role dilemmas in light of the prevailing social forces and pressures with which he must cope. Finally, I will briefly speculate on the consequences, for both individual and enterprise, resulting from the dilemmas that must inevitably arise when there are—as there always will be—dis-synchronies between individual developmental imperatives on the one hand, and the role demands required by historical or situational imperatives on the other.

A conception of adult development

In the view of Levinson (1977) and Levinson *et al.* (1978), adult development is best conceptualized as the evolution of the *Individual Life Structure*.[4] Their research suggests that the life structure neither remains static, nor changes adventitiously. Rather, they argue, it goes through a sequence of *eras* which last roughly eighteen to twenty years (*Early Adulthood*, *Middle Adulthood*, *Late Adulthood*, *Late, Late Adulthood*) and within these *eras* a sequence of alternating stable and transitional *periods*. The stable *periods* ordinarily last for approximately six to eight years and the transitional *periods* from four to five years (see Figure 5. 1).

For Levinson *et al.* (1978), a developmental *period*—stable or transitional—is defined in terms of its major primary tasks, which require a man to build, modify, and rebuild his life structure. It is not defined in terms of significant external or marker events, such as marriage, divorce, birth of a child, job change, though these will, of course, give the developmental *period* its essential content and quality. Specifically, they note that 'the primary [developmental] task of [a] stable period is to build a life structure: a man must make certain key choices, form structure around them, and pursue his goals and values within this structure' (p. 49). Each stable period has its own distinctive tasks. Further, while

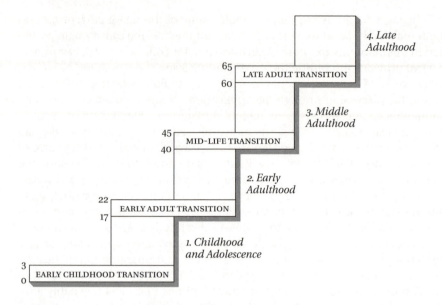

Fig. 5.1   Eras in the male life cycle
Source: Levinson *et al.* (1978: 20).

many changes may occur during a stable period, the basic life structure remains relatively intact. They further note that:

the primary tasks of [a] transitional period are to question and reappraise the existing structure, to explore the various possibilities for change in self and world, and to move toward commitment to the crucial choices that form the basis for a new life structure in the ensuing stable period. Each transitional period also has its own distinctive tasks reflecting its place in the life cycle. (ibid.)

Three particular aspects of Levinson's theory need be highlighted in order to make the ensuing discussion meaningful. First, it is an age-stage theory. That is, not only does it formulate a predictable developmental sequence for the male adult life course, but it postulates a normative chronological matrix for each period. Secondly, the theory places a particular emphasis on the nature of a man's *Dream* or its absence and on the role of *Mentoring* in shaping the quality and character of a man's development—as distinct from its structure. And thirdly, the primary concept of *Individual Life Structure* refers to the patterning or design of the individual life at a given time. It refers in the broadest terms to self-in-world; to the continuous engagement and interplay of the individual in society. In essence, then, it is a general conception of person in role in group at a particular stage of life.

The Mid-life Transition: an overview

Let me turn now directly to a consideration of the mid-life transition and outline its salient aspects from the perspectives of Levinson, Jung, Jaques, and even
White (1962), the author of the charming and wise modern version of the
Arthurian legend—*The Once and Future King*. While these various conceptions
of mid-life and the mid-life transition differ somewhat, they are, in general,
remarkably similar in substance and tone.

Levinson defines the *Early Adult Era* from roughly the age of 20 to the age of
40, and the *Middle Adult Era* from 40 to 60. The basic task of a cross-era transition—for example, the *Mid-life Transition*—is to terminate the era just ending
and to create a basis for the next era. Specifically, the *Mid-life Transition*
centres on the task of terminating the second early adult life structure, which
takes shape at the age of 32 or 33 and persists until the age of 39 or 40. During
this period—which Levinson terms *Settling Down*—a man tries to build a life
structure for the culmination of early adulthood. He seeks to realize gratification, esteem, and competence in the major components of this structure, such
as family, work, friendships, and community, and to realize his youthful aspirations. Levinson notes that during this period the two major tasks are: to establish a niche in society and to work at making it—planning, striving to advance,
proceeding towards a goal, and so forth. The imagery of the ladder and the role
of ambition are central to the *Settling Down* period.

Towards the end of the *Settling Down* period, starting ordinarily at the age of
37 or 38, there is, according to Levinson, the beginning of a distinctive and identifiable sub-phase he calls *Becoming One's Own Man*. The acronym *BOOM* connotes an important aspect of what a man wants in this phase: to become a
senior member in the world, to speak more strongly with one's own voice, and
to have a greater measure of authority. Levinson notes that a crucial dilemma
during *BOOM* is that a man wants to be more independent and more true to his
own wishes, even if they run counter to external demands. But he also wants
affirmation, respect, and reward from his world.

BOOM, which represents the onset of the *Mid-life Transition*, brings a new set
of developmental tasks and challenges. Now, according to Levinson, the life
structure itself comes into question and a man may begin to ask: What have I
done with my life? Is it really satisfying? Do I want more of the same? What are
my real values and deepest wishes? My *Dream*—am I, in fact, living it out? In an
effort to reappraise his life a man often discovers the extent to which it has been
based on illusions and he is faced with the process that Levinson calls *de-
illusionment*. This is the reduction of illusions and the recognition that long-
held assumptions and beliefs about self and the world are faulty. Since illusions
play so vital a role in our lives, this process merits special attention. And to
Levinson's notion of *de-illusionment*, I would add the concomitant process of
re-illusionment—which forms the basis of a new or revised mid-life *Dream,* as

distinct from the youthful *Dream* of early adulthood. I will return to this point as it relates to Cromwell's leadership.

Further, most theorists—differences in emphases and detail notwithstanding—view the mid-life transition as bringing with it the desire to reclaim, to recontact, and to live out parts of the self that were denied, neglected, or given short shrift in the struggle to succeed and establish oneself and to restore the parts of the self corrupted by ambition and the unconscious activation of infantile envy and greed. Erikson, for example, postulates the polarity of *generativity* vs. *stagnation and self-absorption,* and Jung speaks of the desire for harmony and the longing for the lost feminine parts of the self during this time. Jaques (1965) notes that during the mid-life transition there occurs a reactivation of the dynamics of the *depressive position* outlined by Melanie Klein (e.g. 1935; 1940) to describe the period of early childhood from approximately six months to two years. In conceptualizing the mid-life version of the *depressive position*, Jaques argues that a man comes to experience more acutely the mixedness of life and, if development is felicitous, comes to both a greater humility and a fuller appreciation of the mixedness of self.

White offers a similar view. In an extended aside regarding the foibles and follies of youth, he comments on the development of 'the seventh sense'—'knowledge of the world':

a thing called knowledge of the world, which people do not have until they are middle-aged. It is something which cannot be taught to younger people, . . . by which both men and women contrive to ride the waves of a world in which there is war, adultery, compromise, fear, stultification and hypocrisy—this discovery is not a matter for triumph. (1962: 374–5.)

Like Jaques, I would add to this a parallel knowledge of the self, informed by negative, damaged, or imperfect parts. And such discovery is also hardly an occasion for triumph, but it is the basis for new possibilities of wholeness, authenticity, and further development.

Adult development and leadership

In an attempt to relate the aforementioned conceptions of adult development—with an emphasis on mid-life and the mid-life transition—to the nature and dilemmas of leadership, I would like to make the following proposition:

that the nature of leadership, like any other mode of human activity, should manifest the particular qualities and character of the stage of adult development during which it is exercised. That is, if the general structure and character of adult development is predictable, the nature of leadership should characteristically and predictably display and be informed by normative developmental transformations at that stage of life.

Specifically, if the stages of adult life are viewed as each having appropriate developmental tasks[5]—as Levinson *et al.* (1978) conceptualize them—I am suggesting a sequence for adult developmental leadership transformation which I outline below.

The sequence I postulate is based on an understanding of individual and group 'states of mind' derived from Klein's theory of *developmental positions* (e.g. 1935; 1940; 1945), Bion's *basic assumption* theory (1961), and the correspondences between them (L. J. Gould 1997), as well as on the work of Jung, Jaques, Erikson, and Levinson, noted above.

Early adulthood

I propose that Bion's (1961) *fight/flight valency* (*baF*), with its corresponding *paranoid/schizoid* (*P/S*) states of mind (L. J. Gould 1997), is appropriate to the primary developmental tasks of *Early Adulthood* through the culmination of the *Settling Down Period*, with its imagery of making it, climbing the status and power ladder, and ambition. This developmentally informed motivational constellation is supported (psychologically and behaviourally) by the capacity for splitting, aggression, lack of ambivalence and moral certainty, and an action orientation—all central aspects of the *P/S position* and, if appropriate to the task, sophisticated *baF* mental states.

Correspondingly, through the twenties until the end of the *Settling Down Period* (approximately the age of 37 or 38), a man's leadership will be tend to be undergirded by *baF*. Even from a rudimentary elaboration of evolutionary theory it makes sense to assume that the younger, stronger, and more able-bodied men of the tribe would be the specialized *basic assumption* subgroup carrying the *fight/flight valency*. I would note here that, in common language, the metaphor of 'the Young Turks' gives evidence of a social recognition of this fact. While those in their thirties may seem old to be characterized as 'Young Turks', I believe that the prepotency of the *fight/flight valency* represents a long-term developmental trend which gradually wanes over the course of early adulthood but is still the active (prepotent) state through the mid- to late thirties. That is, I postulate that there are different essential *basic assumption valency* hierarchies at each stage of development or, put another way, different mobilization thresholds for the various *basic assumptions* at different points in the life cycle, with *baF* having the lowest threshold during this period.[6]

The mid-life transition and mid-life experience

With the onset of *BOOM*—at about the age of 37 or 38—the *basic assumption* leadership *valency* undergoes an accompanying shift. As *basic assumption dependency* (*baD*) and *basic assumption pairing* (*baP*), which I argue are appropriate to the primary task requirements of the *Mid-life Transition* and the mid-life itself, begin to become more prepotent, there is a corresponding diminution of *baF*. From a psychological and behavioural perspective, the emergence of the capacities necessary to meet the developmental challenges during this period coincide with, and are the result of, the reactivation and reworking of the dynamics of the *depressive position* (Jaques 1965) and the *early Oedipal period* (Klein 1945) and their respective correspondences with *baD* and *baP* (L. J. Gould 1997). These capacities centrally include a tolerance of ambivalence and uncertainty, realistic gratitude for those who have helped along the way, and a desire to contribute to social and institutional development and reproduction.

Quite complementary views are also offered by Jung (1971), who argues that during this period a man begins to reclaim the *feminine* and lost parts of the self. Levinson *et al.* (1978) suggests the emerging capacity (and desire) to become a mentor oneself and to accept and take responsibility for the dependency of others. Erikson postulates a maturing desire and need for greater mutuality and generativity, which encompasses '*procreativity, productivity* and *creativity*, and thus, the generation of new beings as well as new products and new ideas' (1985: 67; italics in original).[7]

Given the above, one would hypothesize that a man's leadership will display these qualities, which are quite similar to Jaques' (1965) description of artistic creation informed by the reactivation and reworking of *depressive position* dynamics and resolutions during this period. In examining the works of a number of great artists and musicians during the mid-life transition, Jaques found that compared to the work of their twenties and early to mid-thirties, the work of their late thirties and forties undergoes a significant shift in form and substance. He found that it becomes increasingly more sculptured and wrought, with more balance, discipline, and control. And so it is, I will argue, with the manner that Cromwell's leadership was transformed in his late thirties and early forties, resulting in a new ego ideal, a mature and enlightened (for his time) explicit leadership philosophy, and a reworked vision of Parliament—a structure designed to balance tensions and ensure harmony. Simply put, it was a political vision and philosophy newly infused with love, justice, equity, and co-operation.[8]

It needs to be emphasized, however, that the above developmental progression, as I have described it, is rarely seen in anything even approximating its pure form—at least on the behavioural level. This is due in large measure to the complexities introduced by three additional factors.

The constraining nature of task requirements

Much more often than not, task requirements are incongruent with the endogenous developmental imperatives at work within the leader himself. Commonly, for example, especially in the realms of commerce and politics, we see leaders continually acting and speaking in a warlike manner, long into mid-life. That is, many tasks may require the leader to mobilize *fight/flight* states of mind and their corresponding instrumental behaviours. Equally, however, and attesting to the underlying developmental changes during this time, we also often see, if we are not completely cynical, many such leaders—particularly after a fall from power (or after leaving the leadership role for whatever reason)—given to reparative strivings, and having a much greater understanding and perspective about what they have wrought, than we would have imagined them capable of, based on their leadership behaviour. (These issues will be further developed later in this chapter, in the section entitled 'Leadership and adult development: a further proposition'.)

Basic assumption demands of the group

Closely connected to the above is the fact that developmental imperatives as they relate to leadership, or stimulate dynamically synchronous leadership modes of behaviour, are always contravened, to a greater or lesser extent, by the *basic assumption* demands of the group. That is, groups demand leadership that will give voice to the particular *basic assumption* they have mobilized as a defence against anxiety. Needless to say, the developmentally prepotent *basic assumption* of the leader, given his stage of development, may not be congruent with the particular *basic assumption* demanded by the group. In such situations, the leader is the object of the group's powerful projective identifications, which dynamically shape the collective transference field. As a result, he can be counter-transferentially inducted—often for extended periods of time—into modes of leadership not congruent with his stage of development. As we will see below, the tragedy of Cromwell (and many others) is, in great measure, due to such dynamics—that is, when powerful developmental processes in the individual leader collide with powerful group, institutional, and social processes and are subverted by them.

The leader's personality

Although it is beyond the scope of this chapter to discuss this issue in detail, the above propositions are, of course, further complicated by the particular features of the leader's personality formation and his preferred defensive strategies. Kernberg (1980), for example, has written persuasively about the regressions in leadership as they relate to particular personality constellations. In particular, he highlights aspects of leadership where the leader's personality contains marked narcissistic trends (which are quite common in those who ascend to leadership positions). Such powerful neurotic tendencies and unresolved early conflicts distort and impede, more or less depending on their severity, the full flowering of normative developmental trends. That is, following the lead of a number of contemporary theorists (e.g. Settlage 1992), we may conceptualize neurotic conflicts as constraints on development. For example, we may view an individual, at any stage of development, as being pulled between the neurotic, regressive forces of *repetition compulsions* (which are, by definition, anti-developmental), on the one hand, and the powerful, progressive, biopsychological thrusts towards growth and change, on the other (see L. J. Gould 1982).

CROMWELL

Any serious consideration of his personality aside, it is the interplay of the developmental and group forces outlined in the preceding sections, together with the additional factors noted above, that I would like to illustrate with a recounting of Cromwell's leadership transformations from early adulthood through his mid-life transition and beyond. It is too be hoped that this enquiry will highlight, from an adult developmental vantage point, some of the complexities and dilemmas of taking enlightened leadership and hence shed some light on the ever-present possibility of both individual and enterprise tragedy when such leadership fails—for whatever reasons.

From young adulthood to the mid-life transition

Cromwell's late twenties and early thirties are characterized by a conventional and lacklustre parochialism. He has chronic money troubles, appears to be both a stern and indifferent father and a husband who took a wife for convenience and for whom he has little affection. He is a small landowner and in social terms a gentlemen, even if hardly pecunious. Dogmatically religious, he gives obeisance to an unrelenting and forbidding Calvinistic God. Cromwell is also a minor regional member of Parliament, but he does not appear to have strong, well-defined political convictions or passions and in this role he is often out of sorts and almost continuously quarrelsome. His various biographers appear to agree that his most essential characteristics during this period are his tendency to act on impulse, his violent temper, and his preference for *ad hominem* attacks on those with whom he disagrees.

However, in his mid-thirties a number of internal and external changes begin to occur. First, Cromwell's fortunes take a turn for the better when he comes into a comfortable inheritance through the death of an uncle. He also becomes taken, apparently for the first time, by two of his daughters in particular. (He was to have nine children by the age of 40.) Even many years later, in the midst of his weary campaigns, he thinks of them often—his 'little wenches'. And, when his eldest son Robert dies from one of those mysterious and rapid fevers which decimated seventeenth-century households, he is shattered by grief. But, even prior to this, Cromwell has serious bouts of depression and melancholy. He broods a lot and his behaviour is marked by alternating periods of withdrawal and violent outbursts.

The most significant change during this time, however, occurs in his thirty-ninth year and is referred to explicitly by his biographers as a conversion experience, occasioned by a religious revelation. In effect, this revelation is of God as bountiful, generous, and forgiving and Cromwell develops the conviction that God loves him and that he is saved. As he himself puts it, 'My soul is now with the congregation of the firstborn', and in a letter to a friend he writes ecstatically praising 'the great mercies of God with a newly uplifted heart'. With this conversion comes a marked shift in Cromwell's religio-political ideology. His earlier dogmatism is replaced by a more ecumenical view of conscience. He begins to feel strongly that all men must have the freedom to live out their conscience, to be free of persecution, and to be able to express their convictions in safety. He, in fact, becomes a religious liberal. In this connection, I hypothesize that Cromwell's 'conversion' represents a more dramatic and explicit manifestation of the powerful, underlying, but normative, developmental processes, described above, that emerge at this stage of life.

Politically, he is still middle of the road—he believes in the King's ultimate authority (the king in question being Charles I), but increasingly comes to feel that Parliament should be a stronger force in sharing the governance of England. So here is Cromwell at the age of 39, in the euphoria of his conversion, newly saved, reunited with his family emotionally, through birth and death, and economically secure. Further, he is more tolerant, loving, and forgiving, and, conversely, he is less tempestuous, angry, or battling, less inclined to tilt at windmills. He is more involved politically at a local level, feels strongly that the voice of the people must be heard, and increasingly takes more mature and effective leadership toward this end. Finally, as mysteriously as they appeared, his melancholy and depression lift entirely. Altogether, I think you will agree that Cromwell's life seems to have taken a decidedly felicitous turn as his fortieth birthday approaches.

By way of a rounding out a picture of Cromwell's leadership, I would like to describe briefly what happened to him subsequently, and the respective *Dreams* we left him with at the age of 40. I would also like to provide some speculations on the *whys* and *wherefores*. Finally, I will attempt to draw some conclusions based on what I believe are relevant parallels to the dilemmas of everyman leaders and their enterprises.

The ensuing years

Let me begin by providing a bridging image between Cromwell's fortieth year and the ensuing twenty or so years. We find Cromwell living in Ely. He is active in local politics and in the pursuit of good works, including prominent membership in the Parson's Charity for giving relief to the poor. His life is that of an honest and independent gentleman farmer who shows his faith in the practical work of helping the afflicted and championing the poor.

If there had been no civil war in England, it is likely Cromwell would have passed the last twenty years of his life in reputable and rural domestic obscurity. He has now reached the age of almost 40 without notably distinguishing himself, and he seems reasonably content, the only darkness in his life being the death of his eldest son Robert, mentioned earlier.

However, in 1640, events set in motion a bloody, seven-year civil war, pitting the King and his Royalists against the forces of Parliament, which Cromwell eventually comes to command. The war ends with the victory of Cromwell's forces and, after a protracted period of negotiation with the King, Cromwell's opinion hardens against him and he is beheaded. The year is now 1649 and Cromwell is almost 50. The war, however, has taken a terrible toll—England is in ruin, an impoverished country, rent apart. On a personal level, Cromwell has also suffered many losses—a son Oliver has died (also of a fever), and many of his closest friends and a favourite nephew (named Oliver, as well) have been killed in battle.

It is worth noting that one of the most remarkable aspects of Cromwell's life during this period is his consistent attempts to live up to an ego ideal that I believe crystallized during his mid-life transition—that is, to be a man of equity, conciliation, and justice and above all a statesman, despite his virtually continuous role as a *fight* leader. And even in battle and with his troops, he was—certainly for his time—an extremely enlightened leader. For example, he created a system of his own for recruiting and training troops and was determined that they should be honourably treated. 'If you choose honest godly men to be captains', he wrote, 'honest men will follow them.' Further, at a time when so many troops were foreigners and mercenaries, Cromwell's intention was to have his men, individually and as a body, conscious of the cause for which they fought. In this connection, many of Cromwell's biographers (e.g. Wedgwood 1966) explicitly note the enduring influence of his conversion at the age of 39 in guiding him through times of war and the almost unabated conflicts that were to be his lot until he died.

Although the civil war is now over, Parliament has failed to restore order out of the chaos, quell internal dissension, and succeed against foreign intrusions. Four years after the beheading of Charles, Cromwell, in utter contradiction to everything he believes and fought for to establish Parliamentary rule, disbands Parliament, and installs himself as Lord High Protector of England and Ireland. In effect, he replaces the King in everything but name. The terrible irony in this act is that, given the circumstances in which he finds himself, Cromwell must rule more autocratically than Charles I ever did.[9] And, perhaps more to the point, Cromwell is all too painfully aware of his own failure and the failure of his Parliamentary vision. Five years later—five years of continual strife, during which time he is offered but refuses the crown—Cromwell finally lays down his burden and dies. And he dies a sadder, wearier, and more experienced man than when he took up the struggle at the age of 40. Yet, despite so many disillusionments, even at the end he hoped for some better foundation for his government than mere force, as indicated by his last prayer, which contained the phrase—'consistency of judgement, one heart and mutual love'. A fitting epitaph for Cromwell who, in death, could once again reaffirm his earlier ego ideals and his vision of a just society—ideals that he mightily attempted to live by, despite two decades of stress, war, terrible losses, conflict, and doubt.

Leadership and adult development: A further proposition

In light of what happened to Cromwell—with the quite mixed picture, in Eriksonian terms, of the antithesis of *despair* vs. *integrity*[10]—I would like to adduce another proposition, and briefly elaborate its implications for the everyman leader and everyman's enterprises—that is, for us, in our institutional leadership roles. The proposition is this:

> Long occupancy in a role that requires the continual mobilization of a particular basic assumption to facilitate task performance will distort natural developmental tendencies, if the basic assumption attitudes and behaviours appropriate to the work-tasks are different from those required for the optimal performance of developmental tasks.

This proposition casts in developmental terms, propositions put forward by Rice (1969) in applying to the individual a systems theory of organization, wherein the individual is conceptualized simultaneously as a sentient being and an open multi-activity system. In his view, and directly connected to my proposition, Rice notes, for example, that:

Individuals have the capacity to mobilize themselves . . . into different kinds of activity systems, and only some of their activities are relevant to the performance of any particular task. (p. 574.)

[Further,] . . . maintaining a role over a long [period of] time leads either to the atrophy of unused attributes or the need to find other means of expressing them. (p. 576.)

The implications of the first part of my proposition, together with the quotations from Rice, are clear in connection with development. With regard to the second part, if the leader attempts to impose the prepotent *basic assumption* behaviours, attitudes, and values, which are congruent with his developmental imperatives but not congruent with the requirements of the task-system, task performance will suffer. Hence, the essential dilemma for individual and enterprise—and writ large in the lives of many heroic (and tragic) leaders—when, due to conscience, for example as with Cromwell, role change, refusal, or abdication are not viable options. Here I would suggest that in such circumstances the *Dream* of the heroic leader takes on particular qualities that have tragic consequences for both the leader and his enterprise. For the *Dream* of the heroic leader who is 'locked' into a role can only be to re-create the world in his own developmental image.

The political visions of heroic leaders are, in part, grandiose externalizations and attempts to impose the *Dream* on the social structure. In essence, they are attempts to establish harmony, and to reduce tension and distance between the role-bound self and the world. To put it another way, it is as if the hero leader unconsciously recognizes that aspects of the self will die, if the world is not transformed to nurture them or at least to provide better opportunities for their expression and enactment. It is in this sense, I believe, that the *Dream* of a heroic leader and its external correlative, the political or institutional vision, also take on particular features. I conceptualize such features as involving a fantastical re-creation of the longed-for, idealized family of origin, in which the self is not spoiled by incongruity, conflict, dissonance, choices, renunciation, and so forth. The political vision is partly, then, a social elaboration of this fantasy and, as such, it is, of course, doomed to failure.

The sad and tragic fate of heroic leaders is that their developmental tendencies, in order to find fruition in the self, must involve grandiose attempts completely to transform the world. So we are brought back once again in this discourse to the archetypal polarity between the individual and society. If felicitous development increasingly involves the desire to reduce splitting both within the self and between the self and world and to find new ways to integrate split-off parts, the quintessential challenge of heroic leaders can be stated simply: to the extent that they experience themselves as 'role bound', they must attempt to transform the system in which the role is embedded, if their developmental potential is to be fully realized. This is the visionary hubris noted earlier in this chapter, and Cromwell's life is, I believe, an all too common exemplar of its fate.

The everyman leader: Summary

But finally, let us return to the dilemmas of the non-heroic everyman leader and his enterprises—for our everyman leader, for the most part, is not 'role bound', or 'locked' into a role, like his heroic counterpart. For him, the issues involve making choices—role change, role refusal, and role abdication become potential options in the face of conflicts with developmental imperatives. Our everyman leader may indeed have the option of finding or creating situations more consonant and congruent with emerging desires, cherished ego ideals, and developmentally appropriate needs. But then there are the needs and tasks of the enterprise in which he is exercising leadership. If he should, in fact, choose to cultivate his own garden, rather than remain to 'fight the good fight' in what may be a developmentally inimical role, the enterprise may suffer from his withdrawal or renunciation of leadership. For our everyman leader, these issues create acutely painful conflicts and the potential for tragedy on a non-heroic scale, but tragedy none the less. Namely, the everyday tragedy of the lack of personal fulfilment, frustration, emptiness, and serious distortions in development, on the one hand, or the disruption and failure of his enterprises, with their attendant social consequences, on the other.

NOTES

1 Earlier versions of this chapter were delivered at the meetings of the American Political Science Association and the Cornell Symposium on Psychoanalytic Studies of Organizational Behaviour.
2 It is of passing interest—no comparison intended—that Freud was a great admirer of Cromwell, who had powerfully attracted him since boyhood. So much so, in fact, that Freud named his second son Oliver, and noted wryly 'how the suppressed megalomania of fathers is transferred in their thoughts on to their children' (Freud 1900: 447–8).
3 See, for example, Bem 1993; Gilligan 1982; Heilbrun 1988; Kantor 1977; Kram 1985; D. J. Levinson 1996; Roberts and Newton 1987; Rossi 1985; Ruffin 1989; Stewart 1976; and S. Taylor 1981.
4 When using specific technical concepts attributed to a particular theorist, or in the context of that theorist's work, I italicize and, if appropriate, capitalize them throughout. I do not do so when I use the same concepts in a general context. For example, *Mid-life* and the *Mid-life Transition* are only italicized and capitalized when used in connection with Levinson's work (D. J. Levinson *et al.* 1978), but not otherwise.
5 The concept of primary task as elaborated by E. J. Miller and Rice (1967) is 'the task that an enterprise must perform if it is to survive' (p. 25). I view as primary those developmental tasks which an individual must perform, in order optimally to meet the emerging challenges at any given stage.
6 In this connection one may speculate that women, for task reasons (the primary responsibility for nurturing the young), may have lower mobilization thresholds for the basic *assumption dependency valency*, than do men, at least during the peak reproductive years. Further, there are suggestions in the literature that women, compared to men, develop a more robust capacity to mobilize aggression (i.e. *basic assumption fight/flight*) later in life. For example, Heilbrun (1988, ch. 7), begins a chapter on Virginia Woolf at 50, with a quotation from Dorothy L. Sayers: 'Time and trouble will tame an advanced young woman, but an advanced old woman is uncontrollable by any earthly force.' Later, she quotes an Isak Dinesen character to the effect that 'Woman . . . when they are old enough to have done with the business of being woman, and can let loose their strength, must be the most powerful creatures in the world.' In a similar vein, Mitchell and Helson (1990), following Jung's view, suggest that women in mid-life more fully integrate the neglected and suppressed *masculine* aspects of the self. And finally, E. J. Miller (1987) offers the hypothesis that there may be more potent counter-transferential pressures on women, compared to their male counterparts, to mobilize them into *dependency*, (i.e. caretaking) leadership roles.

Considered together, these notions may illuminate some of the differences in the macrostructure of the life cycle of men and women—hinted at in the Introduction to this chapter—and the corresponding emotional and behavioural qualities of their leadership at different stages of adult development.

7 This is Erikson's seventh stage of ego development—*generativity* vs. *self-absorption and stagnation*. According to him, 'The new "virtue" emerging from this antithesis, namely "Care", is the widening commitment to *take care of* the persons, the products, and the ideas one has learned *to care for*' (Erikson 1985: 67). This could, in my view, serve as a useful definition of enlightened institutional leadership. Also note that chronologically this stage roughly approximates to Levinson's era of *Middle Adulthood*.

8 As L. J. Gould (1979) has noted, an almost direct parallel can be found in the life and leadership of King Arthur. Towards the end of his thirties, two significant impulses, with their accompanying ideation, begin to emerge: his political vision of the Round Table—the harmony of the circle being the essential metaphor for Camelot—and his active desire to be married. These, in fact, are explicitly linked, and occur within a few pages of each other in *The Once and Future King* (White 1962). There are several other developments in Arthur's life at this time that are pertinent to my enquiry: first, he quite consciously becomes increasingly tired of fighting—victory in the jousts or on the battlefield no longer excites or brings pleasure. Arthur also begins to decry the necessity for being warlike and, in fact, the vision of the Round Table and Camelot— like Cromwell's vision of Parliament—can be viewed quite directly as a consequence of, and a metaphor for, these shifts.

9 The theme of an enlightened leader subsequently having to act 'against his grain' and betray his ideals and cherished beliefs, is almost ubiquitous in the mid-lives, or later, of such men. We see, for example, Cincinnatus reluctantly leaving his farm and being named dictator in 458 BC in order to defend Rome against the Aequi and the Volscians; King Arthur, following twenty years of almost continuous battle, and a crazed preoccupation with restoring the lost idyll of Camelot, on the Plain of Salisbury, sadly awaiting the dawn which will signal the beginning of the final battle with the evil Mordred and his minions; or, Freud, painfully and reluctantly 'feeling forced into seizing control (of the Viennese Psychoanalytic Society) through a "palace revolution" ' in order to ensure its survival (Eisold 1997: 99).

10 In his description of the eighth and final stage of ego development—*integrity* vs. *despair*—Erikson notes that there is a need at this stage for 'a meaningful interplay between beginning and end, as well as some finite sense of summary, and possibly, a more active anticipation of dying' (Erikson 1985: 63). In his view, *wisdom* will be the emergent 'virtue' if development is felicitous, and *despair* the outcome if it is not.

6

Managing the Unconscious at Work

Anton Obholzer

INTRODUCTION

It is a common experience at work, as it is in life, that plans that are made are not carried out, that decisions that are agreed are not enacted, and that time-tables that seem obvious somehow turn out to be unmanageable. All of the above are examples where decisions or plans made on the basis of rational, logical, conscious thought somehow turn out to have been flawed in their planning or execution. It is of abiding interest to us all not only why things go wrong but, perhaps even more importantly, why they keep on going wrong or, to put it another way, why it is so difficult to learn from experience. And it is central to the task of management that the presence of such phenomena is acknowledged, that understanding of them is worked on, and that management has plans for addressing them.

There are many ways of looking at the above problems, and these ways are represented by a great many different schools of thought and theory about management and organizational consultancy. The fact that many of these schools claim to be comprehensive vehicles for understanding, obviating the need for working with other approaches, makes the situation even more difficult for managers to address.

This chapter is about a way of looking at the factors that seem to contribute to the sabotaging of managerial and organizational processes as outlined above. It is based on psychoanalytic and applied group relations theories, and assumes that many of the processes that contribute to organizational difficulties are unconscious in nature. By this I mean that the leadership, the management, and the members are not aware of what the underlying factors are that motivate their behaviour, nor are they in touch with the fact that their behaviour has a destructive effect on the organization. In fact, they often believe the opposite: that their behaviour is in the service, for example, of principle, truth, or good will.

Before I go on to elaborate some basic principles of understanding and managing these processes along psychoanalytic lines, I would like to place this
approach into an overall context. In the widest sense, I believe that all theories
in whatever field are systems of containing our anxiety of 'not knowing'. The
psychological function of a theory is thus, in part, a way of containing our fear
of being lost and overwhelmed. At another level, that of the philosophy of
science (Popper 1934), it is a way of producing a hypothesis that can be put to
the test, and thus modified by experience. The theories that are used as part of
the psychoanalytic model of understanding unconscious processes in organizations are no exception to the above rule. They have the advantage of providing us with a grid of understanding, within which we can interpret our
observations; they also have the disadvantage of holding us down with precon-
ceptions, diminishing our opportunities for seeing phenomena afresh. From a
narrower perspective, I must state that psychoanalytic models of looking at
organizations do not, and should not, claim to be all-encompassing models of
understanding and managing organizations. They have to be applied in conjunction and co-operation with sociopsychological theories, as well as with
management theories and structures based on external reality.

WORK AND THE MANAGEMENT OF WORK IN OUR SOCIETY

In order for us to pursue the concept of unconscious processes at work, it is
important for us to give some thought to the function which work serves in society, for only then are we in a position to manage 'in context'. At its most basic,
work is the activity necessary for society's survival. In Western society nowadays, as the importance of such structures as the extended family and religion
diminishes, work and work institutions (or their lack, in the form of unemployment) are increasingly important as central pillars of our personal identity.
Take away our work, whether through redundancy, retirement, the closure of
institutions, or other factors, and we are increasingly lost, subject to physical
and mental illness, and more at risk of death. Nowadays, much of our work is in
the form of membership of organizations and institutions, so that any changes
in their structure or management threaten to shake the very pillars of our personal and professional identity. To a degree, this explains the ubiquitous nature
of resistance to change in institutions—something that keeps on coming as a
surprise to many a manager.

However, apart from the role of giving us some key building blocks in the creation of our identity, work and work institutions also serve another function
through enabling us to partake in a group and institutional process. They thus
give us the chance to be institutionalized in the sense that Goffman (1961) used
the word. We all know about the negative aspects of institutionalization, as
described by Goffman, E. J. Miller (1993c), and many others. There is less dis-

cussion of the process of members welcoming the process of institutionalization, as it relieves them of the strain of having to manage individual thought and
action and instead allows them to opt into some institutional group norm of
thinking or, perhaps better put, to non-thinking behaviour.

Change in the organization and loss of membership threatens or severs the
bond of belonging, and hence causes resistance or turbulence, such as is wit-
nessed in many work organizations. A manager who thus believes that change
is possible without turbulence and resistance is in my view not in touch with
reality, but is instead in a state of wishful thinking about self and organization,
as well as being in a state of denial such as is described in Steiner's (1985) paper
'Turning a Blind Eye'.

THE ROLE OF ANXIETY IN THE MANAGEMENT OF CHANGE

If we build on the above picture of what function work and work places serve,
we thus come up with two views. The conscious view is that the workplace is
there to perform its work task, and we are there as members to perform our
work roles within the structure of the overall work organization. The unconscious view would be that the work institution is there to give one a sense of personal identity, to take one out of the heat of individual personal thought and
decision making, and to provide one with group membership for the provision
of 'comfort', both personally and in society. The two perceptions are quite obviously in conflict, a conflict that I believe often throws light on some of the difficulties experienced in work organizations. For what is clear is that activity and
work performance that are in the service of the organization's primary task are
not necessarily, in fact are unlikely to be, the same sort of activity that is
engaged in in pursuit of unconscious individual and group processes which further the 'membership' function outlined above.

If we now introduce the concept of management, we find the following. It is
not really possible to speak of management without at the same time coupling
the concept to change. Management without change means managing the status quo, and as the environment is in a constant process of change, management—to keep the status quo—must mean eventually managing oneself out of
existence. Just as management is about the process of change—though naturally there is some choice about the nature and speed of the changes envisaged—so change is inevitably associated with anxiety. At both a conscious and
unconscious level, the management of change is therefore the management of
anxiety and of resistance arising from the anxiety.

If the above hypothesis is correct, namely that management is about change,
which in turn causes anxiety, then it is important for us to understand as
much as possible about the nature of the anxieties aroused. This is where the
essential connection is to be made between psychoanalysis, which is about

understanding unconscious anxieties, and the workplace where these anxieties manifest themselves through unconscious acting out, both individually and on a group and institution-wide basis, with a consequent sabotaging of con-sciously reached decisions.

I use the plural, anxieties, because there are different anxieties operating at different levels. In order to address them adequately in management and in consultancy, we need to make some differentiations. I propose three categories for which I believe there is strong evidence:

- primitive anxiety;
- anxiety arising from the nature of the work;
- personal anxiety.

Primitive anxiety

By primitive anxiety I mean an ever-present, all-pervasive anxiety that is the fate of mankind. A great many authors, philosophers, anthropologists, and psychologists have written about it. Spitz (1957), writing of the work of anthro-pologist and psychoanalyst, Geza Roheim, said, 'he saw in culture a huge net-work of more or less successful attitudes to protect mankind against the dangers of object loss, the colossal efforts made by a baby who is afraid of being left alone in the dark. This was the main stream of his entire work, as expressed in nearly two hundred papers and books.' The network of culture—which fundamentally consists of institutions, be they totemic clans, religious rites, or their present-day counterparts, work institutions—is intended to fend off the dread of the unknown. We do not, however, need to go to Australian Aboriginal studies, as Roheim did, in order to find primitive rituals full of sym-bolism. Anyone with a three-year-old can observe them hop into bed so that the 'monsters under the bed' don't get them, or witness them not stepping on the cracks in the pavement lest some unspeakable horror befall them. And three-year-olds don't 'disappear' with development. They get 'covered' by lay-ers of growing up, but the three-year-old remains as a core, both creative and problematic. And rituals to ward off evil are not confined to children; how many of us walk lightly under a ladder, or don't give Friday the thirteenth a second thought?

Many psychoanalytic authors, including Freud (1913), have written on this theme. Bion (1961: 141) writes, 'I hope to show that in his contact with the com-plexities of life in a group, the adult resorts, in what may be a massive regres-sion, to mechanisms described by Melanie Klein as typical of the earliest phases of mental life.' Esther Bick (1987), who introduced infant observation into the training of child psychotherapists and psychoanalysts in Britain, spoke of the individual's fear of being 'lost in space'. John Bowlby (1969), using yet another language, speaks of separation anxiety. I believe that all the above are writing about the same pervasive primitive anxiety. And just as Australian Aborigines and Kalahari Bushmen band together and create rituals and institutions to hold them together—to provide them with a 'social skin', so to speak—so do we. In our case, however, many of the social institutions of the past, such as those Bion wrote about—the Church, the Army, the Nobility—are no longer generally available, and so we imbue existing everyday work institutions with protective-defensive functions. For the purpose of this thesis, I am therefore suggesting that workplace institutions serve many of the associative-defensive purposes that primitive tribal or religious groupings served in the past. Evidence for this being so can be found when there is severance of the bond, such as in redundancy or retirement. More importantly for management, it can also be found when there is an attempt to change the institution. It is of vital importance for managers to realize that any attempt to change an institution will thus immediately cause a defensive backlash, particularly from those who have 'colonized' the particular institution for the specific purpose of giving them 'containment', in Bion's terms, for their primitive anxieties.

Anxiety arising from the nature of the work

The second category of anxiety is that arising from the nature of the work. Elliot Jaques' (1955) classic theoretical paper, 'Social Systems as a Defence against Persecutory and Depressive Anxiety', was followed by Isabel Menzies' (1960) paper, in which she applied these concepts to a nursing hierarchy in a large teaching hospital. Both Jaques and Menzies built on the work of Melanie Klein, specifically her ideas of the very primitive anxieties and mental mechanisms in the paranoid-schizoid position (Klein 1959). Menzies in her study makes the points that working with patients brings the nurse face to face with very primitive anxieties about death, sadistic attacks on the object, and that the health field in general operates in a way in which taboos about such things as privacy, nakedness, and sexuality are of necessity regularly transgressed. The result is an upsurge of primitive anxiety that has to be defended against, and the resulting defence mechanisms have an 'industry-wide', institutional, and individual component. By 'industry-wide' I mean that defence mechanisms arising in the staff group of, say, a premature baby intensive care unit in Naples, London, Stockholm, and Vienna are likely to have a great deal in common in spite of different social and health care systems, because the nature of the anxiety, namely death in infants, is the common factor in the work.

It needs to be remembered that the concept of work-related hazards, such as silicosis in miners or scrotal cancer in Victorian chimney-sweeps, is a well-established public health concept. What I am arguing for is a widening of the concept to include psychological hazards leading to staff and institutional 'burnout' and thus impaired institutional functioning, with key implications for managers, staff, and clients alike. The assumption is that there is anxiety specific to and arising from the nature of the work and that the institution defends itself against this anxiety in such a way that the emphasis of the structure is on defence-related rather than work-related functioning. In other words, the pressure is for defence-related activity to come to the foreground, with the result that the primary task of the institution is neglected. This represents a shift from 'on task' to 'off task' functioning. If this is correct, then it is important for managers to realize that any attempt to alter the specific way in which work is organized in their institution must, by definition, mean a disruption of the anxiety-holding system, with a consequent release into the structure of anxiety and resistance to change. Most of the work in this area has been done in hospitals and related organizations. It is, however, obvious that there are many jobs in society where the workers are constantly in the shadow of danger. One need, for example, only think of the nuclear industry to realize what a heavy price we might all pay if defensive blindness against the risks inherent in the work were to become part of the work ethic.

The lesson to be learned is not that no change should be envisaged—far from it. The lesson is that change will elicit resistance, that the nature of the underlying anxiety can be ascertained both in principle and by observation, and that addressing this anxiety in the context of an overall process of the management of change can make for a more effective organization, both in terms of work output and in terms of staff morale.

Personal anxiety

The third level of anxiety is the personal one in which external societal and, more commonly, work issues trigger off, in the individual's own inner world, elements of past personal experience, both conscious and unconscious, with resulting disturbance that may manifest itself at work.

An example would be of a nurse in training whose mother had died of breast cancer. Finding herself, in the early stages of her career, with sole responsibility for the night-shift in a female surgery ward where many of the patients had had mastectomies for breast cancer, this nurse suffered a breakdown. In this case, it is likely that a personal, unmetabolized psychic enclave of grief was detonated by the heavy exposure to grief and distress arising from the work. The choice of career in this instance might itself have been determined by unconscious reparative mechanisms in response to the loss of mother. A further example might be of a member in a law firm who got seriously out of role in her handling of a divorce case. The case had many similarities to her parents' divorce when she was 14, an experience that was the unconscious inspiration for her choice of the Law as a career. This is an example of where a personal experience led not only to a career but, for the lawyer who had made no connection between her past experience and her career choice, also to the creation of a professional Achilles' heel just waiting for the 'right' client to activate it.

An additional factor here is the concept of 'valency', a term that Bion (1961) borrowed from chemistry to designate an individual's tendency-cum-unconscious-vulnerability to being drawn into one or other basic assumption type of functioning. The concept is of relevance to understanding and managing institutions and staff groups, because institutions themselves are inclined to one or other type of basic assumption functioning as a result of the nature of the work they are doing and, sometimes, of the leadership culture 'handed down' within the organization. The outcome is that there is often an unconscious 'matching' process between individual and organization, which adds to the quantum of resistance to change, for any change that is then proposed requires not only a change in work outlook and practice but also a concurrent inner world change.

It is clear that, so far, the contribution from psychoanalysis has been about the functions that work and other institutions serve in helping us contain various levels of anxiety. It needs to be clearly stated that these ways of coping with anxiety are essentially defences against anxiety. In other words, the underlying anxiety is not recognized and the defensive structures are unconsciously assembled on both an individual and group basis. To an extent, of course, one 'inherits' styles of defence mechanisms from one's parents, one's family, one's work institution, and one's culture. The essential feature of this way of looking at behaviour is, however, not that there should not be defence mechanisms, but rather that defence mechanisms one unconsciously 'falls into' are not effective, do not address the problem, and often lead to an escalation of the problem. What contribution can psychoanalysis make to understanding such processes? As is clear from the preceding discussion, psychoanalysis can help us to understand and think about the various levels of anxiety and to put in place containing mechanisms for managing the anxieties arising from the work. Without such mechanisms there is the constant risk that the institution is swamped by processes that take it 'off task'.

PSYCHOANALYSIS AND THE MANAGEMENT PROCESS

A psychoanalytic perspective on management would need to take into account not only the anxieties mentioned in the previous section but also the mechanism needed to contain them, in the sense that Bion uses the concept of 'containment'. What is required therefore is a 'state of mind' in leadership and in management which is adequately in touch with the threats to the organization and to its survival. These threats could arise from either side of the institutional boundary—in my view management is thus essentially a boundary-keeping and facilitating function. But this means a great deal more than performing a mere 'gatekeeper' function, for it requires not only judgement about the degree and nature of the 'cross-border traffic' but also judgement as regards timing, symbolism, and the conscious and unconscious elements involved.

By 'cross-border traffic', I mean information about the outside world that needs to be taken in by the institution in order for it to be able to adapt to the changing environment and for there to be an opportunity for this information to be held up against the backcloth of the primary task of the institution so that the necessary adaptation can be made to the mode of working. (I am here using the term institution as defined by Wesley Carr (1996) when he refers to it as the picture we carry in the mind, as opposed to organization which he regards as the bricks and mortar of the workplace.) Equally the outside world needs to be informed about the 'goings-on' in the institution, be they products or changes in the state of mind of the management and the staff.

The timing of these information flows with their concurrent emotional change is obviously a matter of importance and judgement for it involves at times the risk of being overwhelmed by the information flow inward, just as there is the risk of 'acting out' in the information flow outwards. By this I mean that a surfeit of information inward can shift the institution into the paranoid-schizoid end of the spectrum of functioning whereby, via processes such as scapegoating, good and bad characteristics and actions are located in separate parts of the system (for example, in different departments or in 'management' or in 'staff', 'us' and 'them'), rather than being understood as coexisting throughout the system. This is not only counter-productive to the work and thus the survival of the organization but can result in poorly thought out or poorly timed responses that in effect are the institutional equivalent of the 'acting out' process seen in patients. In this latter process, the response is concretely enacted rather than experienced, thought about, and fed back in a way that leads to open dialogue.

The boundary-managing function therefore has to have as a core element a containing function that can take up and hold on to the excesses of the flow that risk overwhelming the system. Information can then be channelled on when conditions are more favourable for it to be heard in such a way that it can be thoughtfully acted upon.

An understanding of symbolic communication or miscommunication is therefore essential in monitoring the flow, for it is not uncommon for a supposedly innocuous piece of information to cause great offence. Likewise keeping a weather eye open for the unsaid, unacknowledged, and sometimes unconscious element of communication is essential as part of an early warning system of trouble in the making.

What is required of management in this 'sitting on the boundary' state of mind is adequate connection with the inside of the organization matched by the equivalent connection with the outside world; a sense of belonging to both systems and yet to neither. I am not, however, advocating an opportunistic 'sitting on the fence' type of role, for the position I am describing is anchored by the need for an acute awareness of the primary task of the organization on the one hand and, more importantly, by the ideas that the management needs to hold on behalf of the institution (Obholzer 1996).

The risk to the manager is to 'give in' to the pull of either inside or outside forces and thus to become identified and 'captured' in a group psychological sense. While being in such a state of capture is undoubtedly more 'comfortable', psychically speaking, it brings with it the risks described so lucidly by Pierre Turquet (1975) in his paper, 'Threats to Identity in the Large Group'. Melanie Klein's concepts of splitting and of projective identification arose from her particular interest in work with children and thus with the most primitive mental mechanisms. It is, of course, these very primitive mechanisms that manifest themselves *par excellence* in group processes. They throw light on the process whereby unacceptable aspects of the self, or of the institution, are split off and perceived in others. The price of employing this defensive mechanism is of course that there is no pressure to review one's own working practices, thus reducing the chance of learning from experience in the service of adaptation.

What is required for the manager is thus what in a clinical sense would be described as a 'depressive position' way of functioning—of being in touch with both inner-world and outer-world phenomena in a balanced, overall, containing way.

To me the most important psychoanalytic concept that contributes to understanding the containing function of management is, however, little spoken about in the management literature. It is the concept of detachment, that is, of careful and considerable observation of what is going on in a framework as free of preconception as possible—something that all psychoanalysts strive for. Put another way, it relates to the story of the man who was observed searching the ground under a streetlight. A passer-by asked him what he was looking for. The man replied that he was looking for a bunch of keys he had lost. 'Did you lose them here?' asked the passer-by. 'No,' said the searcher, 'but the light is better here.'

This phenomenon of searching 'where the light is better', that is, in an area with which we are already familiar, as opposed to allowing ourselves the experience of searching in the unknown dark where we might actually find the answer, seems to me to be a very important management issue. The capacity to stand the experience of not knowing and of not falling into premature pseudo-understanding and action is obviously to be valued and fostered.

It is important not only from the perspective of having a thinking institution but also from the perspective of allowing the greatest opportunity for the creativity of the members and of the institution as a whole to emerge. In order for that to happen the necessary structures for containment need to be in place in the institution—clarity of primary task, leadership, and authority, and the resources, particularly time, so that issues other than and beyond the mere struggle for everyday survival can be addressed.

CONCLUSION

In a recent paper Elliot Jaques discusses and rejects his earlier (1955) seminal paper and adopts a revised view that 'it is badly organized social systems that arouse psychotic anxieties' (Jaques 1995: 343). I agree with him on this, but it begs the question of whether any systems are ever so well organized that anxiety does not 'slosh around in them'. I believe not. As managers it is, however, essential for us to understand that a work organization that has clarity of primary task as a constant in the management process, however difficult to achieve as a definitive outcome, is already half-way there to the process of damping down the excesses of institutional anxiety.

The emphasis on primary task must necessarily be followed by attention to authority and power and to matters of role, role definition, and differentiation of resources, time, and boundaries. All of these are absolutely central components of the concept of containment. The process could be described by analogy with roll-on roll-off ferries. These ships are at risk of capsizing because even relatively little water entering the vessel is not contained and can therefore flow to and build up on one side of the vessel, thus upsetting its stability. The addition of internal partitions prevents the sloshing about and reduces to a minimum the destructive effect of water on board. Symbolically, the ferry is the institution, the water the unconscious and anti-task processes. Where there is no clarity of task and structure, the anti-task processes are allowed free flow; the presence of such structures instead contains the processes and localizes them to minimize their destructive effect and allow them to be tackled.

This brings us back to the concept of containment and to the specific contribution which the psychoanalytic understanding of containment can make to the practice of management. Bion (1962) described a process whereby the mother took in and accepted the child's projections of discomfort and distress, metabolized them, and returned them to the child in an improved and partly understood form. The mother thus acted as the additional purifying agent for the child–mother dyad, a process the child itself was not capable of performing.

The leader and management of an organization in essence need to perform a similar task of containment for the staff. This does not mean the creation of a dependency situation such as is implied by a mother–child dyadic model; it needs to be based on a model of role performance by all concerned in a way that acknowledges both their skills and deficits. By virtue of both role and transference processes, the leader and management should be in the best position to perform the containment functions outlined above. And, as mentioned previously, in order for the containment function to be adequately addressed and for the work to be seen and managed in context, the overall constructs and concepts outlined in this chapter need to be available, in order to provide reference points against which the overall enterprise and its functioning can be evaluated.

The whole idea of managing the unconscious is of course a contradiction in terms. A more accurate phrase might be: managing the organization in a state of awareness of the existence of unconscious processes. There is no doubt in my mind that an awareness of the ubiquitous nature and the destructive quality of unconscious processes in institutions can help to minimize their impact. Put more positively, such an awareness can help to harness unconscious processes in the service of creative institutional functioning.

7

Dependency, Alienation, or Partnership? The changing relatedness of the individual to the enterprise

Eric Miller

INTRODUCTION

The Group Relations Programme of the Tavistock Institute, initiated in the late 1950s, was based on and contributed to the system psychodynamic framework that had emerged from the Institute's early studies of work organization. From 1980 onwards, OPUS (an Organization for Promoting Understanding of Society) used this framework to explore underlying processes in large systems and also at the societal level (cf. Khaleelee and E. J. Miller 1985; E. J. Miller 1986). One prominent theme was the changing world of employment and work at that time. The present chapter draws on studies both of the Tavistock Institute and of OPUS, as well as of others, to review implications of past and future change for the organization and management of enterprises in the contemporary world.

Work has always provided a core identity for the vast majority of adult males. I work, therefore I am. And for a growing proportion of women today work is no longer secondary to motherhood but competing with it as a core identity. Work confers an identity in two ways: through its content and its context. Content covers the activities involved in the job and the skills required to produce them. Since the Industrial Revolution this has normally involved being alongside others in the context of a workplace, with an ordained structure of roles and role relationships; with—often—another role structure of union–management relations; with an informal pattern of interpersonal and intergroup relations; and, both produced by and infiltrating all of these, with that largely implicit set of values, beliefs, attitudes, and norms of behaviour that we call organiza-tional culture. Work identity is commonly experienced and perceived holistically, without recognizing the two elements. However, the distinction is important.

Thus alienation from content and alienation from context are not necessarily correlated. For the individual who is alienated from a job that is repetitive, that uses only a fraction of his/her skills, that gives no satisfaction, and that is experienced as coercive and soul destroying, the workplace, whether overtly one loves it or hates it, may nevertheless through its structures and culture serve a significant function in conferring order, predictability, meaning, and a sense of self. Conversely, if the content of the work is not tied to a specific enterprise, and particularly if the content is challenging, demanding, and satisfying, it is this that confers the work identity whereas psychological investment in the workplace may well be quite low. True anomie, in the Durkheimian sense, is alienation from both content and context (Durkheim 1930).

For very many people in Britain the last twenty years have brought profound changes in both these aspects of work, and especially in context. There has been a significant shift in the relatedness of the individual to the work organization and, along with this, a shift in the place of the work identity in the individual's total life-space. It is the purpose of this chapter to describe these processes and to explore their implications for individuals, for the management of employing organizations, and also for us as a society. It begins, however, by offering a particular perspective on the formation of identities and the meaning they acquire as part of the process of individual development from birth and early infancy onwards.

THE PARADOXES OF IDENTITY

A dictionary definition of 'identity', and one in common usage, is 'individuality'. It represents my self, my way of being and thinking, my name—all the things that mark my specialness and make me unique. The other definition, apparently quite contradictory, is 'sameness': to be identical is to be exactly the same—a twin, a clone. Thus my identity—or, more strictly, my identities, as, say, white, male, British—categorize me as being on these dimensions the same as all the others who carry those labels. Perhaps these two definitions are not so contradictory as they seem: one's individuality can be seen as a unique combination of samenesses on a very large number of dimensions (E. J. Miller 1993b). Nevertheless the ambiguity points us to two paradoxes inherent in our psychosocial being. First, there is the coexistence of the drive to be separate and autonomous and the need to be attached, to belong. That tension and struggle between individuation and incorporation begins in infancy and continues throughout our lives. We are constantly pushed and pulled by these forces within us which are reinforced by pressures from without. Secondly, the experience of sameness is always, implicitly or explicitly, an expression of a difference: in the example of my identities, non-white, non-male, non-British. Inclusion and exclusion are two sides of the same coin. And sometimes the difference is oppositional, as in the 'them and us' of industrial relations. 'We' need 'them' to define 'us'.

There is a further complication: my different identities are not always in harmony with one another. As a taxpayer and as a patient, my views of the health service may be divergent, even contradictory. And those are just two of my almost countless identities. The more complex our society and the greater the rate of change, the larger the number and perhaps degree of such contradictions that one has to cope with.

Here it is useful to go back to our early developmental experience as infants and to consider how far the mechanisms we learned then continue to sustain us as adults. The new-born baby is a bundle of instinctive drives—seeking nurture and safety, avoiding danger or pain—in an unbounded world. It also seems equipped with a need to make sense of it all—a will to meaning (Frankl 1959). Its early experience, mainly in feeding and nurturing, is of fragmented images of whatever it sees, hears, touches, and smells. To survive, the baby begins to split those images into 'good' and 'bad', clinging to the 'good' and pushing away the 'bad'. Only after several months does it begin to perceive a boundary between inside and outside. Initially it is a physical boundary: those toes belong to me; those arms, that breast, are attached to someone else. Thus that first sense of 'me' is coupled with awareness of something other that is 'not-me'—primarily mother. This upsets its earlier sense-making effort, since both 'the good breast', the source of safety and succour, and 'the bad breast', which it had associated with pain and hunger and wanted to destroy, turn out to belong to the same person (cf. Klein 1952; 1959). The baby is now introduced to the experience of guilt and, with it, reparation. But the ambivalent feelings of loving and hating are hard to hold on to, and the early proclivity to split the world into good and bad continues. To keep mother good, the bad must be projected elsewhere.

This is the phase of identity formation. Initially the significant other is mother, and 'self' is essentially the identity of mother's baby. Quite soon we can observe a further differentiation into two identities, as the baby presents itself differently to mother and to father, responding to the different ways they relate to it and learning different ways of manipulating them. These can be seen as two manifestations of its self. Other identities emerge in relation to siblings, grandparents, neighbours and in them gender becomes gradually more significant and the baby learns progressively the behaviours appropriate and inappropriate to each. I find it useful to conceive of 'self' as the function of managing multiple identities in relation to multiple others. As the child expands its relationships, makes new friends, and meets a range of teachers and fellow-pupils at school so the identities multiply and so, too, do the potential discrepancies and conflicts. To cope with these the child applies the defences learned earlier in relation to the parents: splitting, projection, and denial are almost universal. Such individual defences are reinforced by the recognition of samenesses, of 'wes': we siblings in relation to parents; we the family in relation to neighbours; we the classmates in relation to the teacher.

School is the first sustained experience of a system larger than a face-to-face group: it is the workplace of the child. Those shared projections of the pupils on to their teacher—whether positive or negative, and they are usually one or the other—reinforce each child's own use of splitting and projection as defences. 'School' is a social institution in the sense that there are certain expected norms of behaviour that apply to all schools, and as such it has been a significant means of socializing the child into membership of the wider society. Each school, for the children within it, and indeed for the teachers too, also functions as a container. It provides a larger version of the holding environment that the mother provides for the baby—a 'good enough' degree of security and pre-dictability to meet one's dependency needs. This seems to be something that we are always unconsciously seeking: an encompassing mother-substitute—whether as a person or an institution—who can safely contain all our internal contradictions and give us a sense of wholeness.

The proposition that it is a function of social systems to serve as defences against anxiety was put forward by Jaques (1955) and developed by Menzies (1960) and others. Structures—formal and informal—and culture support the defences of members of the organization. Jaques was addressing the defences that we all have and need. Menzies added the notion of supplementary social defences against the anxieties generated by the nature of the task itself. Thus the work of a nurse in caring for severely ill and dying patients can undermine her own defences and resuscitate quite primitive and frightening anxieties of early infancy. This mobilizes additional social defences, such as pushing responsibility upwards, which actually interfere with the task of the hospital. More generally it can be suggested that the number of levels in a hierarchy is an index of anxiety—essentially anxiety about loss of control. Hierarchies supply containment and security.

CHANGES IN EMPLOYMENT AND THE WORKPLACE

During the post-war years in Britain children making the transition from school to employment therefore found themselves in a setting that was experienced as psychologically similar in many ways. The organization was a kind of macro-mother. Structures were defined, boundaries clear. Organizational life offered a kind of ongoing soap opera whose heroes and villains were ready-made for shared projections; individuals' defences were well catered for. Jobs in most industrial and commercial enterprises were as secure as in the public service, and unions were strong enough to keep the employers in line: 'if mother showed signs of being less than generous with the breast, father would be relied upon to keep the milk flowing' (E. J. Miller 1986: 260). And as a backdrop the welfare state was there to take care of one not just from cradle to grave but, it was said, from the sperm to the worm.

In the mid-1970s the backdrop became important: registered unemployment doubled, from 2.6 to 5.4 per cent. After the advent of the first Thatcher government in 1979 the cracks in the dependency culture quickly widened. By 1983, the official figures showed 3.2 million unemployed (13.5 per cent), more than a million of them jobless for more than a year—though the real total was estimated to be nearer four million, to which manufacturing industry had contributed much more than its share.

It has been said that 'the best way to understand a system is to change it' (Kurt Lewin, quoted by Trist and Murray 1993: 30). That is certainly true of employing organizations in the early 1980s. It took the mass redundancies at that time to uncover the full significance—psychological, social, and economic—that employment had acquired in our society. In a study in West Yorkshire in 1983, three themes emerged consistently in the interviews and group discussions (Khaleelee and E. J. Miller 1984).

First and foremost was the equation of employment with respect and unemployment with worthlessness:

- 'People *are* what they *do*.'
- 'the destruction of your whole being.'
- 'rejected and useless; no place in society.'
- 'They shut the front door and go out once a week to sign on.'

Women said that 'a man's not a real man unless he has a job'—and they were referring directly to loss of a gendered identity and to the sexual impotence often associated with it. The second theme linked employment to order and unemployment to anarchy: employment was seen as a moral virtue and as a means of social control. Those still in work dealt with their guilt by stigmatizing the jobless—'they could get a job if they really tried'—and were also anxious about the rising crime rate. Thirdly, employment meant money, choice, and a decent standard of living, whereas the unemployed had lost their status as consumers.

Thus this study revealed the centrality of the institution of employment, which served as a kind of passport to other key institutions—notably marriage, parenthood, and the market economy. I suggested earlier that 'self' could be seen as a kind of manager of the individual's multiple identities. From this study it became clear that for some of these men employment was not just one among many identities: in effect the employment identity *was* 'self', or a substitute for self. For most others it was a dominant identity and the symptoms of depression, loss of meaning, helplessness, impotence, and psychosomatic illness were widespread among the newly redundant. This demonstrated the extent to which they had been dependent on the workplace to buttress—and even replace—their individual defences against anxiety.

Women in general were much less damaged by loss of employment. Most were wives and mothers who continued to have a significant job in running a household, while for the unmarried, future motherhood held out the prospect of a much more significant identity than work could confer. In either case, they were better able to draw strength from their other identities. Some men also had this capacity. Their identity was more linked to content than to context and their response to redundancy was more pragmatic: 'A job's a job'; 'I'll find one: it's down to me'. They were more likely to shift into self-employment or to supplement the dole by working in the black economy. Such men, like most women, had a stronger sense of self and a more instrumental relation to work as a means, not an end: they did not need the conformity and dependency of an employing organization (E. J. Miller 1986; 1993c).

Although many of the victims felt betrayed, those who still had jobs were anxious about their own survival. The workplace was no longer a safe container; as 'mother' it was no longer reliable. Indeed, the experience may have resonated with that much earlier loss of the idealized mother and in some it evoked corresponding defences, such as denial: 'It can't happen to me'. Related to this was a tendency for the survivors to dissociate themselves from their redundant ex-colleagues. Relationships in the workplace became more cautious. Paranoia was widespread: 'management' was not trusted and there was also wariness about some fellow workers suspected of ingratiating themselves with managers to safeguard their jobs. There was a tendency to huddle almost conspiratorially in pairs and small groups that were felt to be safe. So the meaning of the work identity was undergoing a radical shift: no longer was there a sense of commitment to or identification with 'the organization'. As in the wider society there was a shift from the dependency culture to one of 'failed dependency' (E. J. Miller 1986).

The mid-1980s in Britain brought a mini-boom. As more jobs became available, people began to hope and even believe that the economy had simply suffered a temporary blip. Unemployment nevertheless remained high, and so a significant minority of the population remained sceptical. They were proved to be right. The last year of the decade brought the beginning of a much deeper recession. This time it hit a much larger number of middle and more senior managers who had tended to regard themselves as immune, and hence the shock was all the greater. Outplacement firms found an expanding market for their services. Counsellors in one such firm reported that nearly all their clients had to be helped to work though their feelings of shock and betrayal before they could even begin to think about hunting for a new job.

Consequently withdrawal of psychological investment in the employing organization—a phenomenon that had emerged in the early 1980s and then partly receded—has now become widespread (E. J. Miller and Stein 1993). For the majority of people the workplace is no longer felt to be a safe place. This has significant implications for individuals and for organization and management.

IMPLICATIONS FOR THE INDIVIDUAL

Twenty years ago work identity and identity as a member of an employing organization—'content' and 'context'—were for most people undifferentiated. For some, as we have seen, that fused identity was a substitute for self and consequently for them redundancy was traumatic. For many others the process of 'de-fusion' was painful. Whether it was forced upon them by redundancy—the content identity had to be divorced from the context identity if they were to be in the job market—or, as in the case of 'survivors', it may have been a half-consciously chosen strategy for self-protection (quite literally protection of the 'self')—de-fusion meant coming to terms with loss of a significant provider for psychological needs for dependency. Moreover, the actual or feared experience was not just of loss but of betrayal by the organization as 'mother', with 'father'—the trade union—having proved powerless to intervene. Hence the individual would be most reluctant to make a psychological investment in a future employing organization.

Having been the first to put forward the proposition that social systems serve as defences against anxiety Jaques recently withdrew it (Jaques 1995). He now argues that rational organizational design, based on principles that he has developed over the years (e.g. Jaques 1989), eliminates the intrusion of dysfunctional unconscious processes. Up to a point this is supported by the experience of myself and some of my colleagues (e.g. E. J. Miller and Rice 1967): by drawing clear organizational boundaries it is possible to 'design out' some of the ambiguities and discrepancies that cause unnecessary stress and conflict. However, relationships in any system, whether work organization, school, or family, will always be a vehicle for unconscious projections. What has changed, at least in the UK (and Jaques may be partly responding to this), is that because the workplace is no longer a safe container, the individual's relation to it is much more instrumental and hence more guarded, more calculated, and indeed often cynical. It is certainly no bank for depositing one's dependency.

If, as it appears, the individual has withdrawn or reduced psychological investment in the workplace, where has it gone? In particular, what has happened to dependency needs? At one end of the spectrum we have the anomie of the helpless, the drop-outs, unsustained by our social institutions. At the other end is total rejection of dependency on, or obligations towards, anyone else. Self-centred individualism is seen as a product of the Thatcher ideology and is an understandable defence of those who have felt betrayed: trust no one. It is also, of course, a characteristic of psychopaths, who—often because of the experience of betrayal in infancy—do not know guilt. Indeed, intelligent psychopaths seem much more likely to prosper in businesses today, compared with twenty years ago: lack of social conscience is an asset when a company is seen to need radical surgery.

In between these extremes are people with varying levels of dependency needs. Those whose needs are greatest tend to seek an alternative all-embracing identity into which the self can be fused and which can give meaning to their lives. Fundamentalist religions and extremist movements that offer messianic leadership and a supreme cause seem to be attracting a growing number of followers. The rest have in various ways redistributed their psychological investment among their portfolio of identities. Some have transferred investment from the workplace to the family—though paradoxically the workplace which is less able to meet their dependency needs also commands more of their time and energy, so the neglected family may fail them. The most positive category is a seemingly growing number of self-managing individuals, not over-reliant on any one source of emotional sustenance, but at the same time valuing interdependence with others. Many of them are drawn from the increasing proportion of the working population who have no experience of the pre-1980 workplace and who have not been exposed to the severe adjustments that their older colleagues have had to make. Their expectations are probably more realistic, and certainly do not include a job for life. This is not to say that they all have well-balanced investment portfolios—who does?—but they will be less inclined to invest heavily in the workplace identity and more likely to opt for a work-content identity with portable skills. To be an autonomous, choice-making individual who can engage collaboratively with others can be seen as a healthy contrast to the culture of dependency.

CHANGES IN THE NATURE OF 'THE ORGANIZATION'

If the preceding analysis is correct it follows that the 'human resources' in today's work organization are very different from those of twenty years ago. That plainly has implications for models of management, and we shall be suggesting that these implications are not widely enough recognized. But first we need to note that constructs of 'the organization' have also changed greatly over this period.

We have noted the change in the perception of work organizations generally as no longer being reasonably reliable 'mothers'. This undermines the once-familiar sense of 'belonging to an organization', with the connotations of surrendering one's individuality and of being owned, and also of reciprocal obligations to the employee. Moreover, to feel that one belongs to a group or organization there needs to be some consensus about where the boundaries are between inside and outside. In many enterprises these have become much more fuzzy.

Several factors have contributed to this. One is the trend towards outsourcing. Activities seen as not central to the task of the enterprise, including, for instance payroll, printing, maintenance, or cleaning, are increasingly contracted out. Use of self-employed contractors and agency staff has increased. Temporary and part-time staff are also more common and are working alongside a diminishing nucleus of full-time employees.

Another factor is the blurring of the boundary between supplier and customer. Powerful purchasers, such as supermarkets, exert considerable control over the operations of suppliers, extending beyond quality control to insistence on changes in organization and management. Conversely, especially in the manufacturing sector, development engineers from the supplying enterprises are being drawn more fully into the customer's product design, development, and marketing functions, even to the point of directly supplying the production line. Here there is obvious ambiguity about which organization—the supplier or the customer—the engineers 'belong' to.

Organizational boundaries are also disrupted by mergers and acquisitions. Employees suddenly discover that they are part of—or superfluous to—a different enterprise. Globalization means that a unit that seems to be operating viably in one country can be redefined as a liability by the invisible multinational of which it is a part.

IMPLICATIONS FOR MANAGEMENT

These factors combine to reduce still further the psychological investment of employees in the organization, so that their relationship is not much less instrumental than that of the contract or temporary worker; from the employers' perspective ease of hiring and firing seems to be in the interests of efficiency. The recessions at the beginning and end of the 1980s, which undermined the trade unions, gave employers the power to do this, and it is a power that many managements are reluctant to give up: but the costs can be high and are often not foreseen.

A common phenomenon in large organizations today is the increasing distancing of top management from the work-force. It is reflected in the escalating differential between the top people's remuneration and the average wage. The distance permits them to order drastic downsizing while it defends them against the guilt of recognizing the human consequences for the individual victims—a guilt often carried by those who have to carry out this order. The remote leadership often tends to take followership for granted. A fairly senior personnel manager in a large corporation that had made thousands of people redundant said in an interview that top management had no inkling of the effect on the morale of the survivors. Alternatively, followership is seen as something that can be mobilized by the human resources department through suitable 'training' programmes—more accurately described as attempts at reindoctrination—related to a nebulous mission statement. Thus the early 1990s saw a rash of attempts to reverse psychological withdrawal. Given the rage or contempt

towards the leader and top management, it is not surprising that these programmes have often been counter-productive. A follow-up of one such process
revealed increased disenchantment among employees, who labelled it as
'fraudulent' and 'two-faced'—an attempt to brainwash them into becoming
'company persons': 'Indeed, those companies that try hardest to eliminate
negative or ambivalent feelings may instead stimulate the most resentment,
mistrust and suspicion' (E. J. Miller and Stein 1993: 36). To expect that surviving
employees could be persuaded to be loyal to an employer who had been
extremely disloyal to the hundreds of ex-employees who had lost their jobs was
rightly seen as absurd. Cynicism masked by compliance—the term 'calculated
sincerity' has been used—prevailed as the norm.

   These two responses to psychological withdrawal—denial that it is a problem
or attempts to reindoctrinate—reflect two different mental models of the
employees in the minds of managers. The former implies that they are objects
without feelings—interchangeable mechanisms, which can be switched on and
off: echoes of Taylorism perhaps. In the second model they are infants who will
believe what their parents tell them, follow blindly where their leaders take
them. It reflects a wish in management for a 1990s version of the 1970s dependency culture.

   Increasingly, however, managers are recognizing that psychological withdrawal is counter-productive. As a result of the combination of downsizing and
technological advances, particularly in information technology (IT), a growing
proportion of roles are not only beyond the capacity of interchangeable mechanisms or infants, but critical to the performance of the enterprise. They require
what Kahn (1992) has called 'psychological presence': paying total attention,
being fully there, putting all of oneself into the role. Accordingly the question
managers are now asking is how to make psychological presence happen. This
is, of course, a restatement of the perennial question—'How do I make other
people do what I want them to do?'—which has generated the huge literature in
motivation that essentially tries to offer managers attractive packaging for the
carrot and stick. Alongside this is another more relevant body of literature on
workplace organization which indicates that it is counter-productive to try to
make people do anything.

   Kahn (1990; 1992) identifies three 'psychological conditions' for making psychological presence possible. One is availability, by which he means not being
distracted by disturbances in one's personal world which can prevent full attention to the task in hand. The second is the meaningfulness of the task itself in its
immediate context—the psychological 'return on investments' from engaging
in the role (Kahn 1990: 705). The third is psychological safety 'in the sense of
being able to show and employ the self without fear of negative consequences'
(loc. cit.). Kahn refers to safety in the context of the social system of the workplace—relationships, group processes, norms. This is open to misinterpreta-
tion. If one thinks of safety in terms of job security and continuity of
relationships, these are conditions that are decreasingly provided by the

contemporary workplace. Moreover that kind of security tends to generate a sense of dependency which is antithetical to the autonomy inherent in being 'fully there', using one's own authority. Particularly relevant is the authority to speak out, knowing that one will be heard.

Kahn's first condition, availability, is not something that management can influence. The second, meaningfulness, is most obviously met if the work content is intrinsically challenging and satisfying, but even if that is not the case the early Tavistock work on socio-technical systems as semi-autonomous workgroups highlighted the importance of building them around a 'whole task' (e.g. Trist and Bamforth 1951; Rice 1958; 1963; Trist *et al.* 1963; E. J. Miller 1975). This way of working required a profound shift in the conventional definition of managerial and supervisory roles: instead of managing people, their task became to manage the boundary of the system in relation to its external environment by defining the task of the system and making available the requisite resources (e.g. materials and supplies) to enable the people within the system to manage it themselves. Such a way of working is difficult for many managers, and meeting Kahn's third condition, safety, is even more so. Today in Britain, for example, many people in health and education have work that is intrinsically satisfying and they are deeply committed to the tasks that their enterprises are set up to perform but they are alienated from the philosophy and system of management. Although they will be psychologically present in the here and now of the operating theatre or the classroom the ingredient of safety is missing: to speak out may put one's job on the line. It cannot be allowed because the very idea of it makes managers anxious about losing control.

But even if all three necessary conditions are met they are still not sufficient conditions to procure psychological presence; they do no more than make it possible for the individual to choose to give it. This is pivotal. Indeed, I see choice as primary. Whether consciously or intuitively, some managements are recognizing this by providing financial support and time off for the further education and development of staff without insisting that it contributes directly to their task performance. Indeed, it may qualify them to move elsewhere. Paradoxically this can be an effective counter to psychological withdrawal because it gives them that choice: if they choose to stay they are much more free to be psychologically present.

Recognition of the need for a new paradigm of organization is probably especially strong in the smaller hi-tech and other specialized businesses, where psychological presence is essential to survival, and that is where there are signs of its emergence. Very often the people whose skills they need are among the growing number who have opted out of employing organizations in favour of the greater independence of self-employment as consultants and contractors. They have no wish for a dependent relationship, whereas the enterprise requires their competence, not their compliance. The form of association may or may not be a partnership in the legal sense of shared ownership, but it is a partnership based on interdependence and a common commitment to the task: authority derives from competence rather than from position in a structure; leadership is a shifting function; hierarchy gives way to polyarchy.

There are good reasons for moving towards organizational forms that give full recognition to people as autonomous, choice-making individuals as opposed to interchangeable objects. Apart from the moral argument there is the sheer incongruity of assuming that the same person can in the employee role be an object and in the consumer role a choice maker and autonomous. Most important, however, is the failure to make use of 'human resources' as genuine resources that can affect the future of the enterprise. As Stacey (1996) has pointed out, on the basis of his studies of the implications of complexity theory, if an enterprise is to survive and be resilient in the face of increasingly unpredictable change in environmental forces, it needs a capacity for creativity—a capacity to question and abandon taken-for-granted assumptions. As with psychological presence, only more so, creativity is not something that can be made to happen: if it emerges at all it will do so spontaneously. Moreover, it will typically arise on the edges of the system and in relation to management—the dominant coalition—it will appear as subversive (cf. E. J. Miller 1983). Their definition of reality is being undermined; they feel that their managerial task is to provide order and predictability; yet the ingredients of disorder and unpredictability are essential for survival. Thus the internal whistle-blower, for example, who is perceived as a menace in the one context is potentially a valued asset in the other. To sustain such ambivalence seems almost impossible, but structures can help in developing a culture that offers at least some space for more creative thought and action.

A starting-point is to re-examine our constructs of membership of an organization. Even though the relationship of the employee to the enterprise has become less secure and correspondingly more instrumental, the workplace continues to be a significant feature in the lifespan of most people. Interpersonal relationships develop within and beyond role relationships. Happenings in the enterprise, and associated hopes and fears, are a focus of conversation. Implicitly, even though some might explicitly deny it, these transactions express some sense of membership of the enterprise. It certainly has no formal recognition, except perhaps in the employment contract itself. The formal structure, which describes, and indeed prescribes, the relatedness of the individual to the enterprise, is an arrangement only of work-roles. Usually the organization chart presents a straightforward hierarchy and sometimes a matrix, but the language of 'vertical' or 'horizontal' is almost universal. Union membership, as mentioned earlier, may define another role in a second structure of management–union negotiation, at subsystem, enterprise, and sometimes national level, though this has become attenuated since 1980. What is missing in most enterprises is a structure that recognizes that 'human resources' have a stake in the larger system, and individual contributions to make to it, that go beyond the work-roles. Co-operatives and employee shareholding schemes that confer an ownership role are examples, but they are relatively rare. It is argued here that explicit recognition of this third role, as 'citizen of the enterprise', which is implicit in the successful small hi-tech businesses described above, could contribute to the effectiveness and viability of larger systems in the face of rapid change.

The idea of the 'citizen of the enterprise' is not a new one (cf. E. J. Miller 1977; 1993*a*; 1993*c*). It springs from the observation that informally people are acting in this role already, through those interpersonal relations with others both within and outside their immediate subsystem of work-roles. Contained in the 'gossip' is a rich lode of data that is seldom tapped. People at the coalface can see serious flaws in a new computer system, for example, but no one dares tell 'management'; and indeed in an alienated culture with a remote top management there may be a not-unconscious wish that the system *should* fail, to punish 'them'. Or they may identify possible system improvements but refrain from passing them on. Not just through their work-roles but also through their external relations they also garner scraps of information, for example on views of customers and suppliers and even on intentions of competitors. Those scraps when collected are potentially valuable data on the environment of the business. Such data can become available if the third role of citizen of the enterprise is recognized, through setting up appropriate participative structures—for example, cross-departmental and cross-level meetings—and if it is supported by a culture that allows speaking out without recrimination: whistle-blowers welcome! In this respect the 'third role' fulfils a key condition for psychological presence as well as providing a climate for creativity. One could say that a listening organization is a learning organization.

On the other hand, it is a product of the society of the 1970s, when industrial democracy was still in vogue and full employment was seen as the norm. For example, one manufacturing company at that time instituted a regular weekly meeting, open to employees at all levels, to examine the state of the organization (Khaleelee and E. J. Miller 1985). Does it make sense in today's world of job insecurity, psychological withdrawal, and the more instrumental relationship? I believe it may. First, as we have seen, it builds on patterns of informal communication that are inherent in the workplace. Even though the organization is no longer a relatively stable social system for supporting and containing individual defences, the shared 'soap opera' continues to offer an array of opportunities for splitting and projection. Secondly, by treating people as intelligent human beings rather than interchangeable devices it reduces negativity and destructiveness. Beyond that, however, although the picture of the autonomous individual exercising her/his own authority in an instrumental relationship with the enterprise is evidently more healthy than the unthinking dependency of the past, if pushed too far its consequences may be unhealthy, for the individual and the wider social system, as well as for the enterprise. Individuals have, in varying degrees, needs for attachment and dependency that have to be met, while at the societal level we are experiencing the increased inequalities and reduced social cohesion that are produced by the culture of individualism. Some enterprises at least appear to be pursuing cost-effectiveness and the associated instrumental relationship to a point that is counterproductive. One troubled company, which was performing poorly and had low staff morale, gave its workers a guarantee that there would be no redundancies for two years. A far cry from a job for life; but nevertheless the effect was an immediate upsurge in morale, commitment, and productivity. This suggests that although the organization is not able to, and should not, provide the past degree of containment, some increase in dependability and thus of containment can be advantageous to both employers and employees.

CONCLUDING COMMENTS

This chapter has traced shifts in society and the enterprise and in the relatedness of the individual to them. At the societal level the move has been from a reliable dependency culture, through 'failed dependency', associated with rage and alienation, and into a culture of non-dependency, with self-interest as the norm and a widening gap between rich and poor as a consequence. The shifts in the work organization have been similar. For the individual, the work content identity has become more prominent—a passport to economic survival—with correspondingly less investment in context.

We may now be beginning to move into a different phase. The British election results in May 1997 suggested a reaction against the extreme exploitativeness of Thatcherism and a wish for a less selfish and less uncaring society. Enterprises, for their part, are realizing that they need to use people's talents in engaging with an unpredictable environment, while the individual has needs both for autonomy and for a setting that provides a degree of containment. This complementarity points to partnership as an appropriate and desirable form of workplace relationship, in that it mobilizes mature interdependence rather than offering containment of the more primitive anxieties. Thus it would seem to be consistent both with contemporary social values and with commercial expediency.

8

A Fresh Look at Authority and Organization: Towards a spiritual approach for managing illusion

Gouranga P. Chattopadhyay

INTRODUCTION

In this chapter, I take a fresh look at authority and organization by enquiring into the nature of some of the fundamental notions on which our image of authority is based: boundaries, process, hierarchy. Having introduced the idea, fundamental to the chapter, that all boundaries are illusions, I offer a case example which illustrates the damaging effects of treating boundaries as though they are real and fixed, rather than created in the mind. Boundaries that are intended to enable engagement with a task are shown to become a major impediment to its implementation. Since management is largely about creating and providing boundary conditions appropriate for engaging with tasks, it may be considered as the process of managing illusions (Chattopadhyay 1999 forthcoming). In addition, the notion of process is usually lost sight of while managing one's experience as one engages with tasks. As a result, the approach becomes reductionist and many of one's experiences are denied, largely unconsciously.

I then explore the way in which notions of hierarchy, which have their origins in the dynamics of religion and the nuclear family, have become fused and confused in organizations. This is contrasted with the example of Fox society (North American Indian), the religious, family, and societal structures which offer a different perspective on and model for the experiences of authority, hierarchy, and organization.

Finally, I propose a three-fold educational approach to the development of a mindset or disposition that can firmly hold the notion of process as the reality and boundaries as illusions. It is an approach which I describe as *spiritual*. The first approach has been called socio-analysis (Bain 1997; 1998*a*), which is derived from the experiences of participation in group relations conferences (E. J. Miller 1989), and of psychoanalytic, systems, and organizational behaviour theories. The second approach is grounded in an understanding of the basics of quantum mechanics. This proposes that the cosmos may indeed be boundary-less and that human beings 'see' boundaries because of our limited perceptual ability. The third approach is the pursuit of spirituality, which recognizes non-duality as the ultimate reality. This can be engaged with experientially through the methodology of yoga (Saraswati 1984; 1989; Saraswati and Saraswati 1984; Yogananda 1991), or intellectually through the study of the ancient Indian *darshans* (Gambhirananda 1989; Nikhilananda 1987). Each of these approaches or paths on their own, but even more powerfully in combination, can open up fresh possibilities for the experience and exercise of authority in organizations. How fresh ideas of boundaries, such as of time, can be generated through a combination of the second and third approaches listed above can be seen in the dialogue between Krishnamurti and Bohm (1986).

CASE EXAMPLE

I shall illustrate the impact of seeing boundaries as illusions, and thereby being freed to work at process with a new authority, by means of a case example taken from the experience of consulting to a ball-bearing company (see Chattopadhyay and Lawrence 1991).

One way of viewing the process of ball-bearing production is to concentrate on the final stages of production, which begin with cutting metal rods. However, the process could also be visualized as starting with the mining oper-ations and ending as the ball-bearings gradually wear out through use. For the works manager, it seems irrelevant to know about the mines, so long as the metal's quality is compatible with the throughput process. It is necessary to hold in mind a boundary for successfully engaging with the task in hand. The problem, however, is that over time the man-made boundaries become taken for granted. Task-related problems then remain unsolved and escalate because inappropriate boundary conditions keep bedevilling the process.

During the consultation, several boundary problems were diagnosed as lead-ing to wastage. One was the boundary between the cutting and the grinding sections. If the grinders blamed the cutters, the latter would blame the quality of steel, leading to an exchange of memos between the production and the purchase departments. This had become a way of life in the enterprise. The low-skilled cutters were unable technically to point out the problem with the material. The grinders had the requisite skill, but the 'traditional' boundary between the two sections came in the way of helping the cutters. The solution consisted of merging the two sections, that is, removing the boundary, and over a comparatively short period training the cutters as grinders so that the personnel in the section rotated between the two jobs.

This example highlights, overtly, how the notion of process gets lost because we seek to manage it more easily by creating boundaries that are seldom, if ever, reviewed over time. I use the word 'overtly', here, to introduce a more complex, covert phenomenon: the unconscious organizational dynamic.

This ball-bearing company, started as a medium-scale industry, was acquired after ten years of its existence by a large industrial house, which installed a new chief executive officer with the brief to introduce new machinery to increase production without adding manpower. This was perceived by the workers as heralding large-scale automation and downsizing. For the managers there was anxiety about being replaced should they have 'teething' problems with the new machines. However, there was also the hope, or the fantasy, that the new owners would not have made a heavy investment in the company unless they were sure of high returns. These notions led to an unconscious collusion between the managers and the workers that ensured a continued high level of wastage, pulling down profit.

The concrete suggestions for the change of certain boundary conditions (not discussed above) to reduce wastage and increase productivity actually came from a project group consisting of workers, supervisors, and managers. However, what made it possible for all the changes to be effected smoothly was the fact that the new CEO accepted the need to allay the anxieties of workers and managers. For the workers, this was done through negotiating a new agreement with the union. For the managers, a long-range training programme was introduced. For both categories, the creation of a representative project group around the consultants was the first step towards containing the anxiety level because this was experienced as a motion of confidence in the employees by the CEO as the representative of the new owners. Once this happened, they felt free to use their personal authority to suggest changes.

The case highlights how organizational processes can get lost while 'standard methods' of dealing with 'products', such as industrial relations problems and disgruntled or alienated managers, are used. These 'products', or terminologies, are also a kind of boundary imposed on human behaviour from a desire to make it 'manageable'. Words, or jargon expressions, such as structure, blueprint, framework, industrial relations, and discontent, are used to impose boundaries, physical or in the mind, to manage oneself effectively in relation to one's task and environment. But the reality that the boundaries have been imagined in the first place is often forgotten. Consequently problem-solving activities founder, as a result of seeking to remove the symptoms while leaving the function and the functionality of the boundaries unexplored.

BOUNDARIES AS STRUCTURES IN THE MIND

It is best to think of an organization as a picture, or image, within another picture or image in the mind. The larger one is that of the system which one works within and acts from; it has objectives and goals, it imports resources which it transforms by its throughput process and exports across its boundary with its environment. This is the institution in the mind. The second image is that of the organization itself, that is, the way in which all institutional resources are related to one another, including the human beings in a role network, in such a manner that the transformation process takes place with the least amount of wastage, adding value to the end-products. These images are held in the mind partly consciously, whereas aspects of the images that produce high anxiety or fear of pain remain largely in the unconscious, leading to unplanned activities based on unexplored assumptions and images (see, for example, Lawrence 1985a).

The activities by which organizational members bring organizational resources together depend on decisions about whether to engage with, or to disengage or refrain from, various tasks. Each decision on the appropriateness of an activity is based on the authority that one experiences in the situation. This depends on how one experiences and conceptualizes contextual boundary conditions, which are both external and internal. Examples of the former are the aims, objectives, and goals of the institution and of the tasks necessary to fulfil them. Tasks, which are also resources, have to be done within boundaries of time and physical space, utilizing such other resources as material, machinery, technology, and money. The resources internal to the people are skills and knowledge, feelings and emotions, values and attitudes, and assumptions, some of which cannot be checked easily or directly whereas others can be, though for a variety of reasons may not have been.

The presence or absence, the quality and the quantity, of the two sets of resources continually act on one another. For instance, the experience of time as an unlimited resource is likely to prolong the length of the task cycle so much that it fails to meet any objective or goal. By contrast, where it is experienced as a very scarce resource it may generate a high degree of anxiety, leading to a poor quality of task engagement. Conversely, anxiety about engaging with a task may lead to allocating an unrealistic time boundary. Therefore the existence of appropriate boundary conditions within which people engage with tasks is an essential feature of successful organizations. This process of creating and holding appropriate boundary conditions is defined here as the process of 'management'.

The term 'management' is also used to define a number of roles. Holders of management roles are entrusted with the task of providing the requisite boundary conditions and monitoring the organizational processes that follow. They also have the function of controlling deviance. As a group these role holders are usually referred to as 'the management', and they live up to this term so long as they act collectively through sharing authority and responsibility.

HIERARCHY AS A STRUCTURE OF BOUNDARIES IN THE MIND

The notion of hierarchy is of a series of structured boundaries, based on the idea of a number of roles subordinated to other roles. It is taken for granted in almost every kind of organization, operating in veiled forms even where a flat collegiate system is supposed to exist. It is mostly considered as essential for avoiding chaos (a mental construct that describes processes that do not approximate to the picture of ideal conditions held in the mind).

Hierarchy is a construct which is not based only on cognition. It also has a high emotional content. Yet hierarchy in work organizations is presented as an aspect of organizational structure devoid of any emotional undertone. This overt denial of an underlying emotional investment makes the impact of hierarchy very difficult to explore, despite the fact that it contributes significantly to human wastage through built-in contradictions and the potential for destructiveness (Chattopadhyay 1995; Chattopadhyay and Malhotra 1991). In most organizations, such wastage of human potential and other resources occurs because managers more often than not behave as supervisors and controllers, acting out the hierarchy-in-the-mind irrespective of its relevance to the system's tasks.

One of the major manifestations of the dysfunctionality of hierarchy is the separation of authority from task. Secondly, since authority in a hierarchic organization is perceived as a limited resource, distributed, notionally, by the head of the organization, most people lose their creativity to some extent through losing touch with their personal authority to think of and try out more effective ways of engaging with tasks (see, for example, Bain 1982). This is further reinforced by linearizing wisdom. Since skill, knowledge, and wisdom are supposed to increase as one goes up in the hierarchy, the people at the top consciously or unconsciously take steps to have a monopoly over information that is considered important for the organization. As a result middle managers feel unsafe, junior managers feel alienated from the system, and the non-management cadre often get infantilized (see, for example, Pederson-Krag 1951). Since hierarchy also dilutes accountability, many organizations face its consequences only when the bottom line becomes irreversibly red.

Basically, hierarchy obscures the fact that people get to use authority because others give it to them. By accepting membership of the system with all its rules and regulations on joining an organization, one delegates upwards one's authority for such things as time structuring, dress, placement, promotions and demotions, retiring, and even for getting sacked. Theoretically all these manifestations of authority are delegated to the chief executive officer, who then redelegates authority appropriately for engaging with tasks. However, the process of initial upward delegation is largely forgotten because of the picture of hierarchy that people carry in their heads. That picture strongly emphasizes the unquestionability of the system and also blurs the reality that the authority that one delegates upwards is logically related to the organizational tasks that one engages with. This leads to actual abuse of authority as well as to a climate of anxiety about its possible abuse. A glaring example is where employees not covered by industrial laws are made to work without compensation much longer hours than contracted for. Although this is done to engage with organizational tasks, it also hides the fact that people are made to work overtime because the management has failed to create appropriate boundaries. Terminologies, jargon, and myths are created, mostly unconsciously, to buttress the notion of hierarchy.

The almost universal acceptance of hierarchy as an indispensable structural form occurs, I hypothesize, because people carry in their mind, both consciously and unconsciously, its picture as an integral part of interpersonal relationships through experiencing hierarchy in their primary family.

Winnicott (1971) has pointed out the ways in which the infant unconsciously responds to total dependence on the mother, together with extreme terror (and the associated rage) that this one resource for survival may be withdrawn. This kind of feeling is the stuff that later in life nourishes the picture of hierarchy as both nurturing and punitive. At this early stage of life the infant, in its fantasy, creates the breast, through its sense of omnipotence when it is fed on time, but experiences impotence, through extreme anxiety and the terror of annihilation, when the feed is delayed. This is what Klein (1975*a*, 1975*b*) has called the paranoid-schizoid phase. The feelings of both omnipotence and impotence are associated with hierarchy in later life, depending on the position one finds oneself in.

Apart from such experiences, which are lodged in the unconscious and resonate in later life with the experience of hierarchy in organizations, almost all children quite consciously experience hierarchy at home. There is no question either of delegating authority upwards or of making any choice about one's parents! Nor do infants and children understand the logic of getting punished as part of the task of being 'well brought up'. This is the seed-bed for the later fantasy that in organizations people get authority by simply taking up various roles. This fantasy denies the reality of the process of upward delegation of authority related to the demands of organizational tasks, without which the very concept of organizational roles becomes meaningless.

Childhood experience is also fundamental to the mechanism by which discomforts associated with the parental role are later transferred on to other authority figures. As a result, feelings of pleasure and pain are projected on to decision makers, who are then perceived as dispensers of reward and punishment. The systems relating to such things as salaries, bonuses, promotions, and demotions, which theoretically are based on the skills and performance of employees, are then fantasized as systems of reward and punishment. The next step is that the system is actually converted into one of reward and punishment.

Further, I hypothesize that two notions underpin hierarchy as a fundamental basis for modern organizations. The first is that differences cannot be managed. Many efforts at managing differences, for example in interventions by organizational consultants, seem to have only very temporary and contextual impact. This is because they do not take into consideration the basic unconscious connection between difference and internalized hierarchy, which converts most differences into perceptions of inequality. The second notion underpinning the power of hierarchy is the denial that the phenomenon called difference is a matter of human invention based on the limitations of human perception.

The notion that differences are unmanageable is internalized at infancy when the baby experiences for the first time the boundary between the 'I' and the 'not-I' which separates it in its experience from the mother. The infant's desire to possess this 'other' remains unfulfilled forever. When the infant believes that it is in control of this 'other', it feels omnipotent and experiences superordination. When the experience is of loss of control, it feels impotent and experiences subordination. This is how the paranoid-schizoid position lays the foundation for internalized hierarchy. As a result of this first experience of boundary in an individual's life, a process is set up whereby acknowledged or fantasized boundaries represent differences that make objects appear either superordinate or subordinate in relation to the self. From the former one controls the difference while from subordinate positions one gets controlled because of the difference. Hence difference remains as an unmanageable experience in the unconscious. This belief in unmanageability is reflected, for example, in the idiom of 'ironing out differences'; it is a question of perspective: who is holding the iron?

The next hypothesis that I offer is that the unquestioned survival of hierarchy in modern work organizations depends on religion. Religion is a societal feature that strongly underpins transference phenomena in work organizations and provides the structural model that the family does not offer.

RELIGIOUS HIERARCHY AS AN UNCONSCIOUS ORGANIZATIONAL MODEL

Religion and religious organizations existed long before the advent of organized work-forces or governments of any kind. I have hypothesized elsewhere (Chattopadhyay 1994) an unconscious link between religion and the language which the child accepts as the mother tongue. This is related to ego consciousness (Erikson 1968).

The development of ego consciousness, which begins in infancy, continues to be organized, unconsciously, throughout life. Some of the earliest bases of the articulated aspects of unconscious organization develop in the language that the child learns at home. In later life, any attack on that language is likely to be experienced as a threat to the core of one's identity, one's ego consciousness. This results in extremely violent defences, including aggression against those perceived as attacking one's language. At the other end of the continuum death awaits to destroy the ego, along with the rest of what the person experiences, both consciously and unconsciously, as 'I' and 'me'. Belief in a form of 'afterlife' is offered by all religions, supplying, albeit unconsciously, a 'lifeline' to the ego after death. Consequently certain aspects of religion, like many of its organizational precepts, are internalized by people beyond consciousness. This process is so strong that even those who consciously renounce or denounce religion remain part of the process, so long as they do not actually get in touch with their unconscious 'religious behaviour'.

Reed (1978) has hypothesized that religion, through its regular communal rituals, assists believers in regressing to a state where they project the 'divine' in them—such characteristics as compassion and love—on to a Supreme Being. Towards the end of the ritual they are assisted by the priest in reintrojecting those 'divine' qualities, in order to put them to use in society at large. Reed's theory, however, leaves out the equal probability of projecting all that is 'non-divine' (such as the 'seven deadly sins'). For instance, in the Old Testament God has certainly been painted as proud, envious, angry, and perhaps even covetous (see Biran and Chattopadhyay 1998; Fromm 1991; E. J. Miller 1993b). The belief in God's anger and engagement in wantonly destructive behaviour is so strongly held by modern societies that insurance companies have the legal right not to underwrite or compensate for destruction due to Acts of God—which are put in the same category as wars and nuclear explosions!

Thus, through institutional rites and rituals, religion projects both the 'divine' and 'non-divine' in human nature on to the notion of a supreme being. However, religion also articulates the unquestionability of perceived unfair or unjust treatment by the superior role holder (that is, abuse of authority and power), and the impossibility of any appeal against such treatment. These aspects of our experience mostly remain latent and unarticulated in the family as an institution.

As a result of these dynamics, religion as a process becomes deeply and unconsciously internalized (Chattopadhyay 1997a). The philosophies known as dharma, for example, that were born in the Indian sub-continent, such as what are now known as Hinduism, Buddhism, and Jainism, or even the later Sikhism or the Khalsa, were initially propagated by their founders as ideal ways of life and not as the words of any supreme being. However, they have come to be accepted by both believers and the philosophers of later eras as forms of religion. Once the original ideas and thoughts become associated with a supreme being, they also become unquestionable. Retribution for acts contrary to those ideas and thoughts is then expected to be accepted without the possibility of appeal. Subsequently, this extends to the hierarchy of a priestly institution: they

are the managers and the administrators of the laity, who are the 'others' in religious society, just as those in modern work organizations who are not managers
are the 'others'.

This idea that religious organizations provide a model for organizational
hierarchy is supported by W. B. Miller. He makes it clear that, in his view, 'the
pantheon of any society can be seen as a projective system, whereby the essential features of the social organization of the projective society are attributed to
a group of supernatural beings, whose relations reflect those existing among
the people themselves' (W. B. Miller 1955: 278–9). In effect, Miller's views come
very near to my hypothesis. What I have added is that this kind of projection is
actually supported and underpinned by the transference of the infant's relationship with the parents, which is then reintrojected.

AN ALTERNATIVE MINDSET

This idea of transference and reintrojection in the form of organizational hierarchy is very much supported by Miller's description of the Fox (the Central
North American Algonquian) pantheon and the nature of authority distribution
in their society. In Fox society the notion of hierarchy does not enter the
socioreligious system. Even the notions of a hierarchy between species, or the
perceived superiority of humans over nature, or of the living over the non-
living are non-existent there. Nor is there a hierarchic arrangement of supernatural beings. Their beliefs about the afterlife also reflect, as in life so in death,
that a central concern for the Fox remains the ability to use one's personal
authority without being ordered about by anyone else.

However, in Fox society people do feel influenced and do also exercise some
power for co-ordinating collective action. An examination of their myths and
actual interpersonal behaviour brings out their notions of social power and its
distribution. Their notion of power is behind several formalized agencies to co-
ordinate collective activities. Those agencies or roles that have great power
have very limited tenure and those that have some sort of permanence have
extremely limited power. It is a concept of power that is reflected in terms of
authority. Through mobilizing their personal authority, each individual feels
highly   responsible   for   their   behaviour   according   to   societal   norms.
Subordination to others' directives implies one's inadequacy in dealing with
those norms. This capacity is developed through child-rearing practices and is
further underscored by rituals and myths.

For instance, the Fox father does not represent to the child an almost unquestionable, nurturing, and punitive authority figure. Instead, all persons senior in
age are to be respected rather than just obeyed. This kind of 'horizontal' relationship is also underscored in a number of myths that symbolically emphasize
the severance of the father–son dependency tie and lead to the internalization

of the idea of personal authority and self-dependence. The absence of a parent–child hierarchy at home and the progressive internalization of self-dependence mean that there is little likelihood of later transference of unlimited authority and hierarchy in other spheres of life.

This kind of internalization has resulted in three characteristics in the Fox. Every individual can directly relate to the conceptualized source of power. This frees one from the need to be dependent on others' evaluation of oneself to feel self-esteem. Secondly, every individual also relates directly to 'the broadly representative social decision-making agency'(ibid.: 287). This in its turn develops both individuation and consensus-making skill. Lastly, the individual also has direct access to and the knowledge of 'the body of procedural rules governing interpersonal interaction' (ibid.: 287). This adds self-confidence to self-esteem, leading to the freedom to make one's choice because no one person monopolizes information.

I am arguing that logically hierarchy should be replaced in modern organizations by a different system of levels of authority that will eliminate the built-in conflict and destructive potential of hierarchy and greatly release creative energy. This is where the discussion of the power and authority structure in the Fox society becomes relevant.

In Fox society, at the two poles of an individual's life there are societal mechanisms to underscore the absence of a hierarchic form of authority. The individual is psychologically released in the family from parental authority which therefore does not get internalized to be later transferred in other institutional contexts. At the end of one's life too, one anticipates as a 'good' Fox an 'afterlife' where one 'lives' according to one's choice based on personal authority. In almost all other societies, by contrast, what is internalized in infancy is subordination to one's parents. This is then emphasized by religion through the idea that after death—even if one had succeeded, as a grown-up daughter or son, in questioning one's parents' authority—one's 'I-ness' (soul, in some form or other) submits to the unquestionable infinite authority of the unknowable Supreme Being or of a series of supernatural beings. The internalized hierarchy at home gets societal recognition through religion, with the backing of all the force of anxiety, both conscious and unconscious, of the altogether unknown.

Later on, in the depressive position, one feels potent enough to be able to repair the fantasized damage done to the mother in earlier infancy. It is this experience of potency that in adult life leads one to mobilize one's personal authority and actually deal with differences to the extent that one does not feel totally impotent or powerless. In all hierarchic organizational situations one thus moves between omnipotent and impotent stances, occasionally relieved by the feeling of potency.

Reed's (1978) treatment of the process of religion as a form of oscillation in a sense draws one's attention to the process of how one's potency may be recharged, despite the routine uncertainties and other kinds of anxiety-provoking experience that people face in life. Part of the oscillation process is the fantasized unity with a divine form or power, which in every religion (other than among the Fox, so far as we know from available anthropological literature) is superordinate to all beings. This temporary unity emphasizes the permanence of difference which is unmanageable. Since no average human being is devoid of the fear of the unknown, the seeming emptiness beyond death, even those who do not partici-pate in religious activities unconsciously leave the task of religion in their own lives to others.

Hierarchy therefore, on fresh examination, also appears as a social defence (on social defences, see Krantz and Gilmore 1990; Harding 1996). Briefly, such defences are probably (a) against the anxieties that result from being account-able to the many subordinate role holders for decisions that misfire and from recognizing the price that one logically should pay for taking such decisions, and (b) against the anxiety caused by having to deal with the trust of subordi-nate role holders. This trust is implicit in the upward delegation of task-related authority. For the 'others', hierarchy is a defence against the anxieties associ-ated with possible failed dependency and the consequent disillusionment that always hangs as the sword of Damocles. Viewed from such a perspective, social defences may well operate in a 'global domain' (Bain 1998*b*).

Further, Chapman's (1996) concept of task corruption opens the way to examining in a new light the hierarchy present in the family as an institution, in religion, and in work organizations. Chapman explores the extent to which these practices have incorporated phenomenal tasks (that is, unconscious engagement with tasks that actually counter the stated, normative primary task) that in fact hinder the development of minds that can creatively con-tribute towards change. It is possible to hypothesize two reasons for this. One is the vested interest of the parental generation in retaining their authority and leadership. Secondly, bringing up children according to cultural prescriptions also means glossing over the uncertainties that culture rationalizes in every society and reinforces the idea, for both parents and children, that the former always know best as long as the latter are at a 'tender age'.

It is hypothesized in this context that the task of bringing up children to be creatively contributive in society becomes corrupted into producing 'chips off the old block', rather like slightly faded carbon copies of the original, in order to block the possibility of change. One could think of the latest scientific 'develop-ment' called 'cloning' in this context as the hope of the establishment that they may be able to freeze time and thus once and for all stop the process of societal change by replacing carbon copies with photocopies!

In religion the phenomenon of hierarchy defends both the priests and the laity from the anxiety which accompanies the recognition of a Supreme Being that is unknown and unknowable. A religious hierarchy by definition manages the absurdity of knowing and understanding the will of the unknown and unknowable Supreme Being or gods. In work organizations, likewise, the chief executive officers seem to know another manifestation of the absurd. This is what the 'others' are trusting the CEO for, or are entrusting the CEO with.

Hierarchy takes care of it by removing the possibility of exploring the nature of the emotion-laden upward delegations made by the subordinate role holders.

I have indicated a possible phenomenal task that emerges in the family as an institution. In the same way, one could think of the processes of differentiation and exclusion present in most religions (Fromm 1991) as phenomenal tasks in religious institutions. In work organizations, these phenomenal tasks appear in the processes that act as barriers to learning and transformation (or proactive change).

Despite the intellectual recognition that the logic of hierarchy leads to wastage of human potential, and the acknowledgement that differences need to be managed for creativity to flourish, in the end unmanageability of differences as a characteristic of hierarchy prevails. As a result, people in organizations oscillate, at best, between the infantile paranoid-schizoid stance and the adult potent stance. In the paranoid-schizoid stance adults can be, and often are, very destructive in order to defend themselves, albeit largely unconsciously, from the anxiety of annihilation. Further, the infantile need to possess the 'other' in the adult, manifested in the acquisition of both power and material objects as quickly as possible, has resulted in the use of modern technology in ways that are clearly destroying the earth and its atmosphere. It seems to be an unconscious process of being driven to capture the 'good breast' and destroy the 'bad breast', which may well end by destroying altogether the metaphorical mother—creation as we are capable of perceiving it—who owns both the good and the bad breast.

THE ACTION CHOICE

The answer proposed here lies in integrating three kinds of educational approach. One is to popularize the basic notions of quantum mechanics through familiarity with the experiments that have led to the formulation of the hypothesis that all the boundaries that we experience are the result of the limited nature of human perceptual ability (see, for example, Heisenberg 1974; Zukav 1982). This really means that the entire cosmos is boundaryless. Boundarylessness means non-duality, and differences are therefore matters of perceptual limitation. To view things in this way immediately reduces the possibility of investing emotion on either side of the boundary between perceived differences, or on the boundary itself. Emotions will nevertheless be invested, but the strength of such emotional investments may then be low enough to allow the kind of exploration that can show some of the boundaries as irrelevant to the objectives and tasks for which they stand.

The second step is the experiential learning of group processes. With a skilled consultant highlighting the processes that are usually filtered out by the majority, it is possible actually to experience how, beyond one's consciousness, individuals and groups relate to one another, take in from and also put into other individuals and groups ideas, thoughts, and even feelings. That is, one may actually get in touch with the experience of how one unconsciously takes in other people's emotions and ideas, and acts them out on others' behalf, and also, after the first unconscious step, keeps getting influenced by or keeps influencing others (Ogden 1992). Further, it is also possible to get in touch with the otherwise largely unconscious experience—of relating to groups in fantasy—that colours actual intergroup relations (Biran and Chattopadhyay 1998); and with how one's relationship with various organizations to which one belongs are affected by the picture of the institution that one holds in the mind (Armstrong 1991; Chattopadhyay 1997b).

This kind of experiential work goes under the generic name of 'group relations conferences'. Understanding of their theoretical bases (Bion 1961; Rice 1965; E. J. Miller 1989; 1990a; 1990b) and repeated participation in those conferences have resulted in the development of theories, concepts, and methodologies subsumed under the term of socio-analysis (Bain 1997a). Socio-analysis, like other related approaches, is used for helping work organizations to diagnose unconscious dynamics that throw up problems, and to fashion or invent interventions and redraw various boundaries for greater task effectiveness. This kind of experience of the relationship between boundaries of tasks with various other kinds of boundary is an important learning experience that becomes very relevant in step three, below. Such experiences also put people in touch with some of their unconscious defences and strongly point towards psychic boundarylessness. For the thinking person who has the courage to accept the possibility that other perceived boundaries may also be questioned, these experiences open the door for further exploration into the nature of boundaries in general.

The third step is the most important one and also a logical extension of the other two steps. This is the step of developing spirituality.

I make a clear distinction between religiosity and spirituality. Religion strongly upholds the notion of frozen boundaries through introducing the notion of duality—the difference between man and divinity that underscores the notions of hierarchy and of unbridgeable inequalities. Further, the primary task of institutionalized religion often gets corrupted (Chapman 1996: 16), leading to the creation of another kind of hierarchy. This hierarchy is between people belonging to different religions, or even sects, where the religious boundary is used to project unbearable realities of one's own on to another (Biran and Chattopadhyay 1998). Spirituality, on the other hand, is about discovering connectedness and managing perceived differences.

Religion can also be treated as the result of the institutionalization of spirituality. Alastair Bain (personal conversation) suggests that such figures as Buddha and Jesus, and also the composers of the Upanishads, intended to assist people to experience and internalize whatever the seers experienced as 'God' (as a metaphor). Buddha, for example, avoided answering all questions that focused on a Supreme Being; Jesus talked about the 'Kingdom of Heaven' being here, which Bain interprets, following his understanding of Bion (1970), as the internalized picture of cosmic oneness in the mind. Such phenomena of internalization would obviously mean the mobilization and exercise of personal authority for one's action choices and activities. This, in its turn, would pose a great threat for the establishment that represents vested interest. This was one of the reasons why the early followers of Buddha, Jesus, Guru Nanak (the Khalsa or the Sikh), and the Sufis were ruthlessly suppressed.

To survive and spread the ideas of these great seers their followers had to organize themselves, which inevitably led to institutionalization. Their ideas became ideals which could no longer be explored, faith became belief, and many boundaries, both abstract and concrete, were created so that religion became separated from spirituality. The process of religionizing the Upanishadic ideas is buried in the unrecorded history of several thousand years when, in the Indian sub-continent, education was based on experiential learning and verbal discourses by the seers, memorized by their pupils once they had accepted the logic.

A paradox was thus created by institutionalizing spirituality. Whereas spirituality is about experiencing boundarylessness, the followers of the spiritual seers had to create strong, highly structured organizations with both external and internal boundaries in their effort to safeguard the message of boundarylessness. In the course of time this process of survival and growth for religious organizations became internalized as a social defence against spirituality. Yet it is spirituality that questions the very existence of boundaries and can pave the way for reviewing and exploring boundaries of various kinds for greater task effectiveness in organizations. Thus, in reality, religion not only freezes boundaries, but also gets people to internalize the process of freezing boundaries, which can even lead to glaring acts of destructiveness, such as genocide.

Further discussion of spirituality and of how, in practical terms, its pursuit can be made part of management education is beyond the scope of this chapter. All that may be indicated here is that it is worthwhile considering the theoretical basis (the tantric philosophy) and the practice of yoga (both the eightfold system recorded by Patanjali and other forms of raja yoga), as methodologies for pursuing spiritual education for increased managerial effectiveness.

CONCLUSION

This chapter began by pointing out that although managing effectively essentially consists of creating boundary conditions appropriate for engagement with tasks, that very act paradoxically often leads to mismanagement through losing touch with process. This largely happens because of the unconscious dynamics of groups and organizations that remain unexplored.

It has been shown through an examination of some of the basic characteristics of the nature of boundaries in modern organizations that the religious organizational model, with its assumptions and associated emotions, has been unconsciously adopted for work organizations. This has not only contributed towards human wastage in work organizations, but has also led to other kinds of destructive activities, including abdication of personal authority. This leads to the conclusion that alternative models of conceiving and building organizations have to be sought or invented in order to create conditions where people can take more authority for engaging creatively with tasks.

One aspect of this discussion is of particular importance: since management as a process is concerned with creating and holding appropriate boundary conditions for engagement with institutional tasks, it also requires managers to understand that the process is in fact one of managing illusions by mobilizing one's personal authority. In fact, this understanding needs to be developed in every individual in all kinds of institutions, since it is difficult to imagine anyone who has no responsibility whatsoever in relation to organizational processes. If one is responsible for a process, one is also managing some boundary, however insignificant it may appear compared to others with far greater responsibilities.

As a logical extension of this discussion, I have argued that for more effective management of organizations the educational curriculum for managers and entrepreneurs needs to incorporate three steps: familiarity with the basic notions of quantum mechanics; experiential learning through participation in group relations conferences; and development of spirituality, as the term has been defined in this chapter.

9

On Being Frozen in Time

Alastair Bain

1 Everything else is a defence against the experience of the present moment.

1.1 The failure to realize the experience of the present moment results in the creation of time.

1.2 When a group comes together to study the experience of the present moment, anxiety about catastrophic change is aroused.

1.3 The catastrophic change that is feared is being one with creation (that is, without time).

1.4 The anxiety concerning catastrophic change causes a dispersal of group members into the past, the future, and what is 'known'.

1.5 In this they can become frozen.[1]

In an editorial in the *New York Times* at the end of the First World War it is argued that a fit punishment for the Kaiser is 'Time without limit, unending time spent in torment without any respite'. The editorial is entitled 'The punishment of Wilhelm', and it reads in part:

for he is the world's greatest animal and even the most terrible statutory penalties fall miserably short of his desert . . . But suppose he were tried, found guilty, and executed. Would not then end his sufferings? Retribution would cheat itself if so soon his sufferings were ended.

we cannot well know the mental and spiritual nature of this incomparable malefactor . . . He knows that the earth's millions detest him, hate him with a hatred never visited upon mortal man.

Time without limit, unending time spent in torment without any respite, ceaseless, hopeless, that is the punishment appropriate to the crimes of Wilhelm, of Hohenzollern, for sins altogether inexpiable, sins that appal, that outrun experience and overpass the powers of imagination. (*New York Times*, 13 November 1918: 14).

The editorial concludes: 'Yet some men say there is no GOD!'

At this distance in history a small doubt may have entered the mind of readers—'Does Wilhelm *actually* feel all this?' It is believed that he does, that he has identified with the views and feelings of the editorial, hence the punishment of having to live in 'unending time'. And this is perhaps the clue, that Wilhelm is the recipient of the projections of a culture, that it is believed he has identified with these projections, and his punishment is to be frozen in time by these projections.

At one level the phenomenon of being frozen in time is well known. There are numerous political and technological examples, such as the Maginot line philosophy that led to fortifications for the Second World War being prepared to guard against dangers experienced in the First: the enemy, however, came by air. Or the Luddites. Or the shock the West received when the Soviet Union abandoned communism.

But what does being frozen in time mean? From the Wilhelm example it appears to mean being consigned to a present that cannot change. And it is a present that only contains the past. There is no future except for repetitively remembering the past as though it is the present, in every single moment of existence. One is reminded of Dante's descent into hell, and the unceasing repetitive punishments he witnesses.[2] Wilhelm's world, as envisaged by the *New York Times* would be a hell: 'Let no man say there is no GOD!' Indeed.

I have found when writing this chapter that what I want to say is in the form of fragments drawn from different experiences at different times. Except for the theme they seem disconnected. And perhaps they are. Rather than a moving present, which has a reality in a human meaning which provides the connection, they are images of experiences linked by the theme of 'being frozen in time', that are seeking connection through the reader. They can be considered as fragments of a hologram, each of which contains an outline of the original image.[3]

There are four fragments. The first concerns the freezing of an individual and a group in the past; the second explores a problem of institutional freezing; the third sketches an outline of the three 'International Events' in the Bion-Tavistock tradition held in 1988, 1990, and 1993, and is entitled: 'Towards institutional unfreezing'; the fourth explores experiences within group relations study groups of being frozen in the past, the future, and what is 'known', as a defence against the anxiety of catastrophic change which is aroused by being in the present moment.

FRAGMENT 1: INDIVIDUAL AND GROUP FREEZING

I first became conscious of the phenomenon of 'being frozen in time' during the Global Event at the International Group Relations and Scientific Conference in Lorne, Victoria, Australia, 14–19 August 1993, sponsored by the Australian Institute of Social Analysis.[4] It was the third such International Event (see Fragment 3, below).

The theme of the conference in Lorne—'Exploring Global Social Dynamics' —was explored by means of seven different events, one of which was the Global Event. The task of the Global Event was 'To explore Global Social Dynamics using one's learning and experience as derived from the Bion-Tavistock tradition'. There were five sessions. The Event was introduced by two members of the conference directorate, who then joined with the seventy other members[5] in working at the task. Rooms had been allocated to the various national 'groups' represented in the conference, and some rooms had been left vacant for uses to be determined during the Event.[6] People were free to work on the task in whatever way they chose.

I decided to begin the Event in the room allocated to India. (I was born in India and had spent the first four years of my life there.) During the Plenary it had been said that India and Israel were to share the same room. There was one 'official' Indian at the Conference, a black man, and one 'official' Israeli, a black woman. A white woman who lives in the United States and has dual US-Israeli citizenship was the fourth member of this original group.[7]

Why were we there, and what was the meaning of allocating the one room to be shared by India and Israel? We were soon joined by a white German man who said he was a 'refugee' from the German territory, which was occupied by two Americans (who live in Germany). At the end of the session a white American Jew announced that it had been decided in the US room that a meeting of Jews would take place in the Israeli territory. No permission was asked. It seemed to be assumed as a right. The symbolic lineaments of past and present white colonialism (British[8] and American), the holocaust, being a refugee from 'oppression', and lumping Asian, 'black', 'Third World' countries together were awakened in this room in the first session.

On a personal level, my being in the 'Indian' room was a pilgrimage to my early childhood and land of birth. Although I had been warmly welcomed I had not intended to stay more than a session or so, and during the early part of the second session I moved to the Australian room, where I remained for the rest of the Event. There were about 20 people present in one very large room (called the 'Ballroom' by the Guest House). The atmosphere in the Australian room was quite tense. There was talk of people having left and there had been tension around their leaving.

It was during the next few sessions of this Event that I gradually became aware that when people came back to the Australian room there was rarely any space allowed for exploring the experiences they had had in other countries' rooms. On one level this was understandable as people who remained in the Australian group wanted to continue working on their own issues rather than be 'interrupted'. But the experience of relatedness was more than this. The group in the Australian room related to the returning Australians as though they had the *same identity* as when they had left, which was sometimes two or three sessions in the past. It was *remembered* how and when people had left and the tension that may have emerged during their leaving—and for the group that was their identity when they returned. The group behaved as though the returnee could have had no experiences since he or she left. Similarly the returning Australians tended to relate to the Australian group as though it was the same group that existed at the time of their leaving—that is, full of tension—and as though no development could have taken place in the interim. Both 'groups' then were behaving as though the 'other' was frozen in time. There was no space in the experience of 'returning' for learning and growth.

At the time when the returning Australians met the Australian group the present moment collapsed into a collusion that the past was the present. Both were ghosts for the other. But both were 'known' for the other. The collapse of the present moment into a mutual projection of the past, however unpleasant, created a feeling of safety. What was denied in this behaviour was the possibility of a present without the projected ghost of the 'other'. The possibility of this kind of present moment I would hypothesize precipitated unconscious anxiety of catastrophic change.

Letting one's boundaries be defined by the 'other' results in being frozen in time. The problem of letting the 'other' define one's identity, and therefore boundaries, and acting out the projective identification of the 'other' as a phenomenon of group behaviour and of colonialism has been acutely observed and analysed by Gouranga Chattopadhyay (1998; also Biran and Chattopadhyay 1998).

FRAGMENT 2: THE INSTITUTIONALIZATION OF THE BION-TAVISTOCK TRADITION

Just as individuals and groups may be frozen in time, so too can organizations and the management of organizations. In Fragment 2 and Fragment 3 the focus is on organizational freezing and unfreezing, being frozen in a managerial role and in the management of multiple roles. The examples are from organizations working in the Bion-Tavistock tradition, but they are illustrative of phenomena with which readers are likely to be familiar from their own managerial and organizational experience. Fragment 2 begins again at the Global Event in the 1993 International Conference.

Like me, many people in the Australian room had decided during the Global Event to explore their roots: the countries and the people they and their families had come from. Thus some people visited the UK, some Eire, Denmark, Africa, Israel, the USA. Although their experiences varied, three people who visited the UK territory reported an experience which is germane to the theme of this paper. One person who had a message for the people in the UK room was told by a member of the group that the message wasn't wanted and that they wouldn't have been interested in hearing it anyway. Another person found that he couldn't speak in the UK room, and a third felt like a 'convent school girl'. A delegation from Sweden and Norway on entering the UK room also found they couldn't talk and were only able to find their voices in their *own mother tongues*. A common feature in all these experiences was of feeling, or being made to feel, like a child, which is perhaps some support for the hypothesis offered by the delegation from Sweden and Norway that the UK group was acting as a parent for the conference.

One conference member, who was from the UK but not institutionally linked to any of the organizations where the group relations approach developed—the Tavistock Institute, the Tavistock Clinic, the Grubb Institute, the Scottish Institute of Human Relations (all represented in the UK room)—has written:

In the end I have to say it was like being in the Boardroom of a family firm fighting over history, present, and future. The members sitting round the solid oak table of ideologies with the guilt-framed [*sic*] portrait of Bion visible from every part of the room. It was, Oh so English!

The patriarch, the dowager duchess, the brother who had left to set up his own business, with his son the new pretender, the rebellious son of the family (screaming loudly with his surly silence), various nephews and nieces (some of whom had set up their own firms, some together, some not), and somewhere in the background the son who had emigrated to Australia to seek his fortune there and build up his own family business.

This was the parent Company or holding company hypothesized by the Swedish/ Norwegian contingent as acting as a container for the Global Event . . . It seemed that many of these people were hiding their emotions and feelings behind a language and framework of the Bion/Tavistock tradition and for some behind a self authorized role of consultant that they were unable or unwilling to relinquish.[9] (Nutman 1995: 8.)

The frozen institutional splits within the UK membership may have thawed a little during this conference. On an individual level, however, there is also a 'frozenness' in a managerial role, due to projection and identification. Within the group relations world, no role attracts more projections of an institutional kind than director of the Group Relations Programme at the Tavistock Institute, held from 1969 to 1997 by Eric Miller. His experience of the first couple of days of the conference was of being in a 'gilded cage'. This feeling disappeared as the conference unfolded. However, feeling one is in a 'gilded cage' is perhaps linked with his 'commenting with a wry smile as to whether he was going to be "killed off" during one session of the Global Event' (Nutman 1995: 7).

The problem of the institutionalization of the Group Relations Programme at the Tavistock Institute—the Establishment for the 'keeping' and transmission of Bion's idea—has been recognized for some time. Gordon Lawrence, a former co-director of the Programme, writes:

The paradox is that the disruptive ideas he [Bion] first presented have resulted in an Establishment(s), i.e., the group relations training institutions to which I have already referred . . . The Establishment 'in the mind' is the ideal-typical institution purveying the very best of Bion's thinking and those who were immediately associated with him and who began the various institutions for group relations training. Here, I suggest, a number of individuals have been put into the role of representing the untarnished truth of Bion, Rice *et al.* (Lawrence 1985*b*: 309.)

In the same paper, he writes about the pressures on the organization of the Tavistock programme:

To put my concern in concrete terms: the felt pressure on the programme at the Tavistock is never to be innovative; it must be saddled with stability, certainty and preservation. But it must never disappear, as this would leave other comparable institutions with problems of rivalry for succession that would have to be fought out. So the idea of the Tavistock programme as a dead, hollow container or spittoon easily comes to mind, even though individuals as agents may feel differently within themselves. (Lawrence 1985*b*: 310.)

In the Preface to *The 'Leicester' Model*, Eric Miller writes: 'Ascribed to me, therefore, is a symbolic role as *custodian of the tradition*. The paper that follows refers to some of the consequences of the "institutionalization" of the conferences. What is relevant here is the institutionalization of me. My utterances tend to carry more weight than they often deserve.' (E. J. Miller 1989: 1, italics added.) He concludes the Preface with the hope that 'Whilst . . . it [the paper] will be useful, I feel the need to emphasize that this is not the gospel: it is simply one person's picture, shaped by the perspective of the roles he happens to have been in' (E. J. Miller 1989: 2).

What has working in the Bion-Tavistock tradition come to mean? Has it perhaps become a mantra? Is it something that is repeated in order to gain access to a good spirit, that of Bion? In fantasy is the Tavistock the keeper of the good spirit—the Holy Grail of the group relations world? And as 'keeper' does this enforce repetition of behaviour in the 'keeping' and thereby prevent learning, innovation, and growth?

In elaborating his 'container–contained' model, Bion wrote of the fate of the mystic or genius—the bearer of the creative new idea (the contained)—as being tied to their relationship with the Establishment (the container). He described the explosion—the danger to the group—caused by the mystic idea and the resultant struggle of the emergent establishment to contain the idea and to be recognized (in my terms) as its 'keeper', with responsibility for its preservation and transmission (Bion 1970: 72–82). Bion was a genius. And it has so far been the Tavistock Institute's fate to be frozen in the institutionalization of a few ideas suggested by him, by Kenneth Rice, Pierre Turquet, and one or two others.

There are two strands that I would like to open up. The first is that a new idea provokes within the Establishment a fear of catastrophic change, and that the 'keeper' is mobilized to prevent the intrusion of the new idea. And the second is that the person and role of 'keeper' of the Tavistock group relations tradition has perversely become confused with the 'idea' that is being kept. Hence Eric Miller's comment about whether it was time for him to be 'killed off' during the Global Event, and the subsequent 'acting out' of a death by a woman member of the UK group: 'Another member came to the conclusion that it was necessary for somebody to die and become extinct in order that something could change. She said she was leaving the event, a symbolic representation of extinction' (Nutman 1995: 7). Bion has written that in order for a new idea to be born an old idea has to die. I don't think he writes anywhere about the necessity for a person having to die in order for a new idea to be born. It is the fusion—or freezing—of person, role, and 'idea' through massive institutional projections which makes leadership of the Group Relations Programme at the Tavistock Institute so difficult, and organizational and managerial change almost impossible.

FRAGMENT 3: TOWARDS INSTITUTIONAL UNFREEZING

While at a 'local' organizational level freezing may be occurring (as Fragment 2 indicates), at a different system level unfreezing may be taking place. Fragment 3 explores this process of unfreezing at an international systems level. There have been three International Events sponsored by organizations working in the Bion-Tavistock group relations tradition: Keble College, Oxford, 1988; Spa, Belgium, 1990; and Lorne, Victoria, Australia, 1993.[10]

Keble College, Oxford, 1988

Oxford was the venue for the Tavistock/A. K. Rice International Symposium, co-directed by Eric Miller and Margaret Rioch. It was the first such Event to be held and some 200 participants from around the world took part. The design focused on the presentation of scientific papers and there were deliberately no 'experiential learning' events.

Spa, Belgium, 1990

The second International Event, a 'Temporary Learning System', was organized by AIM, an acronym for the three European organizations involved in the planning—AGSLO (Sweden), IFSI (France), and MundO (Germany). Thirty-five people who had been on the staff of a group relations conference participated. Members were mainly from Western European countries, but also Israel, the USA, India, and Australia. There was nobody from the Tavistock Institute and only one person associated (marginally) with the A. K. Rice Institute.

The 'Temporary Learning System' (TLS) was called a 'collegial system' by the organizers to distinguish it from a conference (Boalt Boëthius 1992: 2). To further this aim the organizers deliberately gave up their staff role before the event started. The TLS programme consisted of a Social Dreaming Matrix, a Praxis Matrix, and a Monitoring Matrix. Unlike the first International Event at Oxford it was entirely experiential. Everybody was a member and there were no consultant roles: 'What we wanted to do was to provide opportunities for using the different experiences in Europe to develop something new *with the possibility to go some day beyond Bion*' (Boalt Boëthius 1992: 2; italics added). Part of the *Zeitgeist* of the TLS was of being trapped in the group relations tradition, or in the Establishment text of Bion, and the need to invent something different. Oddly it did not seem to be publicly recognized that the very events went well beyond Bion and that their origins and conception were largely the work of Gordon Lawrence, one of the representatives of IFSI on the organizing group.

As a participant in both International Events it seemed to me that one was the obverse of the other. One was a Scientific Symposium organized by the Establishment (represented by the Tavistock and A. K. Rice Institutes), and the other an Experiential Event organized by a group who wanted 'to go some day beyond Bion'. To exaggerate a little, the Oxford Symposium was almost all 'container', with little space for the interaction between the 'container' and 'contained', and the Spa experience was almost all 'contained', with the hope for an emergent 'container' arising from the membership role.

While both were, in their different ways, absorbing and worthwhile events, the exploration and the experiences were limited to what was generated in a small number of roles: the roles of presenter, listener, and questioner at the Oxford Symposium, and the role of collegial member at Spa. It was the possibility of exploration and experiences generated by *managing oneself in multiple roles* that formed a major part of the thinking in the design of the third International Event. But this thinking would not have been possible without the learning and experiences generated by the first two Events.

Lorne, Victoria, Australia, 1993

The conference took place on the beachfront at Lorne. Perhaps more significantly, Australia is on the other side of the world from Oxford and Spa and this allowed us a certain freedom to innovate.

The Executive of the Australian Institute of Social Analysis (AISA) authorized a directorate to organize the conference. The directorate initially consisted of three Fellows of AISA: Gordon Lawrence, Laurence Gould, and the author of this chapter. Susan Long, Kathleen White, Siv Boalt Boëthius, and Allan Souter (Conference Administrator) accepted invitations to join the directorate. I was authorized by the directorate to direct the conference. The directorate met in New York in February 1993 and then again over a few days prior to the conference starting in August. This experience was very significant in developing a way of working which was not hierarchical and allowed for an 'evolving consciousness for task'.

The design of one of the conference events, the Global Event, illustrates this evolving consciousness. At the New York meeting, we had the idea of starting the Global Event with the directorate sitting in the middle of a 'fishbowl' and working at the task of the Event. Watching and interacting in 'national groups' would be the other participants in the conference. The Event would unfold from this beginning. In the staff meetings held immediately prior to the conference we began from this notion. Questions were raised, however, as to why we thought we were better qualified than the other participants in initially working at the task of an Event which had never been held before. In addition, all of us wanted to work as members in the Event and with the national groups of which we were part. I also began to feel anxious about the role I seemed to be cast in: that of a *de facto* 'world CEO'. In our own thinking, as a management group, we had also become frozen in models—in particular the Institutional Event in a Group Relations Conference—that were not relevant for the task of this Event.

At a staff meeting at Lorne prior to the conference I indicated I was not willing to proceed on the basis of our planning and in particular I did not want to be present in the Event as conference director. As a result, we then began the planning afresh, and the initial start of the Global Event was agreed the night before the conference began. Two members of the directorate would introduce the Event and allocate rooms for national groups and they would then join as members of the Event. The model we eventually arrived at promoted the idea we had of this Event, and of the conference as a whole, being 'held' systemically by all the participants in the conference through the management of multiple roles.

The primary task of the conference was:

To explore, identify and interpret the global relatedness of conference participants using the experience of their own and others' national identities and aspirations, as framed by the Bion-Tavistock tradition.

The conference consisted of the following events:

1. *Opening Plenary*, including an address by Eric Miller on 'The vicissitudes of identity'.
2. *The Global Event*.
3. *Social Dreaming Matrices*. There were four matrices, each with two consultants.
4. *Dialogues and Scientific Exploration Event*. There were nine presentations during the conference in parallel sessions.
5. *Interactive Systems Event*, with the task: 'to study the interactive process between other events and within the conference as a whole'. There were eight consultants.
6. *Prospection Event*, with the task: 'to be generative of ideas in the Bion-Tavistock tradition for further exploration of global relatedness'. There were no consultants.
7. *Closing Plenary*. As in the opening plenary members of the directorate were present in role.

There were seventy-two participants in the conference, and over one-third of the participants had consultant, director, convenor, and presenter roles at different times. All of us were in member roles during most of the Events. For example, as director of the conference, I was in this role at the opening and closing plenaries, during directorate staff meetings which were held each day to consider our experience of managing multiple roles, and very occasionally in dealing with member queries. Another role I had was director of the Interactive Systems Event. But for most of the conference I was in a member role: in the Social Dreaming Matrices, Dialogues, Global Event, and Prospection Event.

The management of multiple roles is not an easy task. In this instance, it was perhaps made both easier and harder through the previous experiences of group relations conferences we brought with us to this new experience. Easier, in the sense that one was exploring and struggling with unfamiliar realities, with colleagues who had some understanding of unconscious processes. But it was also harder as one projected into this new conference expectations and fantasies about authority and roles based on a model of conference learning, which Krantz (1993) has characterized as 'The military model of bureaucratic hierarchy'. In this usual conference model the director, consultant staff, and members have clearly delineated roles, and the staff pay particular attention to the transference and counter-transference feelings which are evoked between members and staff. At Lorne there was neither director nor staff, in the usual sense, and the management of the conference was dependent on all participants taking up their authority appropriately for task; that is, managing themselves in multiple roles and allowing an evolving consciousness for task to develop. In this sense the conference was held in the mind systemically. The difference took some participants a few days to get used to.

FRAGMENT 4: THE STUDY GROUP EXPERIENCE OF FREEZING IN THE PAST, THE FUTURE, AND WHAT IS 'KNOWN'

Fragment 4 explores experiences in group relations 'Study Groups' of being frozen in the past, the future, and what is 'known'.[11] The groups in question were sponsored variously by the Australian Institute of Social Analysis, the Department of Psychology, University of Melbourne, and the Department of Psychological Medicine, Monash University. The groups met weekly for one and a half hours, for ten-, fifteen-, or twenty-week sessions, or formed part of a group relations conference. The task of the study groups was: 'To study the behaviour of the group as it occurs'. The author worked as a consultant with these groups.

A major part of the work of a consultant in a small or large study group is to enable members to gather in the present. In my experience, this is strenuously resisted by members of the group, who prefer to gather in the past, in the future, or in what is familiar and 'known', indeed at any point where there is no potentiality for change. The following vignettes indicate this phenomenon.

At the beginning of one study group a woman began by talking about how far she had come in order to take part in the group. She had travelled 130 kilometres from Phillip Island to Kew, where the study group was being held. She thought she had the furthest to travel. Another member commented on how far he had had to travel from the suburb he lived in. All ordinary stuff, except that as a member of the group one was diverted from the possibly uncomfortable persecutory experience of *being* in the group to thinking *about* something outside the group that was familiar and known, in this case the relative distances from Phillip Island to Kew and from other suburbs to Kew.

While it is customary for members of a study group to introduce themselves during the first session, sometimes one person will talk and talk about himself/herself. While this apparently gives information to help others to get to know the person, in fact it often has the opposite unconscious intention of defending against the anxiety of experiencing one's identity in this new experience, the group. The group is kept at bay. Who one is in the group is unexplored and one's identity is frozen in a shape that derives from outside the group. On introducing himself at the beginning of one study group, for example, one man spent about ten minutes telling us in detail what his job involved and the business his company was in. He emphasized that he was here to learn and he wanted people in the group to tell him what he was like. He insisted that people do this. The following week he was frustrated that the group didn't seem to be making any progress. Although he had not been in a group of this kind before he seemed to be certain about the direction it should be going in and the absence of progress that was being made. The following week he continued the refrain: 'Please tell me what I'm like so I can make a better contribution to the group'. This for a period became his 'group' identity—and one notes that the paradoxical effect of his repeated wish to be told *about* himself was precisely to keep the experience of the group at bay.

In another study group, members of the group who already knew each other from their work had more than the usual difficulty in the first session in concentrating on the task of the group: they were in constant flight from it. The second week, when I arrived for the session, a coffee percolator was sitting on a chair in the middle of the circle of chairs, with a plate of chocolate biscuits on the floor. There was nobody there. I sat looking at the coffee percolator and biscuits. The coffee smelled delicious. People began to arrive in the next few minutes. I was asked politely if I would like a cup. It turned out there weren't enough cups so people were told to go out and get clean cups. Members of the group started to swap papers and journal articles concerning outside work and to talk with energy about outside things they shared. There was no attention to the task of the group. I felt as though I wasn't there, and it was, as I said later, like a Coffee Klatch. At the time I interpreted the group's behaviour as flight from the task, with the coffee percolator and biscuits representing an enactment of flight in bringing the outside physically into the group. On reflecting I think I was wrong and that it was an early instance of 'Basic Assumption Me' (Lawrence, Bain, and Gould 1996).

Another way of not being in the group at the time when it is taking place is to concentrate on a past or future event. In one study group, the members had all introduced themselves at a pre-study group session the week before. There was little opportunity then to talk at length about one's outside identity. Instead, members of the group concentrated on how they were at the pre-group session the week before, the anxieties that were felt, and what one might have mistakenly conveyed. What was avoided in this way was their anxiety in the current session. After the discussion of how one was the previous week one member said, 'I hope I will be seen in the group as . . .', with the emphasis on future events in the life of the group. How one was and how one will be may be used to avoid the experience of how one is. Similarly, within a session, particularly early on in the life of a group, a person will say well after an event has taken place: 'You know when you said X, I didn't say it at the time, but I felt Y.' Within one session this may occur a number of times with different people reporting how they felt at a time earlier in the session. The time lapse then ensures a separation between feelings and thoughts at the time when they occur and their expression. One is not now as one was. Nor do members of the group know how one is now, they will have to wait.

If one explores the nature of flight from the experience of the present in the study group, one notes that in almost all the examples mentioned the person is fleeing to something he or she knows, such as who one is outside the group, how far it is from Phillip Island, outside assignments, what one felt an hour ago in the study group. These are things one can experience a certainty about and can therefore control. The possibility of experiencing something new in the study group becomes replaced by something that is already known. The unknown causes terror and is coated over by this known thing. This kind of control is dependent on memory. Another form of control in avoiding the present is desire about the future, as with the person who remarks that they hope they will be 'seen in the group as . . .'. As Bion indicates memory and desire can be thought of as two facets of the same thing: 'one is the "past" tense [memory] and the other the "future" [desire]' (Bion 1970: 45).

We have, perhaps, different potentialities or valencies for being in the past, being in the future, and being in the present. For example, one person I know is consumed by the past and also has a valency for creatively pointing to the future. The hypothesis I am offering is that the study group can mobilize one's valencies for being in the past, the present, or the future, and the work of the consultant is partly to do with unfreezing the group from the past and the future. It is to the fear of being frozen in the present that I now turn.

It has already been mentioned that a major part of the work of a consultant to a study group is directed to assisting members of the group to gather in the present (particularly early on in the life of the group). To this end, the consultant is likely to make comments when it appears that the group is, so to speak, gathering in the past or gathering in the future, as a way of avoiding experiencing the group as it is.

Members of the group are likely to feel threatened by this behaviour on the part of the consultant as taking away things they *know*, whether this is something they are remembering or something that is hoped for. In this way, the consultant becomes the embodiment of what is unknown. However, at the same time that the consultant is busy making comments about where or when the group seems to be, members of the group are busy building up a 'known portrait' of the consultant. This 'known portrait' may be far from, or close to the reality of how the consultant experiences himself or herself; what is important is the belief by members of the group that it is 'known'.

Thus there may be a belief that the consultant never replies to a direct question. This appears to members of the group as though it is a rule of behaviour made up by the consultant which they now 'know'. In reality, the consultant is likely to respond if he/she feels that this will further the task of the group, but to remain silent if not. At the first session of one study group, two of the eleven members were there on time. The consultant noted the lateness, and for members of the group who were not on time the consultant's observation later became: 'You are angry with us for being late'. This then became part of the 'known portrait' of the consultant. In another study group, following an incident at the start of the second session, the consultant was thought to have 'made a mistake'. For the next six sessions it fell to the lot of one member to say, as though in passing and in a low voice, that the consultant had made a 'mistake'. He said it in such a way that it went unchallenged, and as though he were speaking a fact about group life. Such perceptions then become added to what the group supposedly *knows about* the consultant, and therefore subtract from or serve as a defence against the perception of the consultant as the embodiment of what is unknown.

As a study group progresses the strength of memory and desire may lessen and members of the group may also begin to realize that rules of behaviour which may have been attributed to the consultant have in fact been made up by them. There is less certainty about the previously 'known portrait' of the consultant. Among some members there may also be a growing capacity to see things as they are, without adornment, without the additions and interpretations that are so often put on what others say and do. As memory, desire, and 'knowing about' decrease the members of the study group feel threatened. One member of a study group asked herself, 'What am I threatened by?' She answered herself, 'Reality'. And I think this is true. The study group experience, like psychoanalysis, can expose one to reality, what is ultimately true, and the unconscious anticipation of this can cause terror, and flight into the past, future, and 'certainty'.

Bion writes that the emotional state of transformations in O (his symbol for ultimate reality) during psychoanalysis is akin to dread; he quotes Coleridge (Bion 1970: 46):

> Like one that on a lonesome road
> Doth walk in fear and dread;
> And having once turned round walks on,
> And turns no more his head:
> Because he knows a frightful fiend
> Doth close behind him tread.

He continues that the 'frightful fiend' represents indifferently the quest for truth or the active defences against it, depending on the vertex. This expresses what I also want to convey about a study group when memory, desire, and 'knowing about' decrease to the point at which reality intrudes. This point is marked by anxiety about catastrophic change which occurs, as Bion indicates, at the point of the transformation of **K** (what is and can be known) into **O** (which cannot be known but only be).

Paralleling this movement away from desire, memory, and 'knowing about' to 'not knowing', there is a final defence against the realization of 'not knowing'. The consultant is put in the paradoxical position by members of the group of being both the embodiment of what is unknown, as well as what is known. He becomes for members of the group an enigmatic 'super knower'. Images used by study group members include, for example, a Sphinx, the Oracle of Delphi, an Egyptian God, an Easter Island statue, and God. The characteristics of the consultant for the group at this stage generally contain this powerful ambiguity: the consultant knows everything but he doesn't tell you in a way that is helpful; he tells you in a way that makes it seem unknowable and mysterious.

Difficulties in thinking in the group are most intense at this time. Indeed, at times, it has felt as a consultant that instead of thought the question that is uppermost for members of the group who are most powerfully affected in this way is: 'What is the appropriate offering or tribute?' Generally the implication is that some terrible vengeance will be let loose unless such offering is made.

At this stage in the life of the group then, rather than experience the unknown in oneself as a member of the group, the consultant is made into the omniscient and omnipotent embodiment of it. In a way, this can also be viewed as the final attempt or bribe by members of the group: we will make you a God if you please don't bother us any more with your questions; just tell us what you want and what to do. In varying guises, this is likely to have been an underlying theme from the start of the group.

In the first of the *Four Quartets*, 'Burnt Norton', T. S. Eliot wrote that 'human kind cannot bear very much reality' (Eliot 1962: 118). By 'reality' I think he means what he writes later in 'Dry Salvages': 'the point of intersection of the timeless with time' (ibid.: 136). He continues in 'Burnt Norton':

> Yet the enchainment of past and future
> Woven in the weakness of the changing body,
> Protects mankind from heaven and damnation
> Which flesh cannot endure.

Time past and time future
Allow but a little consciousness.

It is these forces that are being struggled with in the study group at this time. As a member of the group can one let oneself experience the 'intersection of the timeless with time', which Eliot describes as the occupation of a 'saint'? Better perhaps to have a consultant/God rather than have to recognize these forces within oneself and within others.

1   Everything else is a defence against the experience of the present moment.
1.1 The failure to realize the experience of the present moment results in the creation of time (that is, past, present, and future).
1.2 When a group comes together to study the experience of the present moment, anxiety about catastrophic change is aroused.
1.3 The catastrophic change that is feared is being one with creation (that is, without time).
1.4 Anxiety concerning catastrophic change causes a dispersal of group members into the past, the future, and what is 'known'.
1.5 In this they can become frozen.
2.0 If someone is living in the present moment he/she is regarded as a saint (or mystic genius).
2.1 For members of the group, identifying a saint is usually a defence against the experience of the present moment.
2.2 'I', as a group member, can now live in the past, the future, and what is 'known'.
2.3 Living in the past, the future, and what is 'known' destroys the saint.
2.4 The destruction of the saint is the creation (again) of the 'idea' of the present moment.
2.5 When the group retraces the steps from the past, the future, and what is 'known', at some stage the present obtrudes.

NOTES

1 The propositions at the beginning and at the end of this chapter are shared thoughts with Joshua Bain. I am also indebted to Gouranga Chattopadhyay for his comments on an earlier draft of the chapter.
2 See Dante, *The Divine Comedy*, Inferno, Cantos V–XXXIV, tr. Mark Musa (Indiana: Indiana University Press, 1971).
3 I am indebted to Robert French and Russ Vince for suggesting the hologram analogy and leading me to discard my original snapshot idea. Usually I am suspicious of directly translating ideas of physics into explorations of social reality, but in this case the analogy may be illuminating and provoke some thought.
4 Now the Australian Institute of Socio-Analysis.

5 There were no consultants.

6 Members of the Conference came from the following countries: Austria—26, Denmark—2, Eire—1, Finland—1, Germany—3, India—1, Israel—1, Norway—1, Sweden—5, UK—15, USA—15.

7 For an analysis of the dynamics in the 'India/Israel' room, see Biran and Chattopadhyay 1998.

8 I had UK citizenship and passport at the time of the conference.

9 Two very senior members of this group had had no membership experience of a group relations conference, and this perhaps contributed to the phenomenon described.

10 The fourth such event took place, in Philadelphia, USA, in July 1998 while this volume ways in preparation.

11 Some of the material in this Fragment was originally presented at the Tavistock/A. K. Rice International Symposium in 1988.

PRACTISING THEORY IN GROUP RELATIONS

10

The Recovery of Meaning

David Armstrong

This chapter is written from the perspective of an organizational consultant working within a tradition grounded in the experience of psychoanalysis and the practice of 'group relations'. The link between these two domains, as I see it, lies not so much in their theoretical underpinning as in their method of enquiry which focuses on mental acts of attending to, formulating, and seeking to interpret emotional experience within a bounded setting. In psychoanalytic work that setting is defined by the meeting between analyst and analysand; in group work by the meeting between group members and one or more 'consultants'. In both, the object of study is what happens within this relational space: what is put into it or withheld from it or enacted within it, and why.

I have argued elsewhere (Armstrong 1995) that this methodology can have an analogue in the organizational domain and that the practice of this analogue can yield insights into the dilemmas, challenges, paradoxes, and discontents of organizations and their managers and leaders that may elude other methods of enquiry. In what follows, I want to explore one such area of 'insight' and its potential value for organizational clients, drawing on two recent experiences from consultancy assignments.

Before turning to this material, I need to make one preliminary point relating to the particular context in which the idea of this chapter first came to mind. This was an annual symposium to be planned by the International Society for the Psychoanalytic Study of Organizations, which brings together consultants and practitioners interested in the contribution which psychoanalytically informed approaches (including 'group relations') can make to understanding organizational life and practice. The title of this symposium was 'Organisation 2000: Psychoanalytic Perspectives', and its stated intent was to explore 'the future of organizations and how [these perspectives] can help us understand this future'.[1]

Such a statement invites a certain mental resistance. How can a psychoanalytic or indeed any other perspective help us to understand something that is not yet here? One available answer is contained in Wilfred Bion's evocative phrase, 'the shadow of the future cast before'. This could be taken to mean that the seeds of the future exist now, as an inner resonance or presaging of things to come, something that can be captured and given provisional expression. An example that comes immediately to mind is Fred Emery and Eric Trist's (1972) formulation of the theory of turbulent environments and its implications for organizational development.

However, I do not think that this interpretation fully catches Bion's meaning and its emotional undertow. It is hard in this context, for example, not to hear echoes of Freud's image in *Mourning and Melancholia* (1917), of 'the shadow of the object that falls on the ego'; something impending that heralds loss, abandonment, 'catastrophic change' (Bion 1970). On this reading the shadow that the future casts darkens rather than illumines. It heralds the arrival or return of the not known: a world without something or with something unprecedented.

I want to argue that it is through encouraging our acceptance of and our readiness to receive this darkening that this method of working can most help us, if not to understand the future, at least to take the measure of the present in a way that prepares or attunes us to meet the future, to make it, and to develop with it—organizationally no less that personally.

EXPLORATIONS 1

Some years ago I was invited to work as an external consultant to a one-day meeting of staff working in the Counselling Department of a new university. This department was part of the Student Services Division of the university and was responsible for providing a counselling service for students presenting a variety of emotional or welfare worries and concerns.

The meeting had been planned at the end of the academic year and was intended as an opportunity for staff to reflect together on their experiences during the year and their working relations with each other. (One issue they were facing had to do with a difficulty in sharing and handling anger.) The agenda for the meeting was set by the staff themselves, but at the outset and after a preliminary discussion with the head of department, I proposed the following as a way of getting going.

Each member of staff would find a space in the department's offices where they could reflect alone on their experiences as members of the department: the things they were feeling and thinking in themselves, the patterning of their relations with each other and with the students and staff they met, how they responded to the different situations they encountered. As they reflected in this way, I suggested, they might follow the chain of associations they were making and see if some image or series of images came to mind through which they could visually represent their present picture of the department in the context of the university—with themselves in it and *without using words.*

Large sheets of paper were provided with different coloured pens. After they had drawn their picture staff were invited to come together again and each in turn to present their picture and talk us through it. Other members would share any associations they had to the picture and, if they wished, comment on the impact that the picture and its imagery made on them.

It came to the turn of a very experienced and long-standing member of the department, who worked on a part-time basis, to present his picture. He then said, with a great deal of feeling, that he had been quite unable to find and draw any image. All he had come up with was a list of single words, which he had scrawled across his sheet of paper. A little later he linked his inability to an experience of feeling, as he put it, 'de-centred as a person'. He said that he associated this with the feeling in himself that he was not acknowledged by the university as a person, but only as a 'hired hand'. This in turn, he thought, reflected a number of recent changes and negotiations in respect of his contract.

Things might have been left there: that is, the 'no-picture' might have been seen simply as a reflection of one individual's personal and emotional relation to the department and/or the university. However, I found myself increasingly preoccupied along another direction. Might the experience this counsellor had come in touch with in himself also be conveying or mirroring something of the experience of the students he worked with (a reflection of his counter-transference)?

At the time this was no more than a vague speculation, which reflected something of my own sense of disorientation in the face of his list of words. But subsequently, as we worked through the pictures and what they might represent, it became possible to see that the feeling of 'de-centredness', named in this counsellor's response, had an aptness, an exactness beyond the emotional boundary of one individual member of staff. What students were presenting in counselling was indeed itself describable, at least in part, through this vivid phrase. They too could be said to feel 'de-centred' as persons, unable to discover a relation to their institution except as 'part-objects': consumers, candidates for examinations, inputs to courses.

I do not want to deny the contribution which the dynamics of late adolescence, for example, or the psychological tensions of transition (from school to college, or home to away) may have made to this feeling. But to emphasize just this aspect of the transference/counter-transference relation of counsellor and students risked missing something else, rooted in the organization as a whole and its relatedness to its context. Viewed from an organizational perspective, as a kind of organizational analogue, the counsellor's presented experience registered, contained, and gave expression to a broader institutional dynamic. This dynamic could be seen as one in which the new university's preoccupation, in a rather harsh, competitive climate, with raising student numbers, becoming more 'market oriented' and 'cost effective', was leading implicitly to a construction of students (and by extension of staff) not as members of the institution or the college community, relating as whole persons to the whole body of the institution and its corporate life, but more as 'contractees'—the means through which the institution made its living, the emotional equivalent of the 'hired hand'.

What had begun as an expression of one individual's dis-ease with his own relation to the university could now be reframed and given new meaning as a representation within the individual of a more pervasive experience of dis-ease within the whole institution. This 'dis-ease' I would see, to use a formulation suggested to me by my colleague at the Tavistock Institute, Jon Stokes, as a factor in the state of mind that *was* the organization, there and then. From this vertex, the counsellor's 'no-picture' and its accompanying emotional aura was, one might say, an offering to his colleagues, which through his image of 'de-centredness' paradoxically re-centred all their experience.

I believe it is these acts of reframing that are at the heart of the practice of this mode of consultancy as I understand it. But equally I think they may be at the heart of all creative organizational leadership: which is always moving from 'this is what I feel' to 'this is the feeling I am aware of in myself'—a move which, as it were, creates a space in which the location of the feeling and its possible organizational meaning can be opened up for exploration.

I want to use this experience as a kind of extended definitory hypothesis of what I have in mind by the 'recovery of meaning'. It might be objected that what it illustrates is not so much the *re*covery of meaning as its *dis*covery. But this would be to miss one element of the experience that I have perhaps elided. When I first began toying with the idea of this chapter, I happened to be given a fine account presented by David Taylor, the Chairman of the Adult Department of the Tavistock Clinic, on 'Some of Bion's ideas on meaning and understanding'. At the start of this account Taylor distinguishes 'two approximate general senses' which he intends by the term 'meaning': 'the first is that of general significance—how much or how little, someone or something means to us. An example of this would be the phrase, "life has a great deal of meaning". The second is the way in which systems of representation, be it language or pictures, operate as vehicles of human experience' (Taylor 1996).

I think that these two senses are, in emotional life, intimately linked, in that it is the ability to find or make meaning, in Taylor's second sense, that enables us to recover or restore meaning in his first sense. To return to my illustration, the finding of meaning, and organizational meaning, beyond the purely personal, in the counsellor's struggle with 'systems of representation' seemed also to restore or recover a sense of the meaning of the enterprise of which he and his colleagues were a part: its significance, vitality, and challenge. It mobilized energy, one might say, the energy to address the difficulties and dilemmas that were part and parcel of being a counsellor in this institution in this context here and now—how, for example, to avoid colluding with the tendency to pathologize the individual student, how to work with staff, from the counsellors' position, at the organizational dynamic identified, and how to take appropriate authority for communicating it.

To *dis*cover meaning is to *re*cover meaning, though whether we are able to stay with that recovery depends on more than the moment of insight itself—on our capacity for leadership, for taking risks, for 'thinking under fire', as Bion put it.

EXPLORATIONS 2

I referred earlier to Freud's image of the 'shadow of the object falling on the ego'. I want to suggest now that the approach to meaning, in the senses I am trying to use and illustrate, always starts under the presence, the sway of a shadow: an area of darkness in a client's relation to an organization or an organization's relation to its context—something equivalent to the feelings behind the counsellor's no-picture. It follows, I think, that creative work in and with organizations, whether as consultant or leader—which is not the same thing[2]—turns, sooner or later, on the capacity to entertain such shadows.

For the past four years I have been working with the principal of a large college of further education in a deprived, disadvantaged inner city area.[3] At the time I first started working with her, she had just taken over as principal and was preoccupied with needing, as she saw it, to breathe new life into an institution which in some respects appeared rather closed, embattled, and undermanaged. At the coalface, in the interactions between students and staff, there was exciting work being done, as good as anything she had seen elsewhere. But these interactions appeared privatized, uncoordinated, fragmented, and fragmentary learning encounters. Staff and students inhabited, as it were, a series of dislocated boxes. There was little sense of corporate accountability, lax financial management, and a certain lack of direction. At the same time, within a year, the college would have to face the challenge of incorporation and stand or fall on its own in a much leaner environment.

For the first two years I worked with her, the main themes of the consultancy concerned her thoughts and plans for renewal. A highly imaginative and powerful woman, she quickly moved to recruit a new governing body and to establish a network of political links with actual and potential stakeholders and other strategic allies from the local community, which was itself committed to 'regeneration'. Simultaneously, she began to evolve a very original approach to setting in place a new organizational structure, while constantly maintaining a visible presence throughout the college as a strong and inspirational leader.

New staff were recruited into senior positions, new posts created, new curriculum initiatives mounted. Within two years the college was looking physically and metaphorically quite different. There was a new mission statement, a sharper curriculum focus, new student and staff charters, and a clear sense of direction and purpose.

Half-way through the third year I became aware, as did she, of a sea change in her feelings. She was wondering about the future and being tempted with new opportunities elsewhere. Sometimes she appeared almost depressed and preoccupied with the tension and differences she was feeling between those who still represented the old guard and the newcomers. Yet all the evidence was that the place was flourishing. Opportunities for new building were in the offing, examination results encouraging, and the college establishing something of a reputation locally and nationally.

I felt, a little dimly, that she was wrestling with issues concerning her own relatedness to the college and vice versa. The sea change in her was perhaps a reflection of, and also a response to, the sea change in the college. There was also a parallel between this dynamic and the dynamic around her relation to her own daughter who was on the threshold of puberty; a parallel she would sometimes bring into sessions as a kind of commentary or a counterpart to her organizational experience.

Approaching her fourth year, towards the end of one meeting, she suddenly recalled a striking dream from some years back before she took up this post. In the dream she had taken a baby, wrapped in a blanket, from a brick in a wall which she had removed. She had to fly with the baby in a plane to Israel. All through the flight it remained in the blanket. But when she had landed and unwrapped the blanket the baby wasn't there: it had 'evaporated'.

In recounting the dream in this session, my client was not presenting it in a therapeutic context, as an element in a therapeutic exchange or dialogue between us. It was neither relevant nor appropriate, as I saw it, to probe into its possible intrapsychic meaning for her. She was, I assumed, reminded of the dream and offering it for work now, as having perhaps something to say about the situation she was in and which we were trying to understand.

From this perspective, the dream appeared to me to have an immediate transparency as a realization of her current experience and dilemma as principal. The blanketed baby, taken from a brick she had dislodged from the wall, could stand for the baby she had given to the college from the gap in the wall opened by her appointment as principal. (It is relevant to note here that in the early days of the consultancy she had referred to the college as a fortified castle, inhabited by robber barons.) Israel was the land of promise the baby would inherit.

What then of the 'evaporated' baby? I felt that this image gave expression to a reality she sensed: that the baby she had both found and made, to borrow Winnicott's phrase, the image of the college she had formed and given life to, was no longer *hers*, to be shaped or moulded or cared for by her. It had, in a graphic phrase she used, 'disappeared into the ether'.

This linked to, and in turn helped to shape, a transformation in how she conceived of the task she and her senior colleagues were now faced with. She framed this as a shift from *in*tention to *at*tention, from care to support, from minding to mindfulness, from formation to 'engagement'—a term she herself drew on and offered.

The recalled dream, you could say, was released by her to release her. In so releasing her and drawing on her own formulation, it changed the terms of her engagement with the college as its Principal.

I recognize that there is doubtless far more that could be said about this dream and I am not wanting to claim any priority for the direction I found myself taking in responding to it. But then, I do not see dreams as containers *of* meaning—a puzzle to be solved once and for all; but rather as containers *for* meaning; available narratives through which we negotiate and seek a formulation for the emotional experiences we register. In this sense a dream can be seen perhaps as a probe into the world, something available across time, like a kind of personally fashioned deep grammar through which an indefinite number of statements can be made (see Armstrong 1998).

The dream, I want to suggest, emerged from the shadow side of my client's feeling, which the method of consultancy had enabled us both to contain without pushing for a premature explanation or resolution. Within that space she herself, I suggest, discovered its resolution from the repertoire of her inner world. The dream material gave expression to the shadow, the sense of loss, but at the same time pointed to its mutation and, in so pointing, restored the 'vital' capacity both to think and to act anew.

SPECULATIONS

I referred above to the possibility of seeing dreams and dreaming as 'probes into the world', rehearsals or precursors of meaning. Now I find myself wanting to say that the two experiences I have shared carry something of the same significance for me, as if they were a consultant's dreams, through which one probes the world of one's own collaborative interaction with one's clients.

To put this another way, these experiences have been important for me not so much in exemplifying something I already knew, to be deployed as illustrations or realizations of a familiar concept or line of thinking, but rather as generators of something until now unknown—or if known unthought (Bollas 1987), or if thought not fully acknowledged.

When I first began thinking about this chapter, I recalled from many years back an observation of Charles Rycroft's that psychoanalysis was concerned not with causes but with meanings. But it had not occurred to me that one might perhaps claim the same for a psychoanalytically informed approach to consultancy. And indeed one can look through the literature of this field without coming across much if any specific reference to psychoanalytic accounts of the genesis and significance of meaning in human development. Meaning as a dimension of, or rather as a means of processing, taking the measure of all our experience, that gives life to our relatedness to the worlds we inhabit, that is simultaneously feared, resisted, defended against wherever and whenever it is most needed: meaning in this sense is present in the literature—if at all—implicitly not explicitly.

Alternatively, meaning is relegated to the sphere of each individual's personal inner world, as something that lies beyond the domain of what is specifically public, organizational, or societal. On this view, meaning concerns the nature of the individual's personal relationship to a certain line of work or organization or political standpoint, but not his or her related*ness* to such social objects. I am proposing on the contrary that this social world is itself an arena for finding and making meaning and, by the same token, for the avoidance or denial of meaning, in both the linked senses identified in the quotation from David Taylor's paper (1996) which I cited earlier.

Without reference to this dimension I doubt it is possible fully to understand, for example, the tensions between work group and basic assumption mentality (Bion 1961) or the part played in social affairs by defences against anxiety (Menzies 1960). For it seems to me that the ground in which such tensions and mechanisms emerge is precisely that in which questions of meaning and our capacity to entertain meaning unconsciously arise: out of the shadow of something felt as lost or unavailable, or out of the presence or foreshadowing of something felt as unprecedented or impending.

It is this last point that I want briefly to touch on further. The two experiences I have shared might be taken from one perspective as instances of the finding or refinding of meaning, its discovery and recovery in an organizational context. But it is equally important to acknowledge their origin in the experience of the loss or absence of meaning, with its undertow of feelings of persecution or depression.

To my mind, one of the most signal things we have learnt from psychoanalysis is that what drives development or its counterforce is the way we handle, as infants and as adults, the presence of something absent. For those analysts working under the aegis of Melanie Klein and her successors, meaning is seen as evolving from and within this experience, through the 'interaction and emotional exchange with primary objects' (Taylor 1996). This evolution is, however, never completed, in the sense that experiences of absence or, which I suspect is the same thing dynamically speaking, of unanticipated presence continually arouse the same primal emotions.

Having said that, I need to acknowledge that, as far as I can at present see, there is no real equivalent in the social sphere of the dynamic interplay between self and object, container and contained, out of which the ability to generate meaning, in good enough normal circumstances, naturally evolves. And it occurs to me that this may be why, in organizational and social life, *meaning*—that is, the meaning that attaches to organizational and societal experience as a bounded domain—so often, as it were, slips through one's fingers. The result is that the experience of absence or of unanticipated presence, instead of being reflectively held and processed, provokes flight, action/reaction, or withdrawal.

I am thinking, for example, of the pervasive use in organizational circles now of the language of 'vision', 'mission', 'core values', and of its accompanying punitive undertow, formulated in concepts such as 'downsizing', 'delayering', and 'key performance indicators'. Too often such language and concepts seem to short-circuit questions of meaning, as if they are being superimposed from without, rather than generated from within.

I feel something of the same in relation to the current vogue for so called post-modernist theories or accounts, either of the self or of the organization, and their preoccupation with the virtual, the invented identity or the 'management of meaning'. I do not think the virtual is a category in psychic reality, nor that identity is invented, nor that meaning is managed—although of course its discovery, as my two earlier experiences suggested, has implications for everything one manages. Such usages and vogues, it seems to me, may operate rather as a kind of manic defence against what is unknown in the face of change, as if the answer to 'no x' is 'try y'.

It is not that some of these things are not important. In much of my own consultancy practice I work a good deal with organizations on vision, mission, and values in a context of constant change. But I would also feel that such work needs always to be rooted in, or at least provide space for, the evolution of meaning which is necessarily provisional and transitional but without which such terms risk a kind of emotional degeneration.

My tentative hypothesis is that what drives such emotional de-generation is the precedence we tend instinctively to give to the claims of survival over those of development. I remember, still with a sense of shock, first coming across one of Wilfred Bion's more oracular statements:

I would make a distinction between existence—the capacity to exist—and the ambition or aspiration to have an existence that is worth having—the quality of the existence not the quantity: not the length of one's life but the quality of that life. There are no scales by which we can weigh quality against quantity, but existence is to be contrasted with the essence of existence. The fact that the patient, like the analyst, (like the world) is still in existence is not adequate. (Bion 1978.)

The contrast between quantity and quality, existence and the essence of existence is at the heart of the distinction between survival and development that I am trying to draw. What makes it difficult to sustain, in organizational as in personal life, is perhaps this: that when we venture into the territory of the meaning of an experience, we cannot predict what the outcome will be. From this point of view, both experiences I recounted are, as generalizations, over-optimistic. *En route* to the discovery and recovery of meaning one may confront the unbearable. As with Bion's patient

who was quite articulate, in fact articulate enough to make me feel I was analyzing him rather well. Indeed the analysis did go well, but I was beginning to think that nothing was happening. However the patient checked all that. After one session he went home, sealed up all the crevices throughout his room, turned on the gas and perished. So there was my highly successful analysis—a very disconcerting result indeed and no way of finding out or learning for myself what exactly had gone wrong, excepting the fact that it had undoubtedly gone wrong. (Bion 1978.)

There are occasions when there may be very good reasons for feeling persecuted by the unknown. It is just too surprising. At a time when organizations face unique challenges of globalization, radical technological change, and the increasing discrepancy between available resources and the claims we make on those resources, it would take a puritan not to feel some sympathy with the instincts of survival. None the less in putting development at risk, through denying or avoiding the need for meaning, the cost of survival I suspect will always be the perpetuation of our discontent.

NOTES

1 The symposium was held in New York in June 1996.
2 The difference, in my view, concerns the link between reflective understanding and executive action. While a consultant may need to stay with the client while he or she works through this link, the consultant rarely experiences directly the particular creative challenge involved in the transformation of insight into organizational praxis.
3 Colleges of further education offer a wide variety of mainly vocational courses for post-16 school leavers and for adults. Since 1993, their governance has passed from Local Education Authorities to self-governing trusts, funded by a national Further Education Funding Council.

11

From Envy to Desire: Witnessing the transformation

David Gutmann, Jacqueline Ternier-David,
and Christophe Verrier

This chapter sets out, on the basis of a case example, to discuss the workings of two major affects—desire and envy—as an integral part of the constructive and destructive processes underlying institutional life.

We begin by proposing a definition of desire and envy as both individual and collective feelings, outlining the nature of their impact in organizations. This is followed by an account of a workshop which revealed envy and desire as key elements of the client organization's dominant dynamic. Finally, we offer some concluding remarks on the significance and impact on organizational processes of the transformation from envy to desire.

DESIRE AND ENVY: CONCEPTUAL FRAMEWORK

Desire

Etymologically, the word desire can be traced back to the Latin term *desiderare*, composed of *de-* (privative) and of *sideris* 'the stars'. Desire therefore literally means 'to stop gazing at the stars'[1] and hence 'to feel the loss of', 'to long or hope for'. Thus the etymological perspective underlines the close relation between desire and lack. It also suggests that understanding one's own desire consists in having one's feet (back) on the ground, no longer being 'star struck', moving on (again), being (once again) in reality.

Desire emerges as one of the fundamental affects of an individual's life. Through it we not only exist, but seek to create: families, works of art, buildings, institutions, businesses, relationships. Desire is therefore not only present in institutions, but instrumental in their construction, development, and trans-formation. This desire is, first and foremost, that of the individuals who make up the institution, starting (but not ending) with that of its leaders. Desire is ever present. At times it can erupt like a volcano and is too destructive to allow for any creativity. At other times, it is like stagnant water in which the products of our individual and collective histories ferment and are deposited, but have not the effervescence to generate the dynamics of creation or transformation. How then can it be stirred? How can the inner source of individual or collective desire be awakened? How can one be brought to acknowledge it, to connect it with one's own desire so as to see it as a resource that can lead to transformation and, in the case of an institution, to share it with others or, more precisely, to have one's own desire resonate with that of others?

Consequently, we have come to believe that the primary role of managers is to reveal and bring into interaction the desire—individual and collective—that exists within an institution.

Envy

Envy is another possible response to lack. Unlike desire, however, which can initiate a constructive process, envy harbours destruction. It involves feelings of anger and indeed hate towards the person having an object or quality that one covets, but cannot acquire. The envious person will therefore seek first to destroy the object of envy and then to destroy the person having the object. Envy is directed first at the object, then at the person.

One of the most relevant descriptions of the intimate mechanisms of envy is proposed by Melanie Klein (1975*a*), who describes envy as the most potent man-ifestation of the destructive impulses that 'undermine feelings of love and grat-itude at their root, since it affects the earliest relation of all, that to the mother' (176). Klein stresses the projective nature of envy, by recalling that the word envy derives from the Latin verb *invideo*: to look askance at, to cast an evil eye upon.[2] Finally, she proposes a number of interpretations of attitudes observed in adults and in interpersonal relationships, which are of great relevance to the theme of this chapter. Thus, envy drives the very ambitious individual to 'the inability to allow others to come sufficiently to the fore. They may be allowed to play a subsidiary part as long as they do not challenge [his/her] supremacy. Such people are unable and not unwilling to stimulate and encourage younger people, because some of them might become their successors' (op. cit.: 261). On the other hand, 'where greed and envy are not excessive, even an ambitious person finds satisfaction in helping others to make their contribution' (op. cit.: 261). Here we have one of the attitudes underlying successful leadership.

Living institutions live envy

By nature, institutions that are strong, thriving, and imbued more with the life principle than the death principle do generate within them affects such as envy. Envy can be necessary when—provided it is confined and contained—it contributes to the definition of roles, their structuring, and the demarcation of the boundaries separating them. It is, nevertheless, often a negative process fostering regression rather than progression, destruction rather than construction, if only by colluding with the envy that any thriving institution arouses. It can sometimes completely overwhelm the institution. How then can envy be taken out of the equation when it comes to analysing the processes at work in an institutional context?

Narcissism, envy, and guilt

It is our belief that envy and guilt form and fuel a vicious circle. On the one hand, envy arouses guilt in the person who looks to spoil or destroy the (human) object of envy. On the other hand, however, envy can stem directly from an even deeper guilt. It is the guilt that is experienced by those who know themselves neither to be perfect, nor to conform to the *ego ideal*[3] that their own narcissism continually exalts. Envy is anger at falling short of perfection, irrespective of past successes and satisfactions (see Figure 11.1).

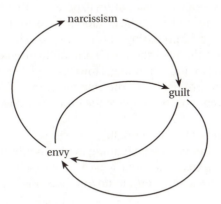

Fig. 11.1   Narcissism, guilt, and envy

In the case of the head of an institution this guilt, associated with the impossibility of satisfying a narcissistic need, has an impact on the institution as a whole. The inability to attain perfection causes a corporate leader to adopt a posture of omnipotence in which he/she seeks refuge, and which the rest of the institution tends to accept. This is, first, because he or she has a degree of power that can make this attitude prevail and, secondly, because he or she places this indomitable and insatiable narcissistic need as a vital issue at the very heart of the institution. Envy thus pervades the institution in so far as each of its members seeks to meet this impossible demand which the leader soon comes to personify. No longer able to 'live up to' the demands placed upon them, everyone is dragged into the guilt process. All that then matters is presumed proximity to the leader's ideal, directly inspired by his or her narcissistic need. Any reference to the profound and individualized desire of the institution's members is then of course impossible. And those attempting to progress by standing in the way of this process are destroyed or rejected.

In this way, the leader in an institution overwhelmed by envy is placed in a position of omnipotence, continually imposing on others a guilt-engendering comparison with his or her own ideal: an ego ideal imposed as a permanent point of reference which has an impact on all other members of the institution. The hold exercised through this imposition of the leader's ego ideal impedes the working of desire within the institution. The institution as a whole lives under the illusion that it can only be transformed through the action of its leader.

WITNESSING THE TRANSFORMATION: AN ACCOUNT OF THE WORKSHOP

In this section we describe a consultation experience that took place in 1993 in order to offer a number of hypotheses about organizational processes. Our intervention consisted of preparing and running a self-contained workshop, and we shall focus on the workshop itself and on its preparation in so far as it also yielded elements of understanding. However, as is often the case with such organizational interventions, it was the actual fact that such a workshop even took place that proved most revealing of the processes at work within this institution.

For obvious reasons of confidentiality, we will not be citing the institution concerned by name, nor will we be naming the main protagonists.[4] The corporation in question, which relocated a part of its facilities to Israel, will be referred to as HT and described only as an American high technology company.

1. The genesis of the workshop

HT Israel is the largest of the corporation's facilities located outside the United States. It includes a production unit employing 700 people and a centre for design, research, and development. Much of its success is due to the remarkable and sustained development it has enjoyed over a number of years, and which today places it at the cutting edge of global competitiveness and ensures its short-term survival.

The considerable—and continual—challenge facing HT is reflected in a constant process of ruthless selection and competition among the people working in each of the corporation's sites. This Anglo-Saxon trait runs head-on into Israel's culture and heritage of courage (HT was the only company to remain operational during the Gulf War), to say nothing of its survival-mindedness. It is also to be noted that HT Israel is headed by its founder S, who invented a process which has largely contributed to the company's success, and which consequently confers added potency to his authority within the Israel-based operation.

M, the Director of the Production Unit, initiated the management's decentralization by reducing the hierarchical ranks from four to three and then two, introduced new work schedules, and appointed a woman, N, as Total Quality Facilitator. And yet this transformation was slow in making its way into the day-to-day running of the production unit. At the time of our initial intervention, David Gutmann, one of our team, had been advising M as an adviser in leadership since 1991.

One of our initial hypotheses—shared by M—was that nothing seemed to be lacking at the Production Unit. All that was needed for its success was in place. But this 'absence of lack' is also an absence of desire. By thwarting transformation of the unit's management, this 'completeness' also prevented the institution and the people in it from understanding, expressing, and giving effect to their individual and collective desire.

In March 1992, M attended the workshop on Authority, Leadership and Innovation[5] organized near Paris by the International Forum for Social Innovation and directed by David. In July 1992, M suggested that David organize such a workshop at the Production Unit for the seventy managers working there. And so this methodology came to be applied *in vivo*, in a corporate setting, and in Israel, the country of miracles and faith (Gutmann, Pierre, Ternier-David, and Verrier 1997).

2. The preparation

The work done in the run-up to this workshop took much time and effort. It involved our Paris-based team of consultants, as well as our British colleague, Jon Stokes. We finally opted for a two-session programme. The first of these was to be a four-day session with three exercises built up around the central theme of here and now.[6] The first exercise focused on relationships between the roles corresponding to the three hierarchical levels at the Production Unit. The second dealt with individual involvement in the Unit's decision-making process, and the third covered relations with management in a competitive context. Transformation analysis groups were set up and regular meetings were programmed between the two sessions to continue this work. The second session, lasting a day and a half, was designed to give the participants some time out after the first, and to measure the headway that had been made in overcoming resistances. (Bion 1961; Gutmann, Ternier-David, and Verrier 1995.)

The project thus presented was approved by M. It was agreed that the consultant staff, headed by David, would be made up mainly of members of Praxis International.[7] Then, in March 1993, just one month prior to the workshop, came a dramatic turn of events: S, the Director of HT Israel, decided to call the whole thing off, refusing to 'bring in' consultants who were not from HT or Israel.

This about-turn led to a new proposal being put forward: if S opposed the idea of having seven external consultants, then the number would have to be drastically reduced. This meant members of the Production Unit management team—that is to say, the dozen Department Managers—had to take all the staff roles.[8] The 'casting' under the original workshop proposal was therefore completely changed: whereas, initially, the Production Unit's managerial team was to take charge of management of the workshop (with M acting as workshop director), it suddenly found itself both in a management and in a consultation role, as facilitators.

Provision consequently had to be made for training these Department Managers in readiness for their role as facilitators to the other participants (the seventy Group Leaders). To this end, we set up a pre-workshop, which was to last a day and a half and immediately precede the workshop itself.

After some tough negotiation, this new proposal was accepted. Only two external consultants, David and Jon, would take part in the workshop. H, an internal consultant from the Human Resources Department of HT was brought in specially from the USA to work with them.

This decision was not, however, taken lightly. In view of the lengthy training needed to prepare members of staff for a workshop of this kind, there was no question of 'letting loose' the Production Unit managers as facilitators, although four people—the Director, N, H, and one of the Department Managers—were more prepared for work of this kind than the others, owing to their earlier participation in here and now seminars. Four measures were therefore taken to provide the relevant back-up and support:

1. Each of the two sessions was preceded by a pre-workshop during which the external consultants 'primed' the managers of HT Israel for their role as facilitators. The working groups in which this preparatory work took place were known as consultation analysis groups.
2. During the workshop and on the fifth day, the facilitators were supervised by the consultants: the consultation analysis groups met twice daily so as to gain a better understanding of the facilitator role of the Department Managers.
3. David, in the meantime, continued to act as leadership adviser to the Director and the staff as a whole.

4. Finally, daily staff meetings were held, alongside the consultation analysis groups, to continue the process of clarification and interpretation of the life of the system as a whole, as well as each of its subsystems. These meetings served to ensure containment of the workshop, that is to say, to guarantee that members of staff did not target other participants with their own projections, and to provide a climate in which individual professionalism could be enhanced by developing mechanisms of co-operation and support between the various subsystems.

These measures were the final elements in the preparation for the programme, called 'Leadership, Competition and Transformation'. As a result of our preparatory work, we had devised an original working approach, whereby professional managers were given a more active part to play in the consultation process. We acted on the belief that achieving success in such a technologically innovative corporation might mean bringing in potential innovation in the area of human development.

3. The workshop (20–24 April 1993)

As our description of the run-up period set out to illustrate, the workshop was a learning experience for all concerned: the participants (Group Leaders), the workshop staff (the Director, M, and the Department Managers), and the external consultants (David, Jon, and H), but also the members of the workshop preparation team who stayed behind in Paris. It would be difficult to chronicle an event as complex and multifaceted as a four-day workshop which eventually brought together seventy-four participants. We shall therefore confine ourselves to setting out the broad lines of our programme.

We framed this workshop in every way as a 'learning institution', if only a temporary one. Viewing an institution as a place of learning for one and all opens up a new understanding—and potentially acceptance—of role differentiation. The institution is no longer perceived as a place where only its leaders hold the truth and are seen as having exclusive access to power and knowledge, but rather as a place where it is possible to imagine decentralized forms of management, and indeed co-management.

During the first part of the workshop, M discovered the role of workshop director. Step by step, he found his own mode of operating. During the 'Competition' sessions, he came up with a very useful working hypothesis when he said 'each Department Manager is its department's gladiator'. In other words, Group Leaders are in the arena of management through a 'filtering down' process, through the 'sacrificial' mediation of the Department Managers. This does shed light on the imaginary relation between these roles, where the Group Leaders 'use' Department Managers while avoiding any direct risk taking or development of their own authority.

With this image, M expressed not only a working hypothesis interpreting the way Production Unit management take up their roles, but perhaps something much deeper about his own condition as manager of HT Israel. It suggested that he himself is the gladiator for the whole system. S, the director of HT Israel, entrusts to him the responsibility for doing battle (first at the Production Unit, and then from 1994 onwards at the Design Centre), each time 'putting himself on the line' professionally, his sole reward being to stay alive, to survive the system, without any special glory or truly recognized merit. Such struggles can be to the death, that is to say, might even involve expulsion from the system.

We shall return to a discussion of the processes which were brought to light during the workshop. At this juncture, however, we would observe that the workshop as a whole showed just how the members of the Production Unit felt 'locked in' to the dominant culture of survival, which seems to foster not only immediate action on long-term strategy, but also a lack of confidence and ill-contained aggressiveness. The feeling of being trapped in the past condemns the future, which is not perceived as an open space where a wealth of possibilities might unfold. The new generation, exposed to the *de facto* cultural domination of the elders, is particularly affected by this (Gutmann, Ternier-David, and Verrier 1996a). A characteristic feature of this sense of being trapped, or locked in, is the blocking of individual and collective desire, which is then not mobilized within the institution. Its members silence their own desire for fear that expressing it might endanger them, have them broach the forbidden, or break a taboo.

This configuration predisposes the institution to accepting and reinforcing the dangerous process whereby one of its leaders is cast in the role of saviour: M, the Production Unit's 'voluntary' director, who represents the new generation, or indeed S, the founding father of HT Israel, so deeply enmeshed in this survival culture. One Group Leader's friendly gibe at M during the plenary closing session, 'We're all coming with you from the Production Unit to the Design Centre!', was highly revealing. It meant that M was seen as the archetypal leader, much like his predecessor in this region of the world, Moses! The question merits consideration as there is an association rooted in tradition between S and Moses within this company. If M is seen as the new Moses, this also raises the whole question of leadership succession.

4. The work between the two sessions

The period between the two sessions was marked by two contradictory tendencies: continuing development versus the (re-)emergence of resistances to change. The work begun in the April workshop was sustained in regular meetings of the transformation analysis groups (twelve Group Leaders, with a Department Manager as facilitator, as at the workshop) and in the working pair built up between M and David.

In July, a half-day meeting was convened, with M, the Department Managers, a few Group Leaders, and David, to assess the progress initiated by the April workshop. As it turned out, some of the groups had made real progress, whereas others had met only once or twice, and some not at all.

It was as though the element of surprise experienced in the workshop had now worn off. Being caught by surprise or 'off guard' can often be a way forward, for it overrides a good many resistances—if only for a moment. Indeed, surprise was one of the processes in April that went some way to making the workshop run smoothly. The seven-month gap between the two sessions seemed to have given everyone space to take time out, to 'shut off', and to re-erect their resistances. The work was also made more difficult by the absence of the external consultants.

Secondly, however, the work between the two sessions was significantly marked by the appointment of M as head of HT Israel's Design Centre. His departure from the Production Unit was scheduled for 1 January 1994, when he was to be replaced by J, his predecessor at the Design Centre. This decision on the part of HT Israel's Director had a number of consequences. There is no denying that it undermined the process set in motion by the experience of the workshop: it was as though this changeover of managers was, consciously or unconsciously, intended to neutralize the results that were starting to come through. The Production Unit therefore found itself preparing for a changeover of leaders just as the transformation of its organization and culture was pursuing its course, and it was undergoing an unprecedented learning experience under the Leadership, Competition and Transformation programme.

As a result, it was deemed essential to have the fifth day focus on this central event of the changeover between M and J. The latter was consequently invited to join the workshop staff alongside his predecessor. The objectives being pursued under the programme also had to incorporate this transition in the continuity of action, that is to say, the continuity of the transformation and the learning process.

The period between the two sessions was also a time of preparation for the fifth day. During this stage, N seemed to take it upon herself to speak on behalf of the institution as a whole, expressing focused resistances, which in this instance concerned the scheduling and duration of the December session. The tension reached such a point that the second session of the workshop nearly did not take place. An agreement as to the working approach was nevertheless arrived at.

A particular manifestation of resistance appeared in the behaviour of many Department Managers. Most of them were clearly determined not to be taken by surprise again, and therefore attempted to prepare for the second session in their own way. Some went to great lengths to try and find out about any unexpected exercises, although they did, of course, know what was on the programme, as they had themselves helped to define it at the July working group. Some entered into a process of collusion, even going as far as rehearsing what they would say and do on the fifth day. This 'conspiratorial' behaviour, about which J had serious misgivings, accentuated the diminishing power of M, who was then just one month away from leaving the Production Unit (Gutmann 1989; Gutmann, Ternier-David, and Verrier 1996b).

5. The fifth day (2 and 3 December 1993)

It was the recognition of these events and attitudes which led David to realize on the evening of the fifth day, at the staff meeting following the work done with the Group Leaders, that everything had ground to a halt under the effect of these combined resistances. At this point, he took the decision to withdraw from the meeting, taking Jon and H with him. In so doing, he forestalled M, who was on the verge of walking out, but found himself instead left with J and the Department Managers.

This instantly brought down resistances, though not completely and only for a time. Our experience in fact shows that resistances rarely give way gradually, but yield all of a sudden, like the onset of a catharsis, or the collapse of the Berlin Wall in 1989. In the dynamics of the workshop, the consultants' departure was also 'Un acte de passage prévenant un passage à l'acte' (Balmary 1986), an action or act of transition preventing an acting out. In other words, by taking this action (act of transition), the consultants were able to get the system past deadlock and got the director off the hook. They avoided his early departure from the scene, if only symbolically (transition in action), given that M was handing over power to J on 1 January 1994, and not 2 December 1993. The consultants were at the same time able to pull out of the maelstrom and take time out to distance themselves from the situation.

Upon their return—forty-five minutes later—the mood was one of distress and foreboding. This situation was very telling, and brings us to the core of our working hypothesis, which we shall be discussing again later on. What had happened was that the feeling of lack had allowed desire to express itself more fully and to some extent override the envy that was dominant at that moment. The transformation that had taken place could thus be seen for what it was: it was not about the managers taking over from the consultants, or one manager taking over from another (J from M), but the transformation from envy to desire.

And so, upon their return, M again took charge as workshop director, with J at his side, facing the troops—the Department Managers—some of whom were in full regression. The following day, as planned, J took over as workshop director during an open work session. The transition phase had well and truly started.

During this second session of the programme, H, who had made a real and enthusiastic contribution in April, seemed to show greater resistance, going as far as to cancel a meeting scheduled with Jon 'so she could get some sleep'. Confronted with David's desire to continue—with her—his work at HT, she reinforced her resistance by implying that this kind of process was useful in Israel, but impossible in the United States. She acted as though coming up against this process of discovering a desire, or a host of desires each stronger than the others, should remain a happy experience, but be 'done with' at a certain point, as though it had to be 'wrapped up' at all costs. It was as if these desires triggered her envy in the face of the success of the process and her fear of having to take authority for spreading word of this transformation in the United States.

This second session was therefore an opportunity to mark the changeover from M to J. And yet, judging from the gibe made at M at the end of the April session—'We're all coming with you from the Production Unit to the Design Centre!'—the personal 'handover' between M and J did not seem to be perceived as conforming to the biblical metaphor referred to above, where Joshua succeeds Moses—who dies—and enters alone into the Promised Land heading the people of Israel. This is why the work done at the Production Unit on a day-to-day basis, combined with the workshop, no doubt made for a smoother handover, also in terms of technological and industrial efficiency.

In a manner of speaking, reality confirmed this intuition. As soon as he took over, J found an institution that was in 'good shape' (shape as in form, as in transformation). It was a transformation which, irrespective of this manager's action, was unquestionably not only in progress, but set to last, with a creative momentum that brought excellent tangible results. M, for his part, spent some time at the Design Centre where he faced a considerable challenge, which he pulled off with success, before leaving HT in 1996.

It was possible to trace the impact of the workshop in three main areas:

1. Day-to-day working relationships within the Production Unit improved, as a result of reduced resistance to the recent delayering in the senior management team from three to two. The idea or fantasy of a 'shadow third rank' in the management hierarchy was removed.
2. Most participants were enabled to discover a new understanding of their role and authority within the system. In particular, they were able to increase their capacity to act with authority in relation to the primary task of the factory.
3. Although the workshop was not entirely appreciated by either the Director of HT Israel or by J, many participants were able to gain a sense of distance from the company and to reduce its hold on them. After M left, some other participants also left the Production Unit, indeed some left HT altogether.

One intended effect which did not occur, because of the interruption to the process, was the transmission of the learning from the Group Leaders to the Production Unit workers.

FROM ENVY TO DESIRE

This—for us exceptional—experience in Israel led us to wonder about the content of the workshop and about the working hypotheses that had emerged from it, to say nothing of the processes involved in its preparation and implementation. What were the determinants and consequences of such a workshop? Could one pinpoint the main conscious and unconscious processes that had woven their way through the institution during it? It was such *a posteriori* considerations that led us, four years later, to formulate a number of working hypotheses concerning the whole issue of envy and desire in institutions.

As stated earlier, envy and desire, whether at the individual or institutional level, are two possible responses—albeit in fundamental opposition to one another—to lack and, more generally, to a sense of void, imperfection (or the desire for perfection), and to incompleteness. But whereas desire may drive one to fill this void through creativity, which is a vital life impulse, envy, by contrast, leads to the destruction of the object of envy and the person possessing that object.

Both these affects play a major role in the life of institutions. After much thought and deliberation following our experience at HT Israel, the main working hypothesis we arrived at was that the fundamental task of managers consists of moving from envy to desire through the process of transformation.

1. An institution dominated by envy

We found HT to be institutionally dominated by envy, as it was long before the actual run-up to the workshop. The resulting dynamics—discreet, veiled, covert, or indeed deliberately obscured though they might have been—were nevertheless at work throughout the run-up to the workshop and during the workshop itself.

S appeared not only to be the institution's absolute leader, but also to be crowned with a glory born of his past successes in research and development. It was he who founded this corporation and was instrumental in making it the success it came to be. In a manner of speaking, he is, additionally, all this and more *vis-à-vis* the State of Israel, for it was he who 'imported' this prestigious American corporation on to its territory. S, on the other hand, seemed so possessed by a desire for eternity, so wanting to stay on as head of HT Israel for as long as possible, that he systematically cast aside any potential successors. All the conditions were right for driving S in search of perfection, which he implicitly imposed on his co-workers, and which is reflected in the intense rivalry they were all caught up in.

One possible interpretation of this demand for unbounded narcissism is perhaps to be found in history: some of HT's main leaders (including S and M) lived through the Shoah or its aftermath, such as post-war emigration from Europe. This may have left them permanently scarred and given rise to a narcissism of compensation. This probably accounts for the desire to be entrepreneurial (especially in a field where technology can give the illusion of omnipotence and omniscience), but it also reinforces the posture of omnipotence which can be found, for example, in the discourse of excellence or total quality management.

Envy appeared to be uppermost in the relationship between M and S, with the added dimension that the succession to the top position at HT Israel was at stake. In a way, the workshop made S face up to this, for he seemed to deny it with all his being. Perhaps this was a reminder for him of his own mortality and the limited nature of life, particularly in relation to the potentially infinite duration of the institution he was instrumental in creating and which, by definition, knows no biological limit. What he envies in M is his—relative—youth and the few years' difference that give him the possibility of taking over a role that has mattered to him so much personally. Naturally enough, this envy has a rebound effect on the institution as a whole.

What appears to have been at issue at the time of the workshop was, therefore, the future of M, the new candidate to succeed S. Would he be cast aside like all the others? Or would he be able to set in motion what is needed to 'release' S from his role as saviour, and the institution from its 'locked in' state?

2. No more star-gazing

Desire arises when the members of the institution stop looking (up) at their leader as a perfect being, like a star, who is out of reach, and thus refuse to be in collusion with his or her narcissism. Comparison with an ideal—and idealized—object then clearly appears as a 'blind alley'. Lack becomes what engenders freedom.

From that moment on, the leader can take a step back, not by relinquishing his or her role, but by partially effacing him/herself, leaving a kind of void at the head of the institution. Space is then made for what is possible. From the lack and the desire engendered by this anxiety stems creativity. From desire arises authority, but an authority expressed by the greater number (critical mass) of the institution's members. With desire 'on the up', plural authority enables a new distribution of roles: a stepping-down, an emergence of co-authors of transformations in progress, generativity, and the generation of new leaders.

HT Israel again illustrates this representation of desire: during the run-up to and the actual workshop, there were two stars (S and M) coexisting in the institution and fuelling processes of identification. And while the one begins gently to wane, the other slowly but surely gains momentum by deploying his or her authority and talent. At the same time, however, this 'changeover' of stars opens up a psychological and temporal space, wherein the rising star has not yet taken over from the waning one: it occurs when there is no one star, and it

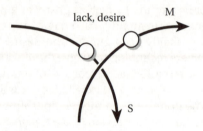

Fig. 11.2   The absence of a star arouses desire

is laden with all the energy of lack and desire (see Figure 11.2). In superseding S as a star, however, M is also running the risk of having to fill this temporary and fragile void that we identify as the main source of desire at this moment in the life of the institution.

3. The transformation from envy to desire

And so, on the one hand, a thriving institution knows envy; on the other hand, the life principle of an institution is nourished by the desire of its members, who can only express it when the leader relinquishes a position of omnipotence. Consequently, one of the crucial transformations to be undertaken by managers consists in moving from envy to desire. As we see it, this occurs in stages, three of which we discuss here: sideration[9] through envy, consideration, and desire.

Sideration through envy

The sideration stage is that of deadlock. Envy has such a strong hold that people are 'star struck' to the point of being paralysed by the (idealized) object of their envy. The ideal of the other (that of the leader), becomes the ego ideal, and vice versa. One's own free will vanishes completely, leaving the way open for the processes of mimesis, repetition, uniformity, and indeed 'cloning'. The world seems to be one of absolutes and of completeness: metaphorically like the world of the exact sciences, repudiating human reality in its complexity, uncertainty, plurality, and diversity.

Consideration

To go beyond the sideration stage, it is essential to move from the singular to the plural. This means going from the contemplation of a single star to that of a constellation of stars. In other words, it is about accepting that processes of identification be directed not towards a single leader, but towards many (see Figure 11.3).

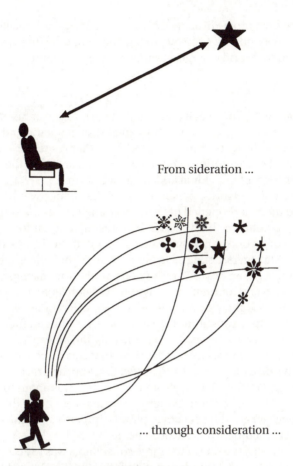

From sideration ...

... through consideration ...

Fig. 11.3   From sideration through consideration

Although this may only be an intermediate stage, the difference is consider-able. The plurality introduced opens up a multidimensional field making dif-ferentiation possible. Identification is no longer about contemplating a single being that transforms you into an object, but attentively observing a diversity of beings so that one is made aware of one's own diversity. This sets in motion interactions between subsystems (external or internal to oneself): it is the re-emergence of life itself.

This can be likened to the development of a young child whereby, in order to discover its own singularity and to progress from the relationship of fusion (that is, to separate from the mother), the infant becomes aware of its father. In so doing, it moves from a situation of identification with a single being—one it has trouble differentiating from itself—to consideration of a two-star constellation. The infant thus discovers the plural, the diversity of the sexes, which it then relates to its own inner diversity, its own singularity. It henceforth exists as a being in its own right. It is not surprising, then, that the infant's interest at this stage turns to the world at large, starting with its own family.

Desire

This life 'regained' allows each and every one to rediscover his or her own identity, integrity, and singularity as a human and social being and to allow his or her own specific desire to come through as another response to the question of void and lack. The institution can then become an arena for the expression and 'working through' of individual and collective desires.

Preparation of the workshop showed how the changeover between the consultants and managers opened the way to a transformation from envy to desire. It is to be remembered that it was S, by refusing to let in foreign consultants, who led to this workshop format being adopted. So it was that the twelve Department Managers, acting as facilitators, took their place alongside M, facing the Group Leaders. By proposing a form of co-management, by showing them that all seventy of them no longer had to converge 'towards the one', M was able to release the paralysis of sideration, wherein he was the only focus (thus making him a substitute for S, 'the star'?), and so enter consideration, where the seventy could consider the constellation of twelve.

However, everything seemed to indicate that this discovery had begun seriously to jeopardize the sole star and its idealization: the process ground to a halt at this stage, just as the next stage—that of desire—was about to come through. The fact that M left to go to the Design Centre made it impossible to get through the next stages where the collective, plural—but also singular—desire of each organizational member could really emerge.

More specifically, the role of the three consultants was to accompany M in his passage from star to human being. Similarly, for the Department Managers, taking on the role of facilitator meant displaying not their 'sidereal archetype' attributes as technicians or managers, but their humanity. They had to do this by starting with their imperfections, just as they were having to take on a role with which they were unfamiliar, despite being well prepared for it. It all seemed as if M had taken the role of Moses, needing an Aaron to take his word to the people, a Joshua to succeed him in the Promised Land, and a Jethro as consultant, for he is not infallible.

The evening of the fifth day of the workshop could be seen as a compressed experience of transformation from envy to desire with its three crucial steps:

1. *Sideration*, when there was a strong temptation to idealize M (or J) as a single star chosen from among the many.
2. *Consideration*, when this process focused on the twelve Department Managers plus the three consultants, like a constellation.
3. *Desire*, when it was finally understood that stars cannot offer more than light.

EPILOGUE

When an institution expresses more desire than envy, transformation is under way. In other words, the transformation of envy into desire is a sure sign that the institution itself is undergoing that transformation without which it cannot survive in its struggle against the entropy that threatens its existence.

The workshop gave the protagonists from the Production Unit the opportunity to live a transformation. It took them out of the day-to-day life of the institution where it would have been impossible, or extremely difficult, to undertake this voyage of discovery. It did not, however, take them into a manipulative pseudo-reality that would have made the whole thing nothing more than imaginary role playing. This workshop, which gave them 'time out' (in spite of nearly being stopped in its tracks), also took them from envy to desire as an institutional configuration. This movement allowed organizational members to recognize their diversity, to form alliances, and actually to undertake[10] work together.

The passage from envy to desire also casts the role of consultant in a different light, especially when he or she accompanies or witnesses to a process of transformation and to the work of the leaders spearheading it. During the workshop in question, the consultants were in the here and now, not only observing but also making the journey of transformation with everybody else.

This experience suggests that transformation requires witness, through a dynamic, cross-referencing presence which encourages it to continue. The consultants of Praxis International provided this witnessing presence, while at the same time being the instruments of the passage from envy to desire. Their role was to re-cognize this transformation and to have the managers share in the experience. They did this by helping the managers take up the role(s) of director and/or facilitator, simply by being involved in the consultation process. They were there, helping M—and the others—to make the journey of transformation.

NOTES

1 *Webster's Third New International Dictionary.*
2 *Dictionnaire historique de la langue française* (Robert 1992).
3 *Ego ideal*: terms used by Freud in his second theory on the human psyche: a condition of the personality resulting from the convergence of narcissism (idealization of self) and identification to the parents, their substitutes, and collective ideals. As a differentiated condition, the ego ideal constitutes a model to which the subject seeks to conform. (See Laplanche and Pontalis 1988: 144.)
4 The abbreviations used denote the following:

- HT: the parent high technology corporation.
- HT Israel: its Israeli subsidiary.
- S: Director of HT Israel.
- M: Director of the Production Unit (and later the Design Centre).
- N: Total Quality Facilitator of the Production Unit.
- J: M's successor at the head of the Production Unit, but also his predecessor at the Design Centre.
- H: internal consultant of HT Corporation (USA).

5 The working conference on Authority, Leadership and Innovation, renamed in 1993 'Authority, Leadership and Transformation', is organized in Paris by the International Forum for Social Innovation (IFSI). For some twenty years, it has been furthering the tradition of human behaviour training, founded on the ideas of Wilfrid R. Bion, and first launched in London in the 1950s by Pierre Turquet and Ken Rice.

6 'Here and now' is an approach whereby each participant works through certain experiences by exploring the methods proposed during the seminar and learning from these experiences. The discussion sessions then help them to assimilate, transform, and relate these to what they experience from day to day within their institutions.

7 Founded in 1989, Praxis International is a company of advisers in leadership, whose role is to work with managers from public or private institutions on the transformation of their roles. It is based in Paris, France.

8 Conference staff: the staff comprised the Production Unit Director (in the role of workshop director) and the Department Managers (who would act as managers and facilitators), accompanied by the consultants. The staff's role was twofold: to 'direct' the seminar and take responsibility for 'boundary management' so that all participants were actively involved. On the other hand, the members of staff were to act as facilitators during certain sessions.

9 'Sideration' (from the Latin *sideris*, meaning stars) is a medical term, indicating sudden paralysis. The word's origin reflects the belief that the attack or condition was caused by the malign influence of the stars. Despite its awkwardness in English, the word is maintained here because of its links to the themes under discussion.

10 The French word *entreprendre*—to undertake—literally means 'to take up together', underlining the extent to which human activity calls for alliance and the 'crossing over' of differences.

12

In the Nick of Time: Reactivating an organization through leader-initiated interactions with members of staff

Siv Boalt Boëthius

The object of this chapter is to give examples of and to discuss some strategies for positive organizational change. I take as my starting-point the critical fact that any leader in any organization will, by virtue of his or her role, often become enmeshed in expectations and demands of various kinds. These constraints, conscious and unconscious, develop by interaction between employees and leader and in relation to the primary task of the organization, the structure of the work activity, and the environment of the workplace. If incorrectly handled, the constraints, by their force, can easily lead to situations in which both leader and employees lose their autonomy, creativity, and effectiveness. In the long run, as individuals or entire groups lose touch with their potential resources as well as with the primary task, the organization, in part or as a whole, may stagnate (Boalt Boëthius 1983).[1]

By way of proposing a remedy, I shall present a case study in which I concentrate on a number of psychological and social measures and processes which may help reactivate an organization, in so far as they contribute to a more open, less defensive work atmosphere and more innovative leadership. In this case and to this purpose, opportunities had to be created for staff and leader, individually and together, to reflect on their work, on their different work roles, and on how the work was carried out. My role in the proceedings was that of leader, and the study was prompted by my own dissatisfaction with my work situation.

My presentation in this chapter is based on my research into groups and organizations, as well as on my experiences as a consultant and as a leader. My aim has been both to increase my own understanding of those experiences, with the help of a theoretical and conceptual schema, and to discover the extent to which my experiences and reflections allow for generalization. My frame of reference has been the psychoanalytically oriented view of organizations developed at the Tavistock Institute or the socio-technical model (Miller and Rice 1967), which comprises of four main assumptions:

1. Organizations can be described as open social systems. This assumes a reciprocity of influences between individuals and their organization.
2. Unconscious processes occur not only within and between individuals, but also within and between groups or social systems.
3. Social events, such as interactions between leader and employees, are important to the organization, just as the group is important to the development of leadership.
4. Interaction between technical and social control systems is of great importance to the proper functioning of work groups or organizations.

THEORETICAL ASPECTS

Projections and introjections: Mixtures of reality and fantasy

Many reactions and attitudes manifested through interaction between leader and employees can be seen as part of a pattern of projections and introjections (Klein 1975a). It is a generally recognized phenomenon, albeit rarely recorded in connection with research, that leaders are, as a rule, the objects of all sorts of fantasies, hopes, wishes, and expectations. These fantasies or expectations, positive as well as negative, may be more or less rooted in reality, and more or less stable over time. They contain both conscious and unconscious elements, and the latter can be described in terms of projections. As leaders, we tend to internalize or introject projections that come our way, and our doing so affects our behaviour and the way we are perceived by others.

By 'projection' I mean the process of ascribing to other people perceptions, feelings, or needs which are really our own, but which for various reasons we are unable to contain within ourselves. By 'introjection' I mean the process of appropriating, as really ours, the qualities thus ascribed to us, and letting ourselves be influenced by them (Klein 1975a). Since projections are not simply conjured up 'out of thin air', but are partly based on actual conditions, it can be difficult to separate what is real from what is fantasy or misconception.

Some leaders, for example, may well see themselves as co-operative, reflective, and keen on reciprocal input when it comes to decisions concerning employees. From the perspective of the employees, however, they may just as well be seen as weak, hesitant and lacking in decision-making powers. The reality is that a leader's behaviour can give rise to different interpretations and, in consequence, the task in an organization is to establish which interpretations will catch the imagination or needs of which individual or group.

As leaders, then, we often find it difficult to discover a sensible way of relating to individuals or groups of employees, a way which does not permit us merely to collude with projections that come our way. It is, of course, easier to embrace favourable expectations and projections—those that idealize us or ascribe omnipotence to us. Adverse projections can be threatening or derogatory, and rather difficult to handle. Either way, there is a dilemma: in order to recognize and understand the 'ensnaring' potential of projections, we must allow ourselves to be 'ensnared' in them.

It is, however, important not to get too caught up in projections. We may allow ourselves to be seduced by the allurements of favourable projections— but the fall from an idealized position is great, as is the damage to our self-esteem. If, on the other hand, we let ourselves remain ensnared in adverse projections, we will lose touch with much of our potential energy. Incorporating projections and acting as if they are or would be real qualities of ours, may be called 'projective identification' (Ogden 1992). This tendency exposes us to the risk of being 'controlled by the sender'. As we identify with the content of a projection, we may find ourselves in some respects manipulated, at least for a while, by the 'sender'.

Projections and introjections are normal occurrences in all social situations. They are therefore at large not only in our personal relations, but also at work in the interactions between people in a working group and in the relationship between leader and employees. In all these relationships, our ability to distinguish between rational and irrational, or prudent and imprudent, behaviour is continuously put to the test, not least because we build up our perceptions of the organization in which we work from the position we occupy in it, and from our place in the social system to which we belong. What is realistic and rational to one part of the organization as social system may therefore be perceived by another part of that system as devoid of realistic foundation.

Projection and introjection develop through reciprocal interaction between conscious and unconscious elements in ourselves and others and between ourselves and others. It is not just a case of employees projecting their thoughts, feelings or expectations on to their leader. Leaders, for their part, project on to their employees such things as their aspirations or vulnerabilities. Sorting out projections and introjections, as attributed to individuals or groups, involves reviewing them in order to distinguish reality from fantasy. Such a review is an essentially reciprocal process: both parties must be motivated to carry it out.

If, in the example outlined above, both leader and employee fail to recognize signs of the probable existence of conflicting interpretations, there is little chance of any deeper understanding. Rather, the interaction is likely to result in a mutual lack of trust, and misconceptions about intentions and expectations will serve to increase the distance between the two parties and affect their work in a negative way. If, on the other hand, the interaction between leader and employee allows for a review of alternative interpretations, the misconceptions and projections may be sorted out. As this procedure is followed, some individuals at least will achieve a better understanding of each other and so facilitate conditions for constructive work.

The imperative to sort out projective fantasies from realistic perceptions may also be seen as deriving from a more general proposition. That proposition claims that being in touch with internal and external realities, emotional ones and others, is conducive to better, more realistic decisions and therefore to reducing frustration and bewilderment and to improving emotional health. The ability to remain in contact with both the external and internal world also allows for the development of an intermediate area—a space for reflection and an opening for creativity (Winnicott 1971).

Projection and leadership

In a study of principals and managers in education and industry, Granström (1996: 67) writes that 'staff and leader are inseparably interconnected, whilst at the same time clearly distinct from one another'. He raises the question whether on the whole it is desirable, or even possible, to strip employees of their irrational notions. He considers these to be manifestations of one of the most human and authentic of needs, namely the need for tolerable working conditions—indeed for mental survival. The relationship between leader and employees can be worked out in such a way that it presents a survival strategy, by which groups of employees make use of their leader in a variety of ways. In his study, Granström shows that the leader is often used as a form of defence, 'as somebody to relax with; to escape with; to laugh with, or laugh at; to kick against; to deride or to mock' (ibid.: 67).

The presence of a familiar and predictable leader is important, but he or she should provide more than a structure and leadership that will enable the employees to work purposefully together. In Granström's view, the leader is needed, possibly first and foremost, as a 'container'—a target or protective receiver—for the shared needs, often unconscious, which inevitably arise during different phases in the development of an activity (Bion 1961). One might add here that the leader, too, has expectations and fantasies—for instance about how a certain type of work should be done, how a work group functions, or how best to achieve a certain goal—and that these will, of course, affect his or her perception of the employees' work.

The nature of the projections directed towards the leader is also influenced by the fact that the leader has greater power than others, in part because he or she is privy to a great deal more information than they have access to. They know that the leader has powers over them, because they experience the effect of that power. They do not, however, know its extent, nor what the information is that he or she possesses. All in all, the leader easily becomes an object of speculation and untested assumptions, which typically overestimate his or her power to change things and to foresee the consequences of his or her actions (Whitaker 1995).

This force field of projections and introjections, with its more or less realistic elements, does not operate solely on top leaders of hierarchical organizations.

It also operates at the level of middle management (Boalt Boëthius 1987), affecting, for instance, foremen or work-group leaders, co-ordinators, and course leaders in developmental programmes. Since the process is reciprocal, it is of course not only the leaders who get caught up in these conscious and unconscious events, but also the people who work with them. As mentioned, adverse projections can in the long run lower the general level of performance. Performance levels can, indeed, be raised as a result of favourable projections—but these are likely to break down and bring disaster, when they come up against reality.

When projections between different subsystems are given too much scope to develop, the ability to resolve conflicts, manage confrontations, and find constructive solutions will diminish. Enthusiasm for finding new ways dwindles, and there is an increase in the tendency to shut off from a difficult dilemma or to quit without really trying. One can hope that things will sort themselves out, but this does not often happen. More commonly, the organization stagnates. Its structure congeals, restricting to very little the freedom of movement of both leader and employees. And, as the prospect of taking initiatives diminishes and creativity declines, job satisfaction plummets.

Creativity and social structures as a defence against anxiety

After projections and the dynamic they create, the second major feature that must be addressed, if one is to stand a chance of bringing about a change in an organization, is the formation and maintenance of social structures. Social structures affect the extent to which people have access to their autonomy and creativity. As shown by Jaques (1955) these structures can serve as a defence against insecurity and anxiety, but they can also block creativity and innovation.

One of the best-known examples of this phenomenon is Menzies' study (1960) of a training programme for nurses. In her discussion, Menzies makes a connection between the adverse reactions of individual nurses and their irrational work routines, coupled with their own denial of their individual needs to develop. Similar phenomena are also described in a recent volume of papers on individual and organizational stress in the human services (Obholzer and Roberts 1994).

A comparative study, based on two recent cases from my own work as a consultant and researcher, illustrates one type of social structure that can be seen as a defence against anxiety. By way of background, I should say that an earlier comparison of intergroup relations in a number of organizations had indicated that when the distances beween different subsystems in an organization are too large, or too tight or unpredictable, communication between them often becomes blocked and characterized by projections (Boalt Boëthius 1996).

The focus of that study was on the ways in which such gaps are formed and maintained. This called for an examination of the types of boundaries used by the subsystems, the building of symbolic links between them, and the way these links were able to alleviate the effects of destructive social structures. One of the most important factors at the developmental stage had been the kind of containment provided by the organizations, and the way this was maintained. Young describes, in a similar way, the need 'to find a way of treating mental space as available for containment, a place where one can bear experience, hold it and be able to ruminate over it, metabolize it, reflect upon it, savour it' (1994: 52).

My study, which combined consultation and a systematic collection of data about attitudes towards the work, as well as intergroup relations, was based on a comparison between a symphony orchestra and a childcare organization. The three subsystems defined by the analysis were the top management, the administrative unit, and the field organization, meaning the musicians and the childcare staff, respectively. The analysis indicated a need for a certain amount of space around each one of the subsystems, to enable them to develop their own resources. This space—this 'intermediate area' (Winnicott 1971)—was defined by the boundaries around, and the relationships between, the different subsystems of the organizations. The relations between the subsystems were described in terms of symbolic links, and were dependent on the boundaries around, and the flow between, the interrelated subsystems, as well as on the space surrounding the system as a whole.

In the childcare organization, the main difficulty in evidence at the start of the consultation was that, over time, a wide gap had developed between the field organization on the one side, and the administrative unit and top management on the other. The day-care staff were, for realistic reasons, feeling abandoned, and disappointed and angry with the other subsystems. Due to the systematic and committed work done by the administrative staff to ease the situation, the gap eventually vanished (Boalt Boëthius 1987). However, as time went by and the administrative unit expressed more resolute demands on the top management, a new gap emerged, this time between the administrative staff and the top management. Again, as these shifts in balance were observed and attended to, the different subsystems as well as the organization as a whole became more effective and more creative in developing new strategies for work.

In the case of the symphony orchestra, consultation was initiated by members of the top management. Here, there was distress and worry about the musicians, whose performances were viewed as not up to the expected standard. The musicians, for their part, felt that top management was not really functioning particularly well and felt frustrated by what they perceived as a lack of knowledge about 'life as a musician in a symphony orchestra'. The administrative staff, meanwhile, were almost invisible, and that was also how they were perceived by the other two subsystems. In this organization, then, there were fairly deep gaps between all three subsystems. As time went by, all the gaps decreased a little and some links developed, in the form of a modest mutual increase in understanding and interest. As to the location of the gaps, however, there was no shift, and, although the projections between the three subsystems could to a large extent be dissolved, the long-term prognosis indicated no major changes in the social structures. These had become too fixed to be affected other than briefly, and the motivation for change was too low.

The results of this comparative study show that for a large organization to survive and develop, there has to be some space between the different subsystems. Once these spaces have become too small or too wide, or have turned into gaps, or even gulfs, then there are problems. Provided that the locations of gaps shift over time, so that there can be no ossification into fixed social structures, a gap will serve a useful purpose—as a sign that something needs attending to. It may be, for instance, that the boundaries between subsystems are at risk of becoming too rigid or too loose, or that the relationship between subsystems is becoming flooded with projections. Severe attacks on relationships between subsystems, when these attacks take the form of heavy projections, as above, can be described in terms of 'attacks on linking' (Bion 1959), and these attacks are probably the most difficult features to identify and influence.

It was also evident that the level of creativity, as well as vitality, increased once an intermediate area between subsystems had been established, provided that the general working climate was characterized by a certain amount of mutual trust. This development can be seen as analogous to Winnicott's (1971) theory that a reciprocal relationship between our inner and external worlds is a prerequisite for creativity. Losing one's creativity implies that one is either too focused on the internal world, or too focused on the external world. The same can perhaps be said with regard to subsystems in an organization.

First- and second-order changes

How then is one to function as a leader in this magnetic field of conscious and unconscious expectations, this field of projections and irrational social structures which, for better or worse, entrap one? For a start, we must learn to handle shifting idealizations and attacks, both when they strike us in our role as leader and when the target is ourself as a person. Secondly, we must learn as leaders to guard against the danger of becoming immured in a false sense of security, through lack of internal criticism and a one-sided filtering of information. This danger has been exposed above all by Janis (1972), through his concept of 'groupthink'. Given that the leader, at least in the context of the group he or she leads, has no peers, he or she runs the risk of receiving insufficient authentic feedback.

So what are we to do? Well, thirdly and of fundamental importance, we must as leaders learn when and how to initiate and facilitate changes—changes of the right kind. If an organization is really not functional—if, say, the output is too low, or the quality of work not good enough, or the work atmosphere has hit a low—then a crisis exists. What usually happens next is that somebody, most often the leader, initiates an organizational change. In general, this means a change to some part of the organizational structure, such as the size of work-teams, the delegation of authority, or the information systems. Rarely does it mean a change in procedures or the ways in which the organization and its people interact. If the changes are of the former kind, then they are likely to be drastic for the employees, while minimally disturbing for the leader. The outcome of changes of the latter kind, involving both leader and employees, will depend on the quality of their mutual relationship and on their ability jointly to find solutions to their shared dilemma (Whitaker 1995).

A change of the first type, then, can mean new patterns of leadership, a modification to the composition and size of work-groups, or new decision-making functions and information channels. However, as these are changes to the superficial structure, they rarely entail any real development in the content, that is, in the work activity. Things may improve for a while, but deep down both leader and employees know that the change is for the most part a matter of form, with no real content or consequence. A change has occurred, but the desired return to vigour and long-term increase in productivity both fail to materialize.

Changes to the formal structure with no corresponding change to the content are common, and unfortunately tend to be followed by more of the same. A reorganization with no potential for real change can be described as a 'first order change' (D. Miller 1990). One reason why predominantly structural changes often fail is that they are not related to the core activity of the organization. Clearly, another reason is that they take no account of the issues discussed above, that is, of the interaction between leader and employees or of irrational phenomena such as projections and the use of social structures to ward off anxiety associated with the primary task.

Organizational first-order changes arise from work on the structure and overt aims of an organization, leaving aside the emotional dynamics and covert aims which are at least as important, though possibly more difficult to grasp. Only when both these perspectives are taken into account will the result be a more thoroughgoing change—a 'second-order change' (D. Miller 1990; Mills 1990) or a 'process of transformation' (Gutmann, Ternier-David, and Verrier 1996a). Since second-order changes, or processes of transformation, are brought about by a combination of structural processes and affective feedback, there is a greater probability that they will prove lasting.

In Mills's terminology, we are looking for ways in which an organization may acquire 'not only an awareness of the system's process and structure but also the capability of re-ordering itself and managing its course of action to realize given values' (1990: 203). This kind of awareness is not easy to achieve, and in the attempt much pressure is exerted on all involved not to retreat into conventional or defensive patterns of behaviour.

How, then, does one achieve a second-order change or a process of transformation? Mills's study of how groups change over time found that a crucial difference between changes that could be characterized as, respectively, first and second order, was the difference in the degree and quality of feedback. Only in the groups that underwent a more thoroughgoing and constructive change—corresponding to a second-order change—was there adequate affective feedback. The development of those groups was based on authentic interaction between leader and group members, the two most important components being the group's relationship with authority and the interactions between group members. A characteristic of these groups was that they worked to improve both their attitude to, and their affective relations with, the leadership. They also sought to bring about co-operation within the group and perceived as important the need to find ways of handling competition and rivalry—with the leader as well as between group members.

AN EXAMPLE FROM EXPERIENCE

To put the foregoing ideas into concrete form, I offer an example from experience. It describes the way in which I used my own leadership as the starting-point for a process of change.

The story of the change initiative

For a good five years I had been in charge of an institute with the primary tasks of professional education, clinical activities, and research. The organization had about forty employees on a permanent basis, and a similar number on a non-permanent basis. I thought that, on the whole, I had achieved many of the goals which had been set jointly by the staff, the governing body, and myself, at the time when I was appointed. The work I had done had been clearly appreciated, which was satisfying. At the same time, there were some complaints: my demands were too exacting, and I was not always 'there'. I found the work for the most part pleasant, with good colleagues and interesting new challenges. And yet, I felt constrained—by what I perceived as far too great a dependence on me, on the part of the staff, and by the pressure from 'things that must be done'.

If I were to continue in my job, I wanted greater freedom. I wanted opportunities to reflect and to think my own thoughts. I believed that this desire was part of a reciprocal process, and that more space for reflection would be to the advantage of my colleagues too, and hence to the institute as a whole. I wanted to release my energy, and that of those around me, from the various defensive social structures which I felt were tying up our energies. And I wanted us all to understand more of the projective mechanisms around us.

Then I was offered a renewed long-term contract. While pondering whether perhaps to decline, I suddenly realized that here could be the opening I had been seeking. I would suggest a course of action that might bring about the changes I felt were needed. If there was in the end no indication of change in the right direction, I was quite prepared to quit. But if the result pointed to a freer and more open climate, with possibilities of real change, then, under those new conditions, I would be happy to continue in my post.

The suggestion I made was that an open reappraisal of the leadership should be conducted, designed to go beyond what the staff perceived as important to the promotion of a good working situation, and beyond what I myself saw as enabling me to do good work. It would be a chance for each and every one of us to rethink, to really think through, the kind of leadership functions we would want to see, and the kind of changes that would in the long run truly benefit our own individual work, and so the work of the organization as a whole.

At first, my suggestion met with great scepticism on the part of both staff and governing body. They wondered what it was I believed might be changed, and whether I realized that I had actually opened up the possibility that someone else might be appointed in my place. I also discussed my proposal with other people in leadership positions similar to my own, and with members of an international network of managers and consultants with which I am connected. The proposal aroused interest, but it was clearly perceived to involve considerable risk.

I knew there was great potential for interactive and innovative leadership because, aside from my worries about their over-dependence on me, the staff were well qualified and fundamentally competent, and there was a good governing body. Discussions with representatives of the institute's main work areas showed that if the process were to go well, it was vital to have a well-thought-out and clear structure. This meant that, among other things, the reappraisal of my mandate as leader had to be clearly spelled out.

Since the request for the reappraisal was principally my own, it was also necessary to find effective ways of channelling the apprehension, insecurities, and even anxiety that it was likely to produce among the staff. Other essential measures included the setting out of goals for the operation as a whole, of other functions of leadership, and of the procedures for delegation, as all these areas were likely to be disturbed or affected already in the first exploratory phase.

It soon became evident that both the positive appreciation of my work, and the complaints about my absences from time to time, were firmly rooted in reality. And yet there was an admixture of reciprocal projection, perhaps even a tendency towards projective identification (Ogden 1992), for I felt as if I were at times colluding with those members of staff who, in their subtle way, expressed their dependence on me.

At the outset of my time as leader, I had detected a number of serious economic problems and managed to find ways of solving them. Against this background I felt that the appreciation I had encountered, like the dependence on me, had a basis in reality, as did the annoyance due to my not always being on hand. My work included attending conferences and taking part in various kinds of meeting. In this respect, I had a sometimes more pleasant schedule than did most of my colleagues—and, to a degree, a less constraining one. This fact probably served to reinforce their view of themselves as constrained. My own difficulty was that I felt guilty when I was not around for them. I probably brought this about myself, both consciously and unconsciously. The pressure of responding to their expectations of what I ought to do, and then of meeting those expectations, had become stronger than my own inclinations.

The details of the reappraisal of the leadership were worked out by the institute's consultative group, consisting of representatives of the organization's four principal activities (the training unit, the unit for clinical work, and the administrative unit, plus myself as leader and representative of the research unit). In addition, there were discussions with the governing body and especially with its chairman.

The work was to have three preparatory tasks, namely: (1) the defining of the main subsystems or parties affected by the reappraisal of the leadership, and the delegation of authority to these subsystems and their representatives; (2) the building of an organizational structure capable of channelling and co-ordinating reactions from individuals or groups of staff members; (3) the creation of a sufficiently protective working climate, allowing space for both positive and negative reactions, as well as for reflections about future work strategies.

The first task demanded an initial definition of the main subsystems or parties that would be involved in the reappraisal of leadership. Three main parties were identified: the governing body; the staff—meaning the various professional groupings linked to their local trade unions; myself in my role as principal. The second step in this first task required making sure that the individuals representing these different parties had the kind of mandate they needed, both from their respective groups and from the management. This applied above all to the various staff groups, and to this purpose the relevant trade unions were consulted, as well as the governing body. Once all subsystems had been identified, the three parties began making an inventory of their points of view. Each subsystem of staff maintained a protocol of questions and opinions, arising from their discussions.

I too was in contact with my trade union and professional association, as I worked through the points I wanted to bring up and the changes I was interested in. I found it very useful to formulate, and put down in writing, my perceptions of, for instance, events in the past where I felt there had been some as yet unsettled disagreement. It became evident that this phase of the reappraisal was conducive to thinking about long-term goals and visions relating to the work of the organization, as well as to my own.

Although the idea of a leadership reappraisal was discussed also by the governing body, I was given to understand that the members of the board were confident that the organization functioned well, and that there was no reason to question my leadership. When I explained why I wanted to do this reappraisal I felt they understood the general idea. When the question of co-ordinating the project was discussed by the board, the chairman suggested that he himself take the role of co-ordinator of the entire enterprise. He is a man of vast experience in organizations undergoing change and had, of course, a clear interest in promoting the healthy development of the institute.

The second task called for the development of organizational structures for the channelling of reactions within the institute. A framework was duly built up, accommodating examination and reflection, and integrating into the whole both an organizational and a psychological perspective. The organizational aspect at this stage of the proceedings involved providing opportunities for discussing the proposal and mulling it over thoroughly. Time had to be allocated for all meetings of all groups, and meeting places had to be found. The time had come to develop a concrete proposal, with the starting-point and purpose of the reappraisal clearly set out, together with working arrangements, responsibilities, and a time plan.

With regard to the psychological aspect of the enterprise, group discussions provided opportunities for asking individual staff members to voice their views on my role as principal and leader. Intense discussion developed especially among the psychologists, the social workers, and the psychiatrists—the professional group to which I belong. Quite evidently, the mere fact that everybody was asked to express and reflect on their views on the work and my role as leader had a liberating aspect. At the same time, a certain amount of shame or concern revealed itself. Some people were afraid that I would feel hurt or unappreciated. However, due to the structure that held these groups together, and to their well-defined mandates, the anxiety was contained. When asked how I felt about being thus evaluated, I could honestly say that I thought it was useful and that I believed it would be beneficial, both for me and for them.

It soon emerged that it was important to differentiate between the person and that person in a specific role, that is to say, between how I was perceived as a person and how I was perceived in the roles of leader and principal. As a result of a more conscious differentiation between person and role, a certain amount of confusion arose about other leadership roles within the institute. There were, for instance, questions about who was responsible for what, according to the types of delegation of authority prevailing at the time. It also became apparent that it was important to delimit the role of principal—to set it apart from other functions of leadership and responsibility—in order to increase the understanding of underlying and unspoken chains of events.

As mentioned, the chairman of the governing body took up the position of overall co-ordinator. In this capacity, he met with representatives of the professional organizations in their various groupings, and had talks with the governing body and discussions with me as principal.

The third task involved the creation of a sufficiently protective climate for the reappraisal to proceed smoothly. It was important to provide conditions in which the employees, individually and in their different groups, would be able to discuss their own experiences as openly as possible. It was also important to have as many members of staff as possible participate in the process of reappraisal and reorientation. The idea was that they should be able to 'air' experiences, thoughts, and fantasies, as well as be given space to voice suggestions and ideas about new ways of doing things, and new ways of thinking about their work. Any channels that were created had to be capable of capturing important psychological processes, without becoming swamped or closing up. In other words, they had to be versatile enough to carry not only realistic criticisms and genuine acknowledgements, but also sufficient irrational phenomena for individuals and groups to recognize themselves in the composite picture produced by the combined results of the work.

The staff members responsible for holding their own group together were struck, early on, by the strong need to distinguish between projections, transference reactions, feelings of guilt, and other psychological phenomena. Over time, however, it came to be seen that this task could be shared by the members in each group, where, in addition, it seemed important to analyse their collective reactions. The aspect that I myself was most aware of in this part of the proceedings had to do with my having to be to the greatest degree accessible and available, in the sense of keeping close at hand, and listening to and keeping up sustained interactions with individual colleagues. It also meant being accessible to the representatives of the professional groups, so that they might each feel as secure as possible in their dual role of colleague and representative.

In conclusion, by the time the more explicit planning started, I had a fairly clear idea of what I, in my role as leader, wanted from the reappraisal, but very vague ideas about how to go about involving the entire staff in bringing about the kind of changes I was hoping for. The strategy used was a result of many contributions. Probably the most important one issued from a collaboration between the members of the institute's consulting group. It was their suggestion that the general framework include the three main parties, time for preparation, and discussions with the various staff groups. Including preparation, discussion meetings, and summing up, the reappraisal took about six months to complete.

A follow-up

In brief, the reappraisal went ahead as planned. After discussions with the staff and with the governing body, my appointment was renewed on the terms I had sought. The opinions expressed by the staff contained both appreciation and criticism, with a preponderance of the former. Reading the compilation of the staff's views was not easy, but it was a very valuable experience. It felt good when, in conference with the staff, I could refer to reactions I had received, both orally and in writing. And it felt satisfying to express my own views on their

experiences and ensuing trains of thought, to describe how I had myself perceived the corresponding situations, and to speak of future plans.

A follow-up showed that, in terms of the difference the reappraisal made, this
was probably most notable in myself, at least initially. I felt distinctly freer. But
there was also evidence of a liberating change in the work climate. It became
more open and more tolerant of new ways, as proposed by others, as well as by
myself as leader. As for aspirations, ceilings were higher, both individually and
on behalf of the organization. There was an appetite for trying out new ways,
and for constructive criticism and competition, with me as well as with other
staff members. An earlier pattern of holding back for fear of being criticized
seemed to have more or less vanished and people dared to expose their ideas
and their curiosity more openly.

Even though demands remained high and the aspiration levels sometimes
felt exhausting, nobody blamed anybody in particular. Furthermore, feelings of
guilt in relation to patients and their families were less pronounced. Alternative
methods of treatment were discussed in a more positive way, and new training
programmes and research projects were developed. In my view, these developments were linked to a more realistic perception of the demands from the outside world and to a new appreciation of available resources. These led to a more
realistic appraisal of what could be done within the framework of the institute,
and what had to be left aside. The increased awareness of practical realities
affected my role too. Over time, a more realistic perception of what I could and
could not do as leader developed.

One small group initially reckoned that the reappraisal had made no great
difference, except in one respect, namely that some attention was given to other
questions about leadership and responsibility. In conjunction with the reappraisal of my leadership, other such functions, in various parts of the institute,
were becoming visible. The upshot was that questions of delegation and representation came to be handled with considerably greater awareness than previously. The 'who' and the 'what' of roles and functions, as pertaining to actual
situations, were dealt with openly, as was the question of how boundaries
between different areas of responsibility should be drawn for maximum clarity.

The staff no longer came to me so often with questions belonging to somebody else's area of responsibility. People tried to make use of delegation
procedures that were by now in place, but some still found it difficult to accept
that once a task had been delegated, the responsibility too had been passed on.
Coming to me as principal continued to provide more security for some people.
I also observed that some colleagues became more aware of their dependence
on me, and came to accept the needs it signified. At the same time I noted a
somewhat more open and constructive competition with me, as well as co-
operation. Individual staff members would sometimes take over tasks they saw
I did not have sufficient time for, in a way that was both helpful and relaxed.

CONCLUSIONS

The steps and measures described in the case study above can be seen as a strategy for bringing about organizational change in a long-term perspective. It required me to involve myself, both as leader and member of staff, in a committed attempt to understand what was happening at the different levels in the organization, and to think about the future. This included attention to the primary task and to the structures in the organization formed to deal with that task, as well as to conscious and unconscious processes associated with this area. And generally, it meant creating space for reflection, and time to allow people to keep pace with developments, to think things through, and to plan ahead as effectively as possible.

The reappraisal can also be seen as a way of reducing the fears and fantasies of staff *vis-à-vis* leader, and vice versa. It reduced the risk of the leader isolating him- or herself from realistic feedback, and went on to seek and achieve changes of a similar kind in other areas. Last but not least, the process of reappraisal may serve as an illustration of what 'proaction' means, namely the act of perceiving an event as offering an opening for the far-sighted pursuit of an objective, rather than as an occasion for mere 'reaction' (Whitaker 1995).

Application of experiences in consultancy

The idea of a leadership reappraisal in this particular organization was prompted by the fact that I, in my role as leader, felt tied down by too many demands and by having too little space for thinking, and felt that my level of ambition for the organization was experienced by many employees as too exacting. As this was something I recognized, from my work as a consultant, as a common but nevertheless crucial phenomenon, I thought I could use some of that knowledge, even though the leader of this particular organization was myself. Indeed, my experiences as a consultant proved to be of great help to me throughout this enterprise.

Assuming, as I did, that my feelings of frustration were part of a reciprocal pattern of reactions, then many employees were bound to have similar feelings but not, perhaps, sufficient space to think about the situation. Hence the strategy used, which gave employees the time and space and authorization to fill in common and important information gaps, and to try to understand previously concealed organizational processes. The work should enable rational and irrational affective reactions to be brought to light, and to be traced to actual experiences. And it should be made possible to investigate the connection between these experiences and the primary task of the organization.

I thought it would suit me best to face at once the doubts and concerns I had, not only about my role as leader, but also about myself, and about how I did and did not want the work to be done, if my plans were approved. However, having learned from my experience as a consultant, I first sought support for my idea from my closest co-workers at the institute. They gave me their backing, and the next step was to persuade the board and its chairman. From then on, provision was made for the staff to discuss among themselves what they felt, thought, and expected of and about me and the project. I dealt with what came out of these discussions in a way I hoped would allow new ways of thinking and interacting, both within the institute and in relation to the outside world.

The work on the reappraisal was in part very deliberately thought through, with structures created to give space for discussion and reflection, and to keep anxiety contained. In part, things were allowed to happen along the way, but the combination of strategy and 'leaving things open' worked well enough. As intended, the reappraisal led to changes in the interaction between leader and staff, rather than to changes in the superficial structure of the organization. And through this work, carried out in common, the institute became more flexible and open to alternative strategies of change.

From a more general perspective, the above case study contrasts with what happens in many organizations having to cope with concrete adjustments in the face of harsh demands for increased effectivity and cut-backs. They may manage to find new strategies for work, and may succeed in cutting their financial costs—but the cost in terms of personal motivation is high. Try as they will to keep their aspirations up, they are increasingly worn down and exhausted. Commitment, especially at the lower levels, dwindles, and sluggishness pervades the system. Moreover, for an organization in that sorry state it is, of course, much more of a struggle to carry out the many changes that are clearly necessary if the organization is to have a future at all.

Which brings me to a question I was left with, at the end of the reappraisal. What will be the condition of the organization in another six or seven years' time? In my work as a researcher and consultant I have often seen organizations face, at intervals of between five and ten years, situations in which they must take further far-reaching steps. This is particularly the case for organizations confronted by new conditions due to the demands of their surroundings, or to altered internal conditions where, as a result, they have to take up a position with regard to new goals and to the means for achieving them. My experience as a consultant to organizations and as a manager/practitioner indicates both that far too many organizations use strategies that yield merely superficial changes, and that the theoretical and practical frameworks do exist that can lead to the more thoroughgoing 'second-order changes' or 'transformation processes' on which longer-term change and even organizational survival depend.

NOTE

1 This study was supported by grants from the Bergdahl Foundation. I wish to thank Galvin Whitaker for valuable discussions and Elisabeth Kondal for linguistic help.

13

Mental Health under Fire: Organizational intervention in a wounded service

Mira Erlich-Ginor and Shmuel Erlich

This is the story of a crisis intervention in a mental health service that sustained a most distressing and unusually cruel blow—the murder of four of its staff by a patient-client. We think it is important to tell this story for a number of reasons:

- The events themselves were of such tragic proportions.
- Resorting to the notion of social defence can further understanding of the often enormous strain between mental health delivery systems and their clients.
- Our approach combined reliance on psychoanalytic insight and open-systems theory. It thus clearly derives from and exemplifies the group relations tradition and practice.
- The model of concentric circles we evolved to understand the nature of the systemic injury applies not only to the system and its environment, but also to our relatedness to the clients. The multiple interconnections make for over-determined choices and dense explanations. Writing this story up is therefore also part of its unravelling.

CHRONICLE OF THE MURDER

What follows is the account of the events as reconstructed by the Center's staff.

The patient, a 21-year-old man, applied to the Mental Health Center serving West Jerusalem several weeks prior to the events. Although in this sense he was a new admission, he had intermittently been in treatment at the Center as an adolescent until he was drafted into the army. There he continued to be treated by the army's mental health service, was prone to making suicidal threats, and menaced his superiors and therapists when he experienced them as unhelpful and thwarting. His frustration was often vented in crying spells and raging outbreaks, following which he would calm down. In the thick file that accumulated on him, he was never diagnosed as suffering from mental illness. Nevertheless, he was prematurely released from army service.

Following his discharge, and after a full year without treatment, he contacted the Center and was seen once. The woman therapist summed up the interview with the feeling that this time he was truly motivated and interested in being helped. Another appointment was set up, but he did not keep it.

On the day of the murder he telephoned around noon and asked to speak with the director of the Center or with the therapist who had seen him. He spoke with her on the phone for about fifteen minutes. He sounded angry and upset for having been denied a licence to drive a truck. The therapist did her best to calm him down and to encourage and support him in this moment of crisis. She then invited him to resume his therapeutic sessions. By the end of this telephone conversation, he appeared to have calmed down.

At 2.00 p.m., he arrived at the Center, stood at the entrance to the main office, which was, as usual, full of staff, and without a word indiscriminately opened fire from a pistol, licensed to him in his position as a security guard. Four members of the Center staff, all of them women, were killed. Two other staff members, a woman and a man, were wounded. Three more staff members who were present in the room escaped uninjured. The murderer then escaped to the roof of a nearby building.

The police were summoned, but their efforts to engage him in conversation were unsuccessful. When it appeared that he was about to threaten the life of bystanders he was shot, and died *en route* to hospital.

The entire sequence of violence and horror lasted only a few minutes. Nevertheless, it sent shock waves throughout the community. In the wake of the public outrage, commissions were set up to investigate what happened, criteria for licensing firearms were reviewed, and channels of communication and lines of responsibility between different authorities, such as the Army and the ministries of Health, Interior, and Transportation, were double-checked. One outcome was to place an armed guard and electronic surveillance at the entrance of every mental health facility in the country, a living testimony to the murder that took place, and a reminder of its possible recurrence. The entire mental health system was deeply shocked and upset. The innocent naïveté that had prevailed was gone, probably forever.

In the waves that swept the entire country after the murder, there was a tendency to neglect the Center and its personnel. There was no shortage of new events and tragedies to occupy the public attention of Israel in the 1990s, and the Center's staff were soon left to fend for themselves. It was shortly after the events that the need for help was felt and we were asked by the Center's staff to intervene.

Our past relatedness and relationship to the Center and its staff had been anything but neutral, distant, or anonymous. We worked for many years in the psychiatric hospital, which had created the Center as its community outpost. In our role as senior staff, we played a significant role in establishing and setting up its professional and organizational modes of functioning, through teaching and supervision, actual work relationships, and various organizational and administrative decision-making processes. The entire nature of our intervention was certainly not the well-established one of the consultant *vis-à-vis* the organization, where the role is buttressed by a measure of professional distance and anonymity.

STAGES IN THE INTERVENTION

Our work with the Center can be described in terms of several stages, which may be pictured as concentric circles, starting from the traumatic event itself and gradually moving away from it. At every stage, there was a recurrence or resurgence of the traumatic wound, each time from a different angle, but also at a more advanced level of coping with the trauma. In this sense, the work described may be seen as lasting three months, or a year and three months, or four years.

Our involvement began immediately upon hearing the horrible news on the radio—we instantaneously felt it was 'our' Mental Health Center that was reported on, in spite of our both having left it and the hospital ten years earlier. We found ourselves going again and again to the funeral house, taking part emotionally and personally in a blood-curdling and shocking series of four funerals, of tears, of a deep sense of pain and crisis, of questions, perplexities, and preoccupations which remained without answers and consolation.

The request to intervene came on a Thursday, on the day that marked the end of the mourning.[1] The Director of the Center, in a telephone conversation with both of us, recounted the story of a week of inability to return to routine work coupled with efforts at self-healing. The staff sat for endless hours in small groups, ventilating feelings, focusing on details, collecting and accounting for minutes and seconds in an effort to reconstruct the traumatic chain of events. They tried hard to understand and to analyse: How did it happen? Could it have been predicted? Was it possible to have prevented the events? Eventually, however, the feeling was that they could not cope on their own and needed external help. The request was for 'a focused and short-term intervention'. Several names had come up as possibilities, and following an unclear process of elimination and choice, he approached both of us, leaving it to us to decide who would do what. We obligated ourselves to provide an answer by the end of the weekend.

In retrospect, we appreciated the fact that we had no real question about our positive response. The only issue was around the choice of a course of action. In the three days that elapsed until we gave our answer, we tried to understand the meaning of the request for help to us. Our feelings and thoughts pointed to several explanations. Mainly, however, it appeared that we were experienced as being 'on the boundary'. We were perceived at one and the same time as belonging and not belonging to them, near and distant, next of kin and friendly standbys. Another aspect of the choice had, perhaps, to do with our being a couple: it aroused wishes for a beneficent and constructive pairing, and for parents who might provide the wished-for mending and reparation of the traumatic wound.

We responded, and wished to be responsive, to the wish for pairing and good parenting, which would bring with it healing and relief of pain. In our countertransference, a clear wish emerged: to be capable of actually knowing, entering, and helping the wounded system. At the same time, we also felt overwhelmed by the enormity and uniqueness of the traumatic break. We wondered if we had any knowledge at all that might be relevant to dealing with something of such awful nature and proportions; but then again, who did? Wishing to benefit and gain from the experiences of others, we turned to colleagues with experience in intervening in traumatized organizations—one after Iraqi missile attacks during the Gulf War, another following the bombing of the Israeli embassy in Buenos Aires. We organized ourselves efficiently, thoroughly, and quite speedily, formulating hypotheses and a primary task for our entry into the system. In retrospect, however, it is quite clear that our need to assume the position and posture of 'experts' reflected two things: a sense of being heavily flooded and threatened by our own anxiety and wish to be of real help; and a response to the enormous anxieties and other feelings rampant in the system.

Out of our conversation with the Center's director, several preliminary notions emerged: during the traumatic event, the staff found themselves in an extremely passive position, helpless and deserted victims. Secondly, the description of the events focused around a preoccupation with the question, 'Where exactly was everyone at the exact time of the murder?' From the chronicle that emerged, we gleaned two maps of the staff: one was a picture of the staff arranged by such usual criteria as seniority, position, profession, formal and informal standing. The other map—superimposed, as it were, on the first one—was that of the day of the murder and of each person's whereabouts and location at the precise moment: in the office, on the floor, in the building, on the way to or from the Center, etc. The 'picture of the world' that emerged was one of concentric circles, centred on the office as the focal point of the shock wave.

In view of the passivity that coloured the experience, we decided both to engage the staff in a manner that would allow them to become an active partner in the proceedings, and that our contact with the staff had to be direct and not channelled through the director. We therefore offered to meet with the entire staff, so that they could all be part of forming a work contract. The understanding, which at this stage was largely intuitive, of the need for a shift from passivity to activity, and hence for the active participation of the staff, actually became the theme and guideline for much of the intervention, and contributed greatly to such success as it had. Some evidence for the correctness of this understanding was also provided by the fact that where we failed to abide by these principles and to obtain full co-operation, we encountered crisis and set-back.

First meeting with entire staff: Diagnosis and contract

Three weeks after the murder took place, we attended a staff meeting at the Center. It was the first formal work session of the staff following the event. Because of the considerations we raised above, we felt it was important that our meeting with the staff be within structured work time. During the meeting, any-one who wished could speak freely. We participated from our position at the time of having been invited by the group to do some yet undefined work with it. We were careful not to take the position of leaders or facilitators. The following are brief excerpts from what came up in the course of the conversation:

A lengthy silence, the silence typically met at the beginning of a group, but perhaps also the heavy minutes of silent commemoration.

X starts: 'I feel like I am carrying a heavy burden. This is actually the first time we are silent. Until now, we talked all the time. Now that you came, we can afford to be quiet.'

'The two of you are both inside and outside.'

Many people, though not all, spoke in succession. The subjects that came up were loss of trust and faith in the profession, in words, in people, in patients.

'I expect you to restore these to us.'

Feelings of mourning came up, in heavy swoops of dark waves of thoughts, feel-ings, fears.

Anger and guilt that cannot find a target: A woman says, 'I cannot sit here and talk, make it easier on myself, and derive benefits, when the murdered women are not here with us.'

One member of staff decided to stay away. Others spoke of their wish not to be pre-sent.

Over and over again the theme of inside and outside came up: inside the office and out of it; in the staff and out of it; inside and out of themselves; among themselves and with others.

The first meeting furthered our understanding and enabled us to draw infer-ences from which it was possible to diagnose more precisely the nature of the injury they sustained, and in turn to derive and formulate the primary task and aim of the intervention. It became clear that what was very deeply hurt and injured, beyond the personal losses, was inextricably tied up with the staff's capacity to go on working as professionals. The feeling was that members of staff had lost their faith in themselves, in their ability to assess and appraise, under-stand and cope with what they encountered. In addition, it seemed they had lost faith in the larger society, on whose behalf they worked, and from whom they derived authority and empowerment for the roles they filled. In brief, they were ridden with doubts and disillusionment as to how much this society was willing and able to provide them with adequate understanding and support, as well as the security, protection, and means necessary for carrying out their difficult task.

Diagnosing the injury

In the first place, members of staff had sustained a serious traumatization—the abrupt and devastating loss of significant and meaningful persons and rela-tionships. Moreover, the trauma occurred at the place and in the context of their work and in close conjunction with it. Hence, in each and every one of them a part of their professional 'work-self' was injured or 'killed'. Secondly, we saw the 'client', or the object of our work, to be the Center as an organization, and not the individuals who comprise its staff. We elected to regard the primary injury as the 'wounding' of the entire system. The individuals within this system were, overall, healthy and capable persons who had undergone and were responding to a terrible calamity and coping with it individually as any one would in their stead.

Out of this diagnostic formulation the primary task of the intervention was constructed as follows:

> To provide opportunities for a process of rehabilitation of impaired and damaged professional and personal functions.

The aim of the intervention was defined as assisting the staff in restoring their capacity for work, each in his or her specific professional role in the present, while taking into account the past, without undue avoidance, denial, and split-ting, but also without regression into the patient's position and posture. The focus of the intervention was thus on work and professional role, and not on the ventilation of feelings. This formulation made use of such concepts as resilience, referring to the recovery and rehabilitation of adaptive capacities and resources inherent in the organization.

THE STRUCTURING OF THE INTERVENTION

The intervention took the following structure:

1. We adopted the 'double task' approach, that is, to oscillate back and forth between content and process, between the here and now and the then and there.

2. We opted for distinguishing clearly between work with staff and with the director, and decided to offer the latter personal consultation.
3. We designed a structure consisting of two work groups meeting in parallel, interspersed with plenaries.

The need for two work groups stemmed from the size of the staff—about forty—in order to allow more space for self-expression and active work, and to minimize potential regression to passive participation at the margins of the group. The injury was experienced and referred to in very personal, almost intimate terms. It therefore seemed appropriate to enable the expression, discussion, and experiencing of such feelings in a relatively smaller, more intimate setting.

Assigning people to the two work groups was done in accordance with the two maps referred to above, taking into account the map of role, seniority, and position at the Center, together with the map of the day of the trauma. In this way, each of the two groups had some member who was actually in the direct 'line of fire'—in the office—and others in growing concentric circles of distance from the event, all the way to those entirely at the periphery of the Center.

We also saw a need for plenary meetings, in which the totality of the staff group could find expression, so as not to allow the staff to split, and so that we as a couple could also work together, and be experienced as such.

We proposed a series of eight consecutive weekly meetings: six work group sessions, and a plenary session after work groups 3 and 6. The compact and relatively brief structure reflected our feeling that long, protracted, and open-ended work was uncalled for, and probably counter-indicated as likely to contribute to regression and passivity. We were also responding to the staff's original request for a relatively brief and well-circumscribed intervention. On reflection, perhaps this also reflected our collusion with the wish expressed by the staff that the wound be healed quickly.

The following provides an illustration of the quality, content, and experience of the process in the Work Groups:

First Session

An unsuitable room in the Children's Clinic. A chair with one leg stuck in a toy crib, crushing the face of a doll. Several of the chairs are small—children's chairs. The room is very crowded.

I (MEG) start with a detailed description of the format of our work together and the rationales that went into it.

A long silence.

After several minutes a woman opens, and relates to her injured life: 'I have no patience, I feel no joy. People who know what happened ask me what's going on, and they are amazed when they hear that everything is not all right with me. They have already forgotten. At work I do all the right things, but without being there. The only place in which I feel good is the staff, with the others who know and feel what I have been through.'

A man says, 'We are a ship full of lepers. We don't want to get close to others, but they also don't want to get closer to us.'

Another woman: 'I feel so alone. I was in the office at the time of the shooting.' Later she will speak of the blood-stained floor panels—she looks at them again and again and sees the horrible sights.

The maps of the event begin to be laid out, in terms of one's connection to the staff and to the time and place of the event. The discussion turns into who does and who does not belong to this group. A young resident, who only arrived at the Center a few days earlier, becomes the butt of anger and hostility.

There is much talk of 'inside-outside', and of circles marking distance and time. The 'ship of lepers' may appear like a single mass when viewed from the shore, yet within it there are those who are more severely afflicted than others.

I speak about the internal maps that people see as they look around, maps which mask and hide very elementary things, like the poor conditions in which we meet; like the room full of women and only a single man. They look around, observe, and nod their agreement, as if they see these things for the first time. 'Like in the office [at the time of the event]: All women, and one man.'

Someone says, with tears of sadness and rage: 'Yes, this is how it is with us: we are oblivious of the conditions under which we work. We accept everything. We think we can treat someone like E [the murderer]. We think we can do everything—without proper tools or appropriate conditions.'

A wave of expectations and hopes swells up in relation to us [the consultants], to me: 'You will help me cry'. There are comments about the way that they were allocated to the two groups: 'You will tell us what to do. You know what you are doing, even if it may be unpleasant for us.'

There are also actual references to their work, such as the unbearable feelings—initial concern turning to anger and aggression—between the surviving co-therapist of a group, in which one of the murdered women worked, and members of the group.

I address the way people are not in touch with parts of themselves. So many feelings are present, mixed together, and the wish is that everyone will be able to own some of them, and that these sessions will help them do so.

I experience a momentary difficulty in leaving. Even the customary greeting, 'See you after the Holidays', evokes a macabre response: 'If we live . . .'.

The following work group sessions were moved to a nearby community centre, where conditions were more appropriate. What came up in these sessions had to do with therapeutic burnout and despair, loss of faith in the profession, and thoughts about how they might protect themselves against threats of harm and violence. The feelings of closeness and togetherness, which were so prominent right after the event, all but disappeared, and they felt themselves isolated and far removed. They recounted instances of hypersensitivity to violent events, of being disproportionately moved by them, because the rose-tinted glasses through which they preferred to see the world had been shattered, so that now things appeared as they were. Or had this murder removed the cork from the bottle, letting out the demons? There was a strong wish to turn inward and withdraw. The depression was less on the surface, yet only more deeply internalized. A woman who was in the eye of the storm, in the office, was saddled with the role of the 'living-dead'—to be the carrier of the traumatic memory, without any possibility of movement, and this fixation made it more difficult to get at the present. There were queries and musings: Can one say 'no' to a patient, or set boundaries? Does such rejection mean we are throwing those we would not treat into others' garbage cans? Are we the garbage bin of society? How can we be a treatment centre and not a garbage bin? How can one say 'no' to someone perceived as not fit for treatment, without feeling guilt and impotence?

A CHANGED FORMAT: TOWARDS ENDING

After the fourth work group—the first after the plenary—we felt that the group processes were becoming overly fixated, stuck, and regressive, and that we were moving away from the primary task we had set. We therefore proposed a change in the structure: each of the work groups would divide itself into three 'Very Small Groups' working in open space. Their task would be to share an actual recent event in which hurt or injury was experienced in the personal and/or professional sphere. With this change, we aimed to introduce movement into the fast-rigidifying existing structure by means of a reshuffle that would allow options to remain open; to encourage more autonomous and independent work as we approached the ending of the set work period; and to reframe and refocus the primary task.

The proposal was initially met with considerable resistance and unwillingness to part from the familiar groups. Although the proposal was accepted following some discussion, we were brought up against the tremendous vulnerability of the group and the individuals, expressed as the need to preserve the existing structure. We were also offered an array of counter-interpretations: 'You are anxious, because pretty soon you will leave us, and we are not well yet.' 'Don't worry, we'll work things out at our own pace, even if these meetings are over.' 'Nothing really happened, so you decided to change; actually a lot happened, let things go on this way.' In retrospect, these interpretations hit accurately where we were in our counter-transference at this stage, close to the end of the intervention.

There were also other responses, such as: 'We are pretty fed up with your telling us what to do.' And: 'How good it is that there is somebody who decides and says what to do. You decide what it is you want, and we will do it.'

Two meetings took place using this more complex format. In the event, once the debate was over and the work in the new, more intimate format began, it soon felt easier to talk in the new setting of very few people. The new structure enabled a different kind of exchange, which brought about a further change of atmosphere.

Following these two sessions, there was a final plenary and ending. Parting and separation were difficult and dramatic. The central feeling expressed was: 'You found us covered with blood, and in the sessions we cleaned up the blood.' There was also, however, a sense of disappointment and some complaint about what was perceived to be our distance: 'Perhaps we worked together, but we did not cry together.' Sadness and reconciliation, appreciation and unfulfilled hunger were all mixed together. There was a powerful, overarching sense that the trauma that had united them was moving further away, and with it the sense of unity and closeness which had so characterized the first days after the murder. The sense of loneliness grew stronger, and depression and impotence gradually made room for personal mourning and sorrow, as if everyone was returning to his or her place and isolation.

SUBSEQUENT WORK

With this, we had completed our intervention. While the ending was as planned, it was none the less experienced as abrupt. On the one hand, we felt that we lived up to the task, as it had been defined for and by us. But at the same time, and along with this feeling, we had a number of unanswered questions: Did we succeed in healing what needed to be healed? Did the intervention fulfil the expectations of comforting the pain, mending the breach, and restoring the organizational and systemic capacity for work? Such questions continued to plague us. After a while we understood these doubts and preoccupations to reflect our own reaction to the enormous emotional burden placed on us. We had absorbed very powerful projections, which continued, of course, to work within us despite the ending. These projections were largely of parents who had 'promised' security and hope, but whose promises were crushed by the rocks of a harsh and difficult reality, leaving behind a bitter burden of disappointment, rage, and despair.

Over the next few weeks, our feelings of unrest and dissatisfaction grew stronger. It is not entirely clear whether these were feelings of worry for the welfare of the 'patient', a reaction to the silence and disruption that suddenly dominated our relationship and communications with the Center, or our concern for the continuation and development of the work project. In any event, after some six weeks went by, we sent a letter to the management of the Center in which we reviewed and summed up the work that had been done up to that point, with the following addition:

Nonetheless, it seems clear to us that the traumatization still exists. There is room for taking this into account, and to think about a further stage of intervention. In our estimation, there still is a deep wound in the 'professional ego' and the 'ideal self' of the Center. This is, of course, above and beyond existing fears and sense of personal insecurity at the individual level. It seems important to us to follow up and be in touch with this state over the next year.

We suggested work with the leadership of the Center, in order to rehabilitate it from residual effects of the traumatization, and through it the rest of the staff. As part of such a rehabilitative process, it was important to foster the leadership's sense of responsibility for, and resumption of its role in working with the staff. The hierarchy of the Center included the director and a Leading Team (LT) consisting of senior representatives of the various professions. The LT approved our proposal, and for the next eight months work continued along two parallel lines: a series of meetings with the director; work with the LT. This work, involving in both instances a more familiar consultative stance, was carried out by one of us (MEG), with periodic consultations taking place between the two of us.

Our observations gave rise to several hypotheses. The trauma had both legitimized and concretized a number of previously existing problems: feelings of being dissatisfied and disadvantaged; problems with delegating and taking up authority; the prohibition of internal differentiation according to knowledge, experience, or profession. These problems, in and of themselves, were not unique to the Center, and are frequently met in the general culture and in the mental health field. In this particular case, however, they were aided and abetted, fortified and justified by the trauma. Work with the LT focused both on the level of existing organizational difficulties and on those problems deriving from or fixated by the traumatization.

The focus in the work with the LT, as well as with the director, was on several issues related to the trauma and its ramifications. A task force was created to investigate the chronology of the murder, to attempt to understand the murderer, and to evaluate the impressive therapeutic efforts and contacts with him over a long period. The findings were presented and discussed in a number of internal staff meetings, as well as through invited external presentations. The first anniversary of the murder arrived, and its meaning, design, and character required an inordinate amount of time and thoughtfulness from both the staff and the LT. Each such occasion was accompanied by tremendous emotional investment and involvement, and played an important part in the continued working through of the trauma, the mourning, and the guilt feelings that came with it.

The possibility for senior staff to leave the system and the Center proved to be another sensitive issue. Guilt and inhibitions in the person who harboured the intention generally accompanied such wishes, as well as resentment and rejection in those 'left behind'. In all of these, the trauma of the murder was still present in the background, although other events and matters were now occupying centre stage. Certain occurrences could all at once bring the murder and the traumatic fixation to the surface. Consider, for instance, the following event, which took place about a year after the murder:

A young resident doctor met a patient with a history of several hospitalizations. This was their third meeting. The session took place in a room in the Children's Clinic. The patient spoke angrily about something that had happened at work. As he talked, he picked up a toy gun and started to play with it, to aim it at the ceiling, and pretend to shoot. He then aimed it at the therapist. The therapist emerged from the session pale and confused. The director was immediately summoned, and a special meeting was held to determine on medications and a meeting with the patient's parents. The doctor, new at the Center and second generation to the trauma,[2] responded to the hypersensitivity he picked up. The message was clearly that 'We do not play with fire here; we take fantasy in all seriousness. The treatment room can no longer be a sealed room or a safe container. Its walls have been ripped open; there is no freedom or space in it for play, since playing with fire might end up in actual death.' The expectation of the patient in question, however, was quite different. He said afterwards, 'In every other place I have to be all right, do what I am told and expected to do. I thought that here it is allowed to be as I wish, not so controlled.'

The sad truth is that here such play was no longer possible, because the illusion set up by the treatment room had been shattered, and the elusive boundary between fantasy and reality, between wish and action, did not exist any more. Working at the boundary between the psychic and the real, between internal and external worlds, is, of course, what makes psychotherapy possible, and provides one source of its potency and efficacy. This boundary and space, however, had been drastically constricted by the impact of the trauma.

The relationship and relatedness of the staff group with the various systems and organizations in which it was embedded repeatedly came up—the psychiatric hospital of which the Center is organizationally and administratively a component part, the national mental health services, the Ministry of Health. This subject was always accompanied by considerable emotional involvement and poignancy. Towards the completion of the work with the LT, this was focused on OFEK's annual International Group Relations Conference on 'Authority and Leadership'.[3] Several members of the Center's staff wanted to take part in the conference, and expected support and reimbursement from the Ministry of Health as their employer. When the Ministry did not accede, a wave of frustration, disappointment, anger, resentment, and accusation was set in motion. What emerged were expectations and wishes that the system should act as a parental figure.

Against the backdrop of such childlike hopes and desires, there surfaced widespread and powerful feelings, which bubbled and sizzled all the time under a thin veneer of compliance, feelings of abuse and exploitation, and of being deserted and orphaned by this 'parental' system. The hurt and vulnerability now centred on the question of whether they were entitled to the support of the Ministry. Did they deserve to be supported as victims of an unwarranted attack, like a terrorist action,[4] or as professionals who wanted to further their own development? Associated with these dilemmas were anger and resentment at the system and the bureaucratic apparatus that discriminated between them and the murdered victims, offering to pay compensation to the families of the victims according to the positions they had held. The LT could not bear this discrimination, and, feeling outraged and repetitively traumatized, sent representatives to wage a prolonged and stubborn struggle with the bureaucracy in an eventually successful effort to abolish what was perceived to be an inhumane decree.

In the course of clarifying this issue, a new formulation was achieved: the system is neither persecutory nor evil-mongering, but it is also not a concerned and nurturing parent. Living peaceably with and within the 'beast-system' requires expending effort to know its ways and habits. Giving up their dependency wishes towards the system was experienced as a real concession, yet it also felt like an emancipation: they were free to think for themselves and of their own interests, and even to separate and leave the system.

Terminating the work with the LT was dominated by the sense that 'the stone that was tied to [their] neck grew smaller, but had not disappeared'. There was more space, and a possibility of emerging from the undifferentiated mass and individuating. There was also a notable feeling of coming out of depression, with greater readiness for acting on their own behalf. The consultant's feeling was also a good one: even if not all expectations were met, there was evidence that new tools and ways of thinking had evolved, and that they would be able to proceed with these on their own. There was the future prospect of a joint writing venture, and a good measure of mutual respect and affection.

Six months after the completion of this phase of the work, we again met with the LT. The meeting was designed to discuss the imminent presentation of this work at an OFEK forum to which they had been invited, not merely in the role of passive listeners, but as counterpart to the intervention—the client, who was to participate in the presentation. The preparatory meeting made it clear that their vulnerability and hypersensitivity had immeasurably lessened. At the same time, however, and in spite of the fact that they took up our invitation and attended the forum, they were unable to make a presentation. They were content to be present and to participate in the general discussion.

Two and a half years after ending the intervention, and four years after the event, we were invited once again to meet with the LT with the aim of thinking together about a symposium, which they proposed, and in which they wished us to take part. Once again, this meeting became an opportunity to reflect together on the relationship and relatedness between them and us, and on the long way they had come, and thus add yet another layer to the work on the injury. The proposed symposium eventually took place, and was actively prepared and led by them.

DISCUSSION

The intervention presented is characterized by the attempt to blend a psycho-analytic approach with an organizational-systemic one. The discussion accordingly integrates these two approaches, focusing first on the psychoanalytic level that deals with trauma and psychic pain, loss and reparation, and transference and counter-transference; secondly on the systemic level that treats the organization as a structural unit with boundaries and functions, and as an open system related to other organizations and the society in which it exists. The discussion specifically focuses on three aspects of this unique blend: the meaning and implications of group trauma; the holding environment and its breakdown; and transference-counter-transference (CT) relationships as a resource and a facilitation in the work.

The meaning and implications of group trauma

The essence and definition of trauma is the rupture of the protective barrier or envelope, thereby flooding the system beyond its capability to process, contain, and absorb. This conception makes sense at the individual physical and even psychic level. When we speak of a wounded social system, however, or of group trauma, as we understood and conceptualized the injury and reaction of the Center, to what are we referring?

As with every social institution, the Center is defined and delineated by boundaries. These boundaries consist of various elements—physical, bureaucratic, and others that derive from and exist in the social realm, such as behavioural norms and expectations. The murder violated these boundaries. Indeed, as has been described above, an immediate response to the murder was the investment in consolidating the physical boundaries. Yet, in this specific case, the murderer entered the system not as a terrorist, a foreign body, nor as a hostile intruder, but as someone known to the system as a patient and recognized by it as its legitimate client. In fact, he did not invade it, but was invited by it.

The traumatic break did not consist of breaking the physical, administrative, or procedural boundaries of the organization. The break in this case was the violation of a social taboo. The taboo in question is the internalized prohibition of hurting or damaging the integrity of the parental figure. The murderous wishes which every infant experiences toward the mother are projected into her and reintrojected by the infant after they have been 'metabolized' through the maternal reverie (Bion 1962). In order to be able to do so, and to have her reverie, the mother must be certain indeed that the infant will not kill her. Otherwise, her anxiety will be of such proportions that she will not be able to tolerate the infant's projective identification, to digest and dilute it for him. Analogously to the infant–mother metaphor, the mental health system assumes the maternal role, containing the violent, aggressive, and destructive projections, feelings, and fantasies aimed at it, and through it at society as a whole. The mental health system can act as such a container, and thus fulfil its unique social role, as long as the taboo against actual damage and injury is maintained. The taboo against raising a hand against it serves it as a protective envelope, and allows the containment and processing of all the rejected, threatening parts directed at it.

The breaking of this taboo was the traumatic wound sustained by the Center, as a mental health unit and a part of this social system. Going beyond the Center, however, this traumatic wound spreads into society. The mental health system serves a critical social function: it is charged by society with containing its rejected madness and insanity, and the measure of violence and aggression associated with them (as distinct from violence stemming from other sources). In this, the mental health system in a modern society differs from other social systems, the primary function of which is to support and help those of limited means and physical disabilities, or with drug and substance abuse. The mental health system contains, in the deepest and most primary sense, the murderous, violent, and mad fantasies and impulses that exist in everybody's unconscious, regardless of external circumstances. Society protects the mental health system through the taboo imposed against hurting and injuring it, and, in turn, is preserved and protected by it from those irrational elements which it cannot contain or cope with. Breaking the taboo, therefore, injures and wounds not only the mental health system, but also society itself, which runs the risk of being flooded by violent wishes and insane and irrational fantasies once the dyke that was to contain them has collapsed.

The holding environment and its breakdown

The violation of the taboo and barrier against madness and violence therefore constituted a rupture and wounding both of the Center as a unit and of the wider society. However, a large part of what surfaced in the course of our intervention, which was brought up by the trauma and in its wake, had to do with the expectations and fantasies of the staff of the Center towards society and the particular social institutions representing it.

What are the nature and the source of these fantasies and largely unconscious wishes? Let us proceed once more from the view that social institutions and organizations are living and vital systems, and as such, they possess strata of unconscious life. Thus viewed, the workplace is also a social organization, which acts as a defence against unconscious fantasies of the workers (and as pointed out above, of society), generally related to the nature and character of the work itself. This is the well-known notion of social defence (Jaques 1955; Menzies 1960). In an organization like the Mental Health Center, the wishes, fantasies, and expectations are related to the fears of the negative and threatening aspects of psychic life, with which the workers are daily in contact and with which they struggle in their work with patients. These include anxieties about psychological alienation and isolation; the dread of regression and fragmentation, and loss of mental and emotional capacities; fear of depression, and of being flooded by the unconscious.

For all of these, the well-functioning mental health organization serves as a sort of oxidation basin—a place where toxic waste matter can be contained, detoxified, and turned into useful materials. This process may, of course, serve to neutralize some of the same dangerous and unwanted products in the workers as well, but that is not the entire story. The analogy to which we referred above, of the infant who projects the difficult feelings he is unable to cope with into the mother, who in turn digests and neutralizes them on his behalf, comes up again in the present connection. Now, however, the infant is the staff, and the Center-organization is the mother. The expectation directed toward the organization-mother is that it would contain and neutralize what the individual worker, or group of workers, project into it and it would, in this sense, be viable, stable, and capable of performing this transformation. The expectation and wish are thus for the Center as social institution to provide stability, durability, and capacities of containment, just like a good mother. Beyond this, it should also look out for the welfare of its employee-child, and be concerned and helpful regarding his or her development and psychological and professional growth.

It is our intention to point out the less conscious aspect of these processes. This finds expression in a sense of entitlement, but even more so in the creation of growing dependency on the organization. At the unconscious level, the organization is expected to act as a merciful and concerned parent, and when it does not live up to such expectations, anger, disappointment, and rage are directed against it. Undoubtedly, the organization can show commitment towards those who work in it. It must be remembered, however, that the system is not an 'other', totally cut off and alienated from those working within it. The meeting and satisfaction of needs is an aim, the achievement of which is also contingent upon the capacities of those who make up the system and are part of it. In this particular wounded system, such feelings of unmet and unsatisfied dependency came up forcefully in the form of frustrated expectations and disappointments aimed at the larger system—the hospital, the mental health services, the Ministry of Health. Indeed, the larger system did respond to such demands from a certain point onward with distance and qualification. The feeling of the staff was clearly that they were 'a ship of lepers', deserted and shunned by everyone. These feelings were better understood in the course of our work as rage over unfulfilled dependency needs, and this understanding opened the door to the exploration of the actual capabilities of the staff, to their activation and better utilization.

Parallel with these developments in the staff, certain changes were under way in the larger system in preparation for a new National Health Bill and its numerous implications and ramifications. The changes instituted demanded a more autonomous, independent, and self-supportive professional and organiza-tional stance. The impact of these demands and new conditions was indeed in the direction we have described, that is, to emerge from a position of depen-dence and move towards greater autonomy. But the coincidence in time of the organizational change in the health delivery system and the residual impact of the trauma was experienced by the staff as yet another cruel, deserting, and alienated demand. It only hurt more where the wound was still open and throb-bing, and increased the staff's feeling of being deserted and standing alone and in isolation against a hostile and threatening world. Working with these feelings of disappointed dependency enabled the organization to regain the energies and capacities dormant in it, to start activating and actualizing them, and even-tually to turn the dependent expectations and demands from disappointments into ideas, the germs of wishes and goals, and the fulcrum of active planning and achievement.

Transference and counter-transference relationships as a resource

Transference-counter-transference (CT) processes are inimical to relationships and relatedness; in fact, they are another mode of discoursing about and con-ceptualizing them. In any systemic-organizational intervention, numerous transference-CT processes are clearly present and active. When the interven-tion is carried out from a psychoanalytic perspective, however, these implicit, typically inferred processes attain such position, presence, and meaningfulness as to render them a central tool in the intervention. Thus, for instance, the understanding, described above, of unconscious dependency wishes in the context of the impact of the trauma, relied entirely on what we experienced in the transference on to us and in our own CT. Although such understanding is very useful, however, it is not sufficient, in and of itself, to bring about change. Change demands that whatever it is we wish to work with must be experienced with a certain degree of actuality within the context of the transference-CT rela-tionship, as in the psychotherapeutic situation.

A central dimension in relating to us was the pronounced readiness to develop dependency on us. We have already alluded to the significance and meaning of the choice made in contacting us: we were well known to the staff, as persons and figures, in a way that enabled them to relate to us as sources of hope. In Bion's (1961) terms, a mixture of two basic assumptions—dependency and pairing—occurred in the group relatedness to us. We, on the other hand, made it possible for the group to continue along these lines by entering into and accepting the role of 'knowers', of people who know what they do, who can diagnose and make decisions. Thus, for example, they wanted us to determine the structure of the meetings and allocations to work groups. At several points, the group evidenced opinions and positions different from ours. Each time, however, after we turned the matter back to them for discussion and determination, it was decided to do as we had suggested. Our declared position and our actual wish were to support the active parts of the staff, and to prevent them as much as possible from sinking into passivity. In fact, it seems that we accepted the dependency on us as a real need, especially at the initial stage, and met them where they actually were.

In the immediate post-traumatic phase, a powerful link can be observed between dependency and hope. As we have already reflected, the trauma set off a deep shock wave, which upset and undermined the staff's capacity to believe in themselves, in their professional capabilities, and in the skills they had acquired and had at their disposal. In this specific area, a severe blow was dealt to the staff's professional ego and ideal self. It was in this context that the transference to us was as parents who had given them professional life, or as teachers and mentors through whom a significant portion of their primary professional identification was achieved. Out of this transference relatedness they turned specifically to us with the wish to restore the faith and hope damaged by the trauma. In our counter-transference, we responded to this part of the dependency and obliged it, out of our own need to restore and rehabilitate these personal and professional aspects of the wounded staff. In the transference, we chose not to interpret or reflect these projections, but to accept and enable this relatedness. By responding in this manner, we made 'sophisticated' use of basic assumption dependency in the service of the restoration of hope (Bion 1961).

This, we believe, is what made it possible to enact within the transference-CT relationship the 'play' around restoring hope. In the post-traumatic situation, there is usually an enormously powerful tendency toward concretization and the fixation of experience. In the context of such increasing rigidification, the free play accorded to transference-CT processes—both relationships and relatedness—made possible a potential play space, within which symbolization processes could once more take place and be reactivated.

ENDING

We were invited to 'do something' in order to help an injured staff group. We accepted the invitation out of a wish to be of use as members of society and as professional colleagues. We marshalled such tools as were at our disposal, and what we did was described in this paper. Have we been of help? We believe so. Was it possible to do otherwise? Most likely, yes.

We cannot end this presentation without paying tribute to and expressing our genuine esteem for the members of this staff, who were hurled into a calamity, wounded, coped with it, and overcame it. Their ability finds expression in their personal and professional stance—the ability to seek help, to recognize the limits of this ability, and their commitment to work on themselves seriously and continuously, without making allowances for themselves, without becoming unfocused, and without sinking too far into the victim's position.

Organizational work, as well as any psychotherapeutic endeavour, is also political action, in that it always aims to alter and change the existing balance of power. In terms of the specific local politics, these staff came out the winner. As far as the politics of society is concerned, however, the question is still open: whether, in what ways, and to what extent the social balance of forces has really been changed as a result of this tragedy.

NOTES

1 The seventh day of the 'Shiv'ah'—the ritual seven days of mourning in the Jewish tradition.
2 In Israel, 'second generation' is a clear reference to the second generation of Holocaust survivors.
3 OFEK: 'Organization, Person, Group', the Israel Association for the Study of Group and Organizational Processes.
4 In Israel, victims of terrorist actions are entitled to full government compensation.

14

The Inner Drama of Role Taking in an Organization

Joseph Triest

Taking a role in an organization inevitably produces an inner drama in which internalized past figures, which are related in some way or another to the 'role in the mind', are brought back to life. These charged introjects meet—sometimes, clash—with the representation of the 'organization in the mind' and therefore influence the perception of organizational reality, the experience of the 'self' in the role, and finally the actual way the role is carried out (Gould 1991; Hirschhorn 1985; E. J. Miller 1985; 1993*d*).

This chapter describes the work of a 'role analysis' group (Barber 1987) of managers from different organizations, which was designed to explore the unconscious fantasies shaping participants' internalized 'object relations' with their respective roles in various organizational situations. The purpose of the following discussion is to explore the special qualities of the group in role analysis and try to establish the type of listening required to identify, within the body of unconscious verbal and non-verbal communication, those events, metaphors, and images which link participants' respective 'inner worlds' with their present and past roles.

From a theoretical perspective, this is an attempt to set the drama of role taking within the conceptual framework of 'object relations' (Bion 1961; Klein 1935; 1959) and 'open systems theory' (Lawrence 1979; E. J. Miller 1976; Rice 1969), with special emphasis on the intrapsychic conflict which occurs when the 'self' is simultaneously (and quite unavoidably) invested in formal as well as informal roles.

The 'self' is understood here mainly by its intuitive meaning. It is the experiencing 'I' to which the subject refers by saying 'I'. The 'self' as a meta-structure is formed in the course of development, emerging from the matrix of internalized 'object relations'. This matrix is based on relationships with significant figures—parents or siblings—which were internalized, sometimes in a distorted way, in different life situations after passing through the 'filter' of defences (Klein 1935; Fairbairn, in Grotstein and Kinsley 1994; Ogden 1986).

Interactions which were ascribed with a traumatic sense or which reiterated patterns of behaving and relating in a consistent and frustrating way will usually exist in the inner world as persecutory introjects, unassimilated into the 'core self', and will tend to apply themselves repetitively on to reality. Through a process of gradual integration and differentiation of various 'representations of the self', a 'self-image' is formed which becomes the sentient functioning and feeling 'I'. The degree of 'self' cohesiveness and 'self' integration may vary among individuals or situations and is influenced, among other things, by the degree of polarization between the various roles the individual is invested in.

The 'formal role' is that aspect of a role which is defined by the organization, regardless of the persona who is supposed to fulfil it; it is directly derived from the organization's 'primary task'. The 'formal role' refers to all of the role's components which are defined a priori by the system, such as the function assigned to the role holder, the definition of his or her authority and rank within the organization's hierarchical structure, the resources at his or her disposal, the norms of communication with subordinates, superiors, and peers, salary and benefits, and working hours. The 'formal role' is shaped in accordance with the system's current organizational culture (Obholzer and Roberts 1994).

The 'informal role' is the role which the individual takes, driven by needs which are more often than not quite unconscious, as part of his or her personality and as a response to the 'call' of the group which is operating on the 'basic assumption level' (Bion 1961). The 'informal role' is associated with psychological functions designed to balance tensions, reduce anxieties, and gratify instinctual and emotional needs. Although these may not be directly derived from the organization's 'primary task', they are quite often necessary in order to achieve it, as in a 'necessary, yet not sufficient' condition. In addition, people have a differential sensitivity (valency) to different basic assumptions and will therefore differ in their preferences for certain roles and in their ability to lead the group to achieve its goals and gratify its needs in any given time.

The organization thus assigns each individual with a twofold role: on the 'primary task' level, the individual receives a 'formal role', whereas on the 'basic assumption' level he or she is 'called' to fulfil an 'informal role'. The inherent tension between these two roles is the primary source of 'the drama of role-taking', because when an individual invests the 'self' in a role, as part of the process of acquiring an identity in the organization (Erikson 1950), the parts of self invested in the 'formal role' may be in conflict with or split off from the parts of the self invested in the 'informal role'. The role and the 'self' mutually shape one another. Different roles enhance or block specific aspects of the 'self' according to projections or social expectations which are directed at the role. The 'self' thus interprets and 'colours' the role according to personal tendencies, identifications, and past experiences.

Summing up, an individual in a role often finds him/herself at the centre of conflicts created as a result of colliding forces operating in the 'intermediate space' in which the role exists.

The individual's fulfilment of the role is eventually affected by a combination of several factors:

1. The definition of the 'formal role', as provided by the organization, in accordance with the organization's culture and 'primary task'.
2. The 'informal role' which the individual is required to fulfil for the organization (covertly and often unconsciously) on the 'basic assumption' level and as a result of the organization's emotional-motivational situation.
3. Internalized relations with significant 'past roles' and past figures (such as parents and siblings), which exist within the individual as sets of 'self representations' and 'object representations' and which are somehow related to the role or the organizational situation. These relations will often manifest themselves through the individual's behaviour patterns and in the ways the system's needs and boundaries are perceived and met.
4. The ability to maintain a differentiation between the needs of the 'self' and those of the role, based on an inner stance of awareness to and separateness from the organization and its inherent pressures.

ROLE ANALYSIS

When the mental pressures on the role holder increase, both from within and from without, so that the integration of the 'self' is threatened, mechanisms of splitting, projection, projective identification, and repression are activated in order to generate false inner consistency, while ignoring complexity or anxiety-producing contradictions. These defences block any possibility for learning or change, and the process of accommodation and assimilation taking place between the 'inner world' and the organizational reality is breached (Saravay 1975). As a result, the processes of validation of hypotheses concerning reality are disrupted and behaviour is mostly dictated by internalized past behaviour patterns transferred on to the present, despite the fact that their relevance to the current situations is often questionable. In organizations and social systems, such a process is expressed in the creation of malignant 'vicious circles' of projections, projective identifications, and splits among the various subgroups making the organization. In such a situation, the boundaries of tasks and roles are shattered and the outbursts of projections and counter-projections are intensified. Because of 'social defenses' (L. J. Gould 1993; Hirschhorn and Barnett 1993) the organization sooner or later operates according to self-fulfilling prophecies, recruits more and more role holders whose skills and qualifications are irrelevant to organizational goals, and is increasingly unable to perform its task (Kets de Vries 1991).

'Role analysis' is designed to break this vicious circle and enable the role holder to regain his or her ability to function efficiently, from a position of separateness and awareness in relation to the 'self', the role, and the organization. From the organization's perspective, a 'role analysis' aims to hypothesize why a particular individual was chosen to fulfil a given role at a specific time and in a particular context (H. Levinson 1991).

The techniques used as part of a 'role analysis' process are numerous and varied and will not be elaborated upon in this chapter; they can, for example, include the use of drawing to describe the role and the organization; of 'critical events' (Hirschhorn 1985); of identifying the relations between childhood memories and management events; of identifying the role in the family of origin and its relation to the current role (Reed 1976).

HOW DOES THIS WORK?

In order to exemplify the work of a 'role analysis' group, an excerpt from a managers' workshop follows.[1] The workshop comprised twelve participants and was held in a 'marathon' format (fifteen sessions lasting seventy-five minutes each). Participants are all considered outstanding managers in their respective fields (industry, hi-tech, communications). The 'primary task' was defined as follows:

- To examine participants' perception of the role and of the organization.
- To explore overt and covert motivations for becoming managers.
- To identify every participant's 'personal leadership style', as expressed in the group's 'here and now', and its repercussions on participants' work in their roles.
- To examine the relations between the roles in the group, in the organization, and in participants' respective families of origin.

At the beginning of the session, participants were asked to describe to the group a management event which has marked them somehow and then to tell the group of a childhood memory. In order to allow for unconscious group processes to 'identify and mark' the 'informal roles', no additional structuring was made apart from this initial instruction.

The first excerpt is taken from the opening session.

The consultant has just finished presenting the 'primary task' and the format, as described above. (His feelings, thoughts, and counter-transference will be expressed in the first person.)

The silence was immediately broken by Mark, an energetic and athletic young man who was wearing fancy 'pilot's sun glasses'. In the last two years he has worked as manager of the development division in a hi-tech organization. His speech and intonation are seemingly arrogant and energetic but actually disclose embarrassment and diffidence.

'OK,' he says, 'Let's not waste time and just start. My name is Mark, I'm 30, married to Lisa, my "better half" . . . and wiser, if I may say so . . . she would have made it OK in this group. Human relations—that's her forte. We have two adorable children—Dan is 8 and Gillian is 4, and I'm very emotional about them, I worry a lot . . . I'm one of those worrying fathers. Oops . . . watch it, it's going to fall.' He catches a glass cup which the participant sitting next to him mistakenly pushed, with a careless elbow movement, dangerously close to the edge of the armrest.

'I came here because I want to improve my management skills. I know that within my organization I'm what you might refer to as a "meteoric success". Forgive my arrogance, they say pilots are arrogant, and particularly ex-pilots like myself. It's not that I have nothing to improve as a manager, but the truth is I have always tried to excel in everything. I skipped grades at school. I went to a prestigious high school. In the army I was admitted to pilots' course and I was a very good pilot. In the last years I moved between organizations every two years. That's the normal rhythm of changeover in the hi-tech industry. Every time I left for a promotion. I've been working as manager of our Development Division for two years now. I actually feel that now, too, I'm on a crossroad and I keep asking myself "what's next". I still don't know exactly. In the meantime I reached a small "peak" in my role, as the manager in charge of the development of an acceleration system of a jet engine. We used a test rocket in our last experiment. It's amazing to see that thing soaring. At first you only pray for a successful lift-off, you're happy with it just not falling back to the ground. But then, within twelve seconds, it reaches maximum height . . . and then it explodes. Hundreds of thousands of dollars going in a bang within twelve seconds. It's unbelievable! All that work and all those painstaking preparations for a single flash of light—and then it's over. I can't get over it. Well, that's it, really. I don't want to take up more time. Let's move on.'

'You didn't tell us anything about your family of origin', says Jacob who sits right opposite him.

'Oh yeah, that's right. Well, I'm the eldest of three brothers. My mother is 72, she lives out of town. She's a real "iron lady". She can barely see or hear anything but she's still independent, alive and kicking. She also demands a lot from others. She's not the warm type . . . she is *strong*! That's it.'

'What about your father?'

'Oh . . . well . . . psychologists would probably say this is no mere coincidence. My father was a pilot, too. He was killed in a flight accident when I was 8. Probably because of some reckless stunt he tried to pull. The truth is I really don't remember him that much. That's it.' (The group is silent.) 'Next.'

Now Jacob joins in. He speaks extremely slowly, with short, pauses, designed to emphasize what he is saying.

'OK' (pause). 'What shall we start with? My name is Jacob, I've been working for twenty years in the production division of the dockyards. Until a month ago I was the workers' representative in the management. I recently joined management as department manager. You probably know that the dockyards are in pretty bad shape. Until recently I was up to my ears in tough negotiations, trying to prevent redundancies. The dockyards must become more streamlined and efficient. There are talks of introducing ISO 9000, which raises a lot of problems' (pause). 'Many problems . . . there's nothing wrong with streamlining and efficiency measures, but on the back of the weak? Over my dead body!' (pause) 'Well, just a bit about myself: My parents live in Tel Aviv—they are very old, almost 90! They live on G Street. That's a very special building—you may even know it—it was designed by the famous architect X in the International architecture style. It's very special. Today it's in a bad shape, the plaster is falling off, but its character still shows. My parents are the last original tenants in that building. All the others have left and were replaced by other tenants.

'I remember my childhood very clearly. The flats in that house are so small it's unbelievable. It's truly amazing how small they are. But my father, who is a carpenter, knew how to use every nook and cranny, every corner . . . He built special cabinets which allowed him to make use of every inch. The beds in which me and my brother used to sleep were put one on top of the other. And since there was so little room, everything had to be very tidy, mess was not allowed. When we took a folded towel out of a cabinet, we put there a folded piece of clothing in its place. My mother used to cook and clean and my father made the furniture. They did everything together and with their bare hands. All the tenants were like a large family. We all used to have dinner together on Friday nights, each time in someone else's flat. This was a truly beautiful time. No one ever locked their doors. We trusted one another.

'In the last years, the neighbourhood grew older. There's a contractor who wants to buy the land and demolish the house, but the owners can't sell before the last of the protected tenants are evacuated. And my parents aren't leaving. They are there and that's it! This is where they lived all their lives and this is where they'll die!'

At that point the door opens loudly and Josh, a boyish-looking man, enters the room (he looks 16) holding a cellular phone to his ear. He apologizes, takes a chair from the back of the room, asks Jacob to move a little, and now the inevitable happens: Jacob moves back, Mark moves back too and says: 'Oops, the cup!' The cup drops to the floor but the 'kid' catches it nonchalantly with one hand, his other hand still holding the chair. In one fell swoop, he puts it on the table with apparent pride. Not a drop spilled. A real virtuoso. The eldest of the group applauds him. 'That's how things are when you're young,' he says. 'Quick reflexes.'

I try to put some order in my impressions. In such a 'role analysis' group, my goal as consultant is to formulate an intervention which would bring to consciousness the dominant group conflict, while at the same time identifying the 'valency' of each participant and the 'informal role' each participant assumes, as part of the group effort to produce a leader who would save it. The participants' contribution represents, in this respect, an unconscious 'suggested solution' which the group can endorse (or reject) as a group solution (Whitman and Stock 1958). The assumption is that there is congruence between the role participants take in the group and the informal roles they assume in their respective organizations.

I wonder about the significance of this obsessive dealing with the falling cup: I find this instance of 'much ado about nothing' fascinating. It is my impression that the group is in a state of great anxiety and that the 'fall' theme is so catchy for good reasons, for it must represent a deep feeling of threat which these (quite literally) high-ranking managers bring along with them.

The task I have given them—to explore personal leadership and management patterns—must have been interpreted as a call for competition: who will be the 'boss of all bosses', a sort of a gladiators' fight designed to gratify my sadistic desire? Failure is experienced as falling from the height of 'my expectations', an irreparable shattering of one's self-image. In spite of their ostensible co-operation, I have an increasing feeling that the group is actually trying to evade the task. True, Mark readily responded and 'hopped on' very quickly, but he also seemed very anxious to 'get off' as soon as possible. (My supposition is that the sexual connotation of this association is not a coincidence.) Jacob interviewed him quite thoroughly, but Jacob's slow speech seemed to be blocking him more than anything else. Where there's no movement, no competition can take place and there are no winners or losers. The group seems to have appointed the former 'workers' representative' to protect it from Mark's 'meteoric rise' in the group, which would have forced everyone to either 'join the competition' or 'be left behind'.

I share these thoughts with the group, and add that now it is my impression that the group found itself an 'omnipotent saviour' in Josh, who not only saved the cup from falling but also saved the group by providing it with a 'cellular safety net'.

Josh looks as though he did not listen, but Mark seems hurt, and says that by volunteering to speak first he felt he had actually contributed to the group.

'The question is whether you have another option inside,' says Jacob.

Mark looks as if he does not understand.

'Let me explain,' says Jacob. 'Let's suppose that the management requires certain performance from you by a certain date. Do you start to put pressure on yourself and your workers or can you just tell them, "Sorry, I can't do it"?'

'Who gives a damn about what the management demands? What matters is what I want,' says Josh.

Josh manages to arouse my anger as well as my admiration. I find myself looking for an opportunity to confront him so that he cannot ignore me and get away with it. I try to work through this counter-transference reaction so that my intervention is not perceived as a threat, which might confirm the fantasy about my role which must already exist in the group.

'Right now,' I say, 'it seems that the group, in its attempt to avoid the danger produced by the "management's demands", is considering getting rid of the consultant. It is like saying that if he were not there, the "mirror" would disappear and no one would have to stare it in the eye and see how they looked. It is my assumption that the three statements heard so far from Mark: "If you're not the first, you're not there at all"; from Jacob: "If everything stops—there can be no competition"; and from Josh: "No manager tells me what to do", are probably, as awkward as this may seem, representative not only of the speakers but also of the organizations in which they "grew up" and are therefore very much worth exploring.'

This structuring intervention is designed to offer work instead of fantasy. For a while it succeeds in centring the group. Following my intervention, Mark and Jacob (and others, too) present the events from their life in their organizations which they chose to share. The working through of these stories is enabled at a later stage of the group work.

Mark's event: 'In our organization,' he says, 'the workers write down evaluations for the managers and vice versa. In the last round of such periodical evaluations I received problematic feedback from both directions. The workers said I was a "pressurizing" boss, that the fact that I was constantly demanding excellence and creativity actually produced the opposite effect. My boss, in the feedback conversation, told me that he was fully aware of my tremendous motivation but that he also felt I was running alone and not really co-operating with the rest of the role holders. Then he said that he mainly felt that I never listened to what he said, which was very odd because I truly admire him.'

In Mark's inner world, the fast advancement (skipping grades, changing jobs every two years) is, I feel, a typical and compulsive coping pattern. The phallic description of the soaring rocket sounded filled with sensuality and excitement but the extinction danger was just as recognizable. 'At the peak of its success', the rocket was destroyed in one bright flash. Just as in sex, the 'peak' is also the 'end'. One must therefore escape such places quickly, 'change jobs every two years', before being devoured and destroyed by one's own organization. I suppose (and as the group work unfolded, this supposition was corroborated) that this explicit phallic attitude was meant to protect him, deep inside, from the 'woman figure' which he experienced as dangerous. The importance of this insight, apart from its 'personal' value to him, lies in the fact that it may clarify the unconscious way in which Mark may have been experiencing the organization—as a devouring woman to which his devotion represented a grave danger of annihilation (demonstrated, for example, by his submissive remarks concerning his wife or his admiring description of his 'cold' mother).

The internalized figures in Mark's inner world naturally affect and form his relationships with his manager and subordinates. No wonder he pressurizes everyone and that his superior feels left out. Mark's attitude towards him stems from the same place of competitive identification from which his attitude towards his father originates. He is totally attuned to him, following in his footsteps, living the same danger which eventually led to his father's death (the fall), failing, however, to acknowledge him. He clearly does not consult with him. His father was never present enough to speak to him. He can only identify with him.

When I think of Mark, I think of *The Unbearable Lightness of Being* (Kundera 1985). Vertigo, says Kundera, is actually the longing to fall. Could this also be

Mark's unconscious longing: 'to fall', so that he does not have to consume him-self in ceaseless acceleration, which is intoxicating and exhilarating but also eroding and destructive? Maybe this is what he unconsciously asks from Jacob—to help him 'fall slowly' without crashing. He wants the values he repre-sents, namely loyalty to workers and to people, to protect him from what he experiences as a cold and narcissistic climate where excellence seems to be the ultimate value and where people seem to be expendable.

Apart from clarifying Mark's inner perception of his role, it seems that his feelings are representative not only of him but also of the general shape of the department he runs. His organization—which is one of the best of its kind—has invested huge sums of money in the development project, although no one knows whether they will manage to reach the finish before their competitors. The development department is therefore under a great deal of pressure to drive the project to 'peaks of success' and save it from a 'catastrophic' fall.

The experience of 'all or nothing' and the tremendous pressure on Mark are not only personal but also organizational. The organization, as seen through Mark's eyes, is a place where achievements are everything, and moreover, today's achievements are no guarantee for tomorrow. Just like the rocket, the organization too, with all its 'investments and efforts', may perish and disap-pear in 'no more than twelve seconds', leaving no trace behind. This is an or-ganization which requires excellence and creativity but whose demanding attitude consumes both these assets. In this organization, no 'term of office' can last more than two years. 'Staying put' means letting new generations of young, brilliant, and ambitious people (or young and ambitious organizations) over-take you. This is similar to the way Mark perceives the hi-tech organizational culture in which he works: either you fly or you fall. If you're not 'brilliant' you don't 'exist' at all. And who can be brilliant for more than twelve seconds con-secutively?

On the other hand, there is Jacob's world:

Jacob tells us later that he is 'a pain in the management's neck'. As a department manager he drives a tough struggle to save his men from being made redundant. The management feels that he is so entrenched in his position that he cannot see the other's side and that his stubbornness may eventually cause the ruin of the organ-ization. In fact, he is perceived as someone who does not identify with the needs of the organization, even in his new role as manager. It is possible that Jacob's loyalty and devotion to his internalized parental figures does make it hard for him to carry out a balanced assessment of the situation.

Jacob speaks slowly, emphasizing what he is saying time and again. His is a ship's rhythm. His description of his parents' house reminds me of a ship. A small and narrow place where each and every corner must be used. The house, like the dockyards, also has historical value. He feels commitment to friendship and a certain disdain for achievement-oriented attitudes. He will not let this 'contractor' (the consultant in the transference) ruin the house that he has built. Like his internalized 'parents within', he heroically and persistently clings to the past, refusing to 'sell himself short'. He will not 'go gentle into that good night'. This is how he protects himself and the group, at the expense of development and learning.

Jacob, too, unconsciously conveys here some of the anxieties and cultural traits of his organization. Many of the workers have been there for many years. Some of them immigrated to Israel after the Second World War. Most of them have no formal education. The organization is now facing changes, as a result of changes in the market and the industry. Many of the workers may find themselves out of a job. Just like his parents' house, the organization in which he works has grown old and is facing a dilemma: 'regenerate or die'. And in this organizational culture, regeneration means the destruction of whatever it is that currently exists.

The conflict which came to life in the group between Mark and Jacob is an inherent conflict in the organizational world, in which constant efforts are required to keep a balance between loyalty and devotion on the one hand and competition, excellence, and achievements on the other.

Increasingly anxious, the group keeps looking for a 'saviour', which is finally found in Josh. Without much ado, Josh takes the familiar role of the 'whizz-kid'. This is not surprising; this is also how he is seen in the communications firm where he is employed as the youngest manager at his rank.

At the beginning of the workshop, he keeps being late to sessions. In fact, only half of him is actually in the session. His other half is hooked to his fancy and quite sophisticated cellphone, which vibrates silently and displays on-screen messages as we go on. In spite of the fact that other participants laugh at that, he seems to be unable to cut this umbilical cord which connects him to the outside.

As for his life story, he tells the group: 'I really don't have much to tell you. I was a perfectly normal kid, a bit spoiled. My parents are just great. Dad's a diplomat. My mom's a lawyer. They were not very young when I was born. I'm their only son. I believe my mom had difficulties having children . . . I think she had two miscarriages before me . . . The truth is I don't know much about their lives before I was born. But anyway, they waited a long time to have me and they were very happy when I was born. Mom quit her work and spent all her time raising only me . . . sorry . . . only raising me.'

I later shared with him some of my feelings for him—appreciation mixed with anger for having seemingly erased me.

For the first time he looks very pensive:

'When I was four, dad went away for a three-year mission abroad. He went on his own because they didn't want to make me move and then return and all that fussing around. Now that I think of it, I grew up most of my childhood without having my father at my side. In fact,' (he laughs, embarrassed) 'the only way I could speak to him was on the telephone.' The group is silent, listening. 'This is the first time that I think that perhaps I may have missed him.' He looks moved but then, as if comforting himself, he says: 'But my mom was always there for me. Even when I messed up at school—and I used to mess up all the time—she always backed me and pulled me out of trouble.'

I ask him whether this pattern of 'messing up and pulling through with mom's help' is still characteristic of him today, too.

He is surprised, and says: 'A few months ago I got a new project and became in charge of the deployment of a wide-area communications network. I'm responsible for a huge budget. As part of my role I need to negotiate with contractors and subcontractors. A few days ago, our negotiations with one of our large subcontractors was terminated. I had a condition which they were apparently unable to comply with, so I said, "OK, then everything is off and we'll just have to find someone else". This made hell break loose. They contacted the General Manger, and they apparently have a lot of strings in the market which they can pull. The manager called me and told me in no uncertain terms to find a way out of this situation, and by the same token he added, "and don't be such a smart-ass". I said: "I'm not being a smart-ass, I'm just very demanding and require excellence. If they can't handle it we'll find others, believe me, we will." And the General Manager said: "Look, this is such a complex operation, I don't want to take my chances with another subcontractor who hasn't proved himself yet. They have renown and experience; it wouldn't hurt you to learn to show some respect to that." '

The experience which Josh insists on re-exploring compulsively is that of 'the whole world awaits him' (just as his mother must have awaited him after her two miscarriages). Yet the ground on which he stands is far from being stable. Ostensibly, what was 'before' is of no 'concern to him'. 'The world started with him' but deep inside he feels abandoned and lives on the ground of his parents' unstable relationship. Time and again he explores the boundaries of his omnipotence—and 'mom' deploys a safety net for him against all the dangerous and revengeful fathers in the world.

In his work, this scenario repeats itself many times. His mobile and eternal cellular phone provides him a sense of omnipotence in that it gives him the illusion of being everywhere all the time. Everybody seems to need him while he seems to need no one. Ostensibly, he casts away each and every father figure which stands in his way but, at the same time, the phone also represents his longing for his father who, he feels, has abandoned him. In this 'inner drama' the mother is replaced by the organization, represented by a forgiving superior who does indeed save him from trouble with the subcontractor.

Maybe in the case of Josh, too, personal characteristics are a mirror image of his organization.

The communications company where he works is a young company which was created by 'renegades' from an older and more well-known firm. It is often seen as the 'whizz-kid' in the communications arena, as it succeeded in entering a most competitive market, and within an amazingly short period of time—and with a stroke of genius in its advertising and marketing campaigns—managed to drive existing market players away and create new market conditions. Soon after that, a 'bug' was found in the system which forced the company to start a large-scale repairs campaign. Some nasty rumours of arrogant and unilateral contracts with suppliers and subcontractors were spreading, which created some antagonism in the industry and made it difficult for the company to score new contracts.

The fourth life story is that of a hard-working man. It dramatically illustrates how important it is to explore how work is perceived in the individual's inner world.

Ben starts by telling us that he has been thinking of something radical. He said this in great excitement: quitting his job. Taking a year off, even taking time off from his family and going to the jungles of South America. A year . . . He has never, in all his life, had a vacation.

Since Ben speaks as a response to Josh's emotional reaction to his work with me, I am first inclined to hear in what he is saying a warning, not to open up, not to show faith or trust. But I suddenly feel ill at ease, and I can't get rid of the feeling that Ben is speaking as if he were parting from life. Hesitantly, I share this feeling with him.

He is very moved and tells the group about his life.

Ben's is a hard-working family. All his life turns, he said, around one dramatic event. 'When I was 13, it was discovered that my father had two children from two other women (excluding my mother) whom no one knew existed. This was an amazing shock, it was inconceivable. Until then I saw him as a friend and a father. But all the trust and faith I had in him broke down that moment.

'This developed into an extremely difficult crisis in our family and I left for boarding school, and actually never returned home since then. In fact, at that moment I not only lost a father but also a home.

'But this was not the end of the tragedy. My father returned home after a period of separation and had to cut off his relationship with the woman he loved at that time. He turned restless, nervous, and gradually became depressed. One day he was gone. They searched for him for three days until they discovered his body in his car. He had committed suicide.'

Ben worked in a company specializing in starting up new factories as turnkey projects for other owners. This was how it went: the promoter would present the purpose of the enterprise he wanted to start up and the budget he had available. Ben and his team undertook all the necessary steps in the start-up process: finding a site, locating the necessary equipment and machines, acquiring know-how, and screening and hiring personnel. When the enterprise was up and running, it was delivered to the client as a turnkey project.

Ben has been doing this work for the last eight years and did it excellently. His job allowed him to switch to a new project about once every two years. Again he would set about the starting-up work—organizing a site, equipment, know-how, and workers, 'turn the key', deliver the enterprise, and move on.

He had recently been promoted to a central role in the firm's general headquarters and became manager of the co-ordination department within the mother organization. In this new job he started to experience many difficulties. The organizational structure was such that each project's manager recruited a team with the relevant qualifications for the job from the company's personnel pool. Due to unclear and unstable professional and social boundaries, this created extremely complex work relationships between everybody and a confused formal and professional hierarchy. Yet, as long as he worked in turnkey projects, Ben felt he was being effective, willing to confront others when he encountered resistance, and, on the other hand, willing to reconcile or please when necessary.

Now that he had been moved to headquarters he found his functioning frustrating. He did not know how to link the different functions. The medium seemed superfluous to him. Did the business not work just fine without this department, too? Moreover, he felt he did not receive the appropriate backing from his superior. He suspected that his superior had moved him to this new role because he (Ben) had accumulated too much influence in his former role and that this new role was really meant to clip his wings.

It is hard not to draw parallels between the childhood world in which Ben's personality was formed and his role in the organization.

In his work, Ben quite unconsciously 'gives birth to other children', for 'other women'. He creates an organization 'for them' and leaves. He thus created for himself a life which was consistent both with his own world and with his organization's needs. The frequent switching between projects provided an outlet for the anger and distress he felt. When he created something new, the feeling of conquest and the surge of adrenalin drove away the underlying depression, perhaps the same experience that his father used to have.

Once he had been promoted to headquarters he felt (maybe similarly to the way his father perceived the suffocating nature of the couple's relationship) that the organization was suffocating and castrating him. He was no longer able to 'hold together' this 'impossible family'; frustration and depression surfaced and rendered him an inefficient manager in his new role. In his fantasy of quitting and leaving, he chooses a solution which had already saved him once in his youth, when he left home for boarding school. But here, on a deeper level, we also discover that he is unconsciously following in his father's footsteps.

Here, too, the personal conflicts are activated because they are 'compatible' with the conflicts derived from the structure of the organization in which he works. The Co-ordination Department, just like its manager, Ben, has to contain the conflictual and unbridgeable needs of different parts of the system. (In this case, as a result of the group's work, a new and more effective organizational structure was later proposed which allowed him to perceive his role in a way which was more congruent with reality.)

DISCUSSION: THE 'ROLE ANALYSIS' GROUP

The 'role analysis' group is a perfect medium for role analysis, since its psychological structure resembles that of the organization. In fact, it provides what Winnicott (1971) called a 'potential space': 'An intermediate area of experiencing that lies between phantasy and reality' (Ogden 1985: 129).

In the 'inner world', taking a role is actually 'getting into the boots' of an authority figure (usually a 'father figure') identified with the role. This process may arouse conflicts between 'self-representations', 'role representations', and 'organization representations'. The group externalizes this 'inner drama' in that various aspects of the 'self' are enacted in various 'informal roles'. The whole process is driven by anxieties and desires, as each individual's personal resolution of the aroused conflicts unfolds.

In the case presented, Mark and Jacob are primarily driven by the anxiety which rose in the group facing its task (exploring personal behaviour patterns being perceived as exposing one's vulnerable spots in front of ruthless and aggressive competitors who will not hesitate to bump into anybody who stands in their way to the top).

The consultant, too, is painted with the shade of massive projections which are thrown on to and into him. At this stage he is perceived as a persecutory and intrusive figure who takes a cruel X-ray of hidden weaknesses without any emotional involvement of his own, not someone trustworthy, certainly not someone from whom one can seek help or even expect empathy and human warmth. These are the characteristics of the relatedness, which drives Mark and Jacob (as well as Josh, Ben, and the other participants) to retrieve personal coping patterns formed in their past experiences with harmful parental figures, which seem to be 'appropriate' in their present situations—Mark 'flies ahead', Jacob 'stops' everything. These internalized relationships come alive in the group through 'vertical transference'—namely, transference from the past to the present.

In parallel, an additional 'force field' to the vertical field operates on the group. It can be imagined in terms of the 'weft' interlacing with the 'warp', creating a sort of 'grid'. This 'weft' is the 'horizontal transference' by which unique peripheral components are transferred on to the group, in this case, the culture of the 'mother organizations' of the different managers (Foulkes and Anthony 1975). This grid actually works as a 'sieve', filtering the memories and associations which form a binding link between the past and the present, between internalized and actual authority figures (Mark's manager, Josh's manager), between the organization's culture and that of the group.

Communication (conscious as well as unconscious) is essentially designed to accommodate the inner world to current objects (Freud 1900; Langs 1976). The pressure to 're-create' the past in the present and to assimilate it in stereotypical behaviour patterns is balanced by a pressure to accommodate the inner world to the present situation. For this reason, only those associations located on a 'junction point' are selected (Freud 1900). The rocket metaphor may very well qualify as such a binding link. It quite concretely represents Mark's work, but at the same time it also symbolically represents his perception of his role and his organization: it is his ambition, his self-image, his driving force, as well as the expression of the catastrophic threat he feels—in the organization as well as in the group. The 'fall' is yet another binding link. It links Mark's childhood trauma of his father's fall to the danger of the possible fall of the rocket; it links the danger of his organization's fall (if the project fails) with the perceived danger of 'falling' in the competition in the group, the falling cup of coffee. Similarly, Jacob's description of the ancient house, doomed to be destroyed and then rebuilt, metaphorically contains his perception of the dockyards' organizational culture, as do Josh's wireless net, Ben's turnkey projects, and so on.

The group has a unique role in bringing 'informal roles' into the light and in externalizing intrapsychic conflicts. The world of 'real' interpersonal relations (relationships) with peers and with the consultant as an authority figure becomes an 'Archimedean leverage point', as it were, from which the world of internalized relations (relatedness) with the role and the organization may be examined.

As interpersonal relationships in the group gain weight and importance, a better separateness is enabled among participants and a clearer differentiation is generated between inner reality, which is driven by fantasy, partial objects, and persecutory introjects, and the 'external reality', which is inhabited by real flesh and blood people; between the formal role as defined by the organization and the informal role as expressed in the group.

NOTE

1 The psychological accuracy and authenticity of these excerpts has been maintained meticulously, although personal identifying characteristics and the facts concerning the organizations have been altered or omitted for the sake of confidentiality.

15

Isolation, Autonomy, and Interdependence in Organizational Life

Vega Zagier Roberts

INTRODUCTION

As the rewards of belonging to or being part of an organization decrease, there is a tendency for individuals and groups to focus more narrowly on their own needs and experience. Both in organizations and in society at large, we can observe simultaneous but opposing trends. On the one hand, there is a trend towards larger, more powerful units—mergers, the European Community—and on the other hand, a shift towards entrepreneurial individualism, small stand-alone units, and separatist nationalism. In organizational life, the psychological contract is changing out of all recognition. The organization is becoming less and less a reliable 'parent' providing permanence and care in exchange for 'good behaviour'. Instead, many individuals, whether employees or contracted workers, feel under pressure to attend to their own short-term goals and performance, without necessarily attending to how these relate to the longer-term or broader aims of the systems to which their work is contributing. If we extend the notion of psychological contract to the societal level, we can see evidence all around us of a similar process: pressure for the citizen to look out for himself, as the state withdraws from its 'parental' caretaking role.

This chapter will demonstrate some of the costs of this at different levels: first between individual and group, then between group and organization, and finally between the organization and its wider context. The chapter goes on to consider some implications of this for leadership, followership, and membership in organizations. The final sections suggest some of the ways in which managers can develop their understanding of group and intergroup dynamics, thereby reducing their sense of isolation and alienation, as well as enhancing their effectiveness.

THE INDIVIDUAL AND THE GROUP

Example 1

Miriam was a community drug worker employed by a drug dependency team. Most of the services provided by this team were clinic based, with clients attending at set times for individual or group counselling, medical appointments, and methadone prescriptions. Miriam's outreach work was outside the clinic, meeting clients in the community, at youth clubs, in local cafes, and in a range of other 'natural' settings. Her manager, Nancy, found it impossible to manage Miriam, who rarely attended supervision sessions or team meetings. Nancy initially felt anxious that she had no way of knowing what Miriam was doing, nor of supporting her in this difficult and risky work. Gradually her concern gave way to anger, as she began to suspect that Miriam was doing very little and might often not be at work at all. She described Miriam as a 'resistant and difficult' person, and saw the problem as due to Miriam's personality.

The outreach post had been set up as an experiment which, if successful, might lead to the team employing further outreach workers to extend this aspect of the service. Now Nancy began to question in her own supervision whether Miriam's contract should be renewed, and even whether the team should abandon the idea of outreach work altogether.

Attributing the behaviour of the hard-to-manage group member to individual pathology is likely to lead to marginalizing and extruding the individual from the group. A more useful approach is to think of the behaviour as representing one aspect of the team's experience of the core work. In this case, for example, one could reconstrue Miriam's stance as expressing something about drug users on the street, those not yet engaged in the clinic's programme. It is well known in drug work that many potential clients are either too suspicious or too chaotic to make use of formal services. The outreach post had been set up specifically to bridge the gap between these hard-to-reach clients and the clinic by meeting them where they were, being accessible and 'user friendly'. Thus, in some sense the very existence of Miriam's post could be experienced unconsciously as a criticism of the clinic, and her relationships with drug users on the streets as a form of competition. The wish to blame and extrude the individual worker might then be understood as a group avoidance of the painful limitations of their treatment programme in tackling one key sector of their client group. Both Miriam and the addict on the street represented powerful threats to the system.

Furthermore, even clients already engaged in treatment were ambivalent about treatment and sometimes sabotaged it, for example by supplementing their prescriptions with street drugs or by missing appointments. Similarly, even those team members who attended supervision and team meetings regularly were ambivalent about being managed and did not always adhere to rules and policies. Locating untreatability in those drug users not yet formally registered as clients of the clinic, and resistance to management in Miriam, may unconsciously have served to preserve the clinic as a 'good' and safe place, while 'badness' and danger remained located outside.

This does not mean that Miriam's personality was not a factor. Personality plays a part in this at many levels. First, one might anticipate that the outreach post would attract a different sort of person than the clinic-based posts, in all likelihood someone with a preference for working independently and alone, and therefore possibly harder to manage. Secondly, Miriam may well unconsciously have responded to an unwritten job advertisement that would have read: 'Wanted: volunteer required to voice the difficult, disowned, anti-task elements of the staff. Both internal and external candidates are welcome, but only candidates with suitably difficult personalities should apply.' (Obholzer and Roberts 1994: 131.)

Gibbard (1975) describes this relatedness of individuals and groups as 'a machinery of intercommunication which is at once a characteristic of groups and a reflection of the individual's ability or even his propensity to express certain drives and feelings covertly, unconsciously and anonymously'. Complex unconscious processes of splitting and projection are involved which allow group members to disown unwanted aspects of themselves by locating them in another who takes on the proffered 'role' unconsciously, with varying degrees of comfort or discomfort.

Example 2

In a therapeutic community for disturbed adolescents, a great deal of time in team meetings was taken up by debates between two male staff members. Rodney was young and 'trendy', wore frayed jeans and an earring, and often defended adolescents who had broken rules, arguing that the staff should overlook minor infractions as 'part of growing up'. Richard, who was older and came from a background in psychiatric nursing, insisted on taking each event very seriously: 'If our boys don't know where they stand, things will get out of hand.' He was regarded by his colleagues as rigid and authoritarian, while Rodney was seen as 'a bit of a flake'. The rest of the staff would generally sit quietly watching, sometimes amused, sometimes irritated at the repetitiousness and time-wasting of the endless arguments between these two men.[1]

The team saw these arguments as due to a 'personality' clash between the two protagonists. However, this way of construing the situation leads to a blind alley, since it suggests that the only solution is for one or both parties to change, which may well not happen. Furthermore, the behaviour of the team in letting these arguments continue fruitlessly week after week suggests an investment on their part in maintaining the situation.

Seeing the individuals concerned instead as expressing something on behalf of the entire team puts the problem into a different framework. What needed to be recognized here was the two sides of an unexpressed institutional debate on permissiveness versus control, a debate which lies at the very heart of the adolescent process with its unconscious struggle between permissive and authoritarian parts of the self.

Institutional dilemmas like this are anxiety provoking and regularly give rise to the kinds of projective processes described in these two examples. These processes can then lead to individual stress and scapegoating, as happened with Miriam. Alternatively, when the unconscious roles particular individuals are pulled into are fairly comfortable for them, as was the case for Rodney and Richard, the impasse may persist almost indefinitely, to the detriment of the organization's primary task.

Wells (1985) used the term 'collusive lattice' to describe this kind of situation, where members of a group accept a tacitly agreed unconscious role to defend the entire group from anxiety. Sometimes, reframing the problem in the way outlined above brings enormous relief, but in other cases it meets with considerable resistance, not least from the individuals occupying the roles of 'difficult' group members. Even when they find their allotted roles uncomfortable or painful, they may well resist seeing the issue as one of relatedness, that is, that their behaviour is determined by forces outside themselves. Relatedness in this sense can present a considerable threat to our habitual way of thinking of ourselves as autonomous and self-determining individuals.

THE GROUP AND THE ORGANIZATION

Example 3

A management team comprising the first-line managers of the five registered care homes and the director of a voluntary sector organization providing care in the community for mentally ill people contracted for four half-days of consultancy over a two-month period. One manager, Tim, had just resigned after a dreadful incident which he felt he had handled very badly. A number of residents in the home Tim managed had become very abusive, the situation had escalated, and Tim and two of his staff had eventually physically forced these residents out of the communal sitting-room and into their own bedrooms. The whole organization was shocked by the incident, and Tim felt unbearably awful, isolated, doubting if he were fit for this kind of work: hence the resignation.

Sarah, sitting next to me during the first consultancy session, was deadly quiet and I could not tell if she were angry or about to cry. I felt under enormous pressure to rescue her, Tim, and the whole management team. But I could not think. I just felt desperate, as if my long and positive relationship with this organization would break down irretrievably if I let them down this time. Partly by calling for a coffee break, I managed to restrain my impulse to say something, anything, to break the tension in the room, and to make a bit of space for myself to reflect and try to get back some capacity to think. During the break, I spoke briefly with Sarah and discovered that my feelings mirrored hers. She had been feeling that her long close relationship with Tim had broken down because she had failed to help him feel all right about his mistake, and this was making her very angry with him as well as very distressed. After the break, the two of us talked in the group about the anxiety and pain we had experienced in relation to what seemed an irreparable breakdown in relations at various levels: between Sarah and Tim, Tim's team and the organization, Tim's staff and the residents. Other managers then could begin to talk about their own feelings, their shock at the incident, but also their hatred at times of the residents in the houses they managed, and their fear that their violent impulses would get out of control. The sense of irreparability began to wane.

Up to this point, Tim had felt isolated because he had felt he had let everyone down. He had felt even further isolated when his attempts to discuss the incident with his peers in the management team led to solicitous enquiries about his feelings, and considerable advice giving. Both sympathy and advice added to his isolation by putting him in the position of the weak needy member of the group, with the problem firmly located in him and his unit. It was only when the whole management team were able to revisit the incident in terms of an organization-wide anxiety about how staff and managers throughout the residential service felt about and responded to hateful clients—their frequent (although usually controlled) impulses to batter clients who pushed them beyond bearing—that Tim began to feel once again part of the group.

Until now, the weekly hour the management team had allocated to 'support' had never felt supportive. I believe this was precisely because it was based on managers taking turns at being the member in need of help. Over the four sessions, we worked at reconstruing the various problems presented in systemic terms, that is, regarding each not as belonging just to the particular manager or team where it had arisen but as belonging to 'us', to the entire organization. Each incident was examined in terms of what it might be telling us about the state of the organization as a whole, about the relatedness of managers and staff, staff and clients, organization and funders, and so on. This made management team meetings much more genuinely supportive to each of the participants, reducing isolation and blame. But this new approach also carried a cost. Problems were no longer comfortably 'out there' but acknowledged as belonging to everyone. Furthermore, ideas for tackling them were no longer the sole provenance of the manager or team most directly concerned, and there were times when this felt to them like a loss of precious autonomy.

One could think of this consultancy intervention as serving to pull the team leaders back to the boundary position necessary for effective management, by holding in mind the relatedness of each team to the totality of the organization rather than focusing only on the functioning of their own teams. I think it went one step further. By reinforcing first-line managers' identity as members of a management team (as opposed to regarding the management team meetings as a coming together of individual managers), they had some opportunity for taking up a position at the outer boundary of the organization, not just at the boundary of their respective teams.

In a paper describing the work of the Grubb Institute over the past several years on using the 'organization-in-the-mind' as a management tool, Hutton says:

This requires working from the *boundary* of the institution and only those who are in a position to relate to the entire organization in this way can build up the idea of 'organization-in-the-mind'. The manager of a subsidiary department can form 'organization-in-the-mind' for that department, but unless he or she is also a member of the senior management team, they will be unlikely to be able to form 'organization-in-the-mind' as a tool of the whole. A junior manager can dream about the institution, can speculate about how it can be changed for the better, and can argue about policy, but his own 'organization-in-the-mind' is likely to prove an inadequate tool to understand the whole. (Hutton 1997: 68.)

In the complexities in which most of us work nowadays, it is increasingly inadequate to hold in mind only one's immediate work unit. The opportunity for managers at different levels to work together at conceptualizing the relatedness of parts to whole are crucial, both for attempting to make some sense of disparate and disturbing experiences, and for effective management.

THE ORGANIZATION AND THE WIDER SYSTEM

This way of thinking can usefully be extended to examine the relatedness of an organization to its context. This may be its immediate operational context, for instance, the relatedness of different care agencies as in the example which follows; or it may be the relatedness of the organization to society, as discussed in the next section.

Example 4

A community mental health team asked for consultancy because of conflicts among different subgroups within the team about what the priorities of the service should be. There was also conflict between this team and other teams providing services in the locality, notably around how clients were referred between different organizations and services.

Neither of these issues, it seemed to me, could be adequately addressed by this team alone since they were neither in a position to determine their priorities for themselves (that is, without reference to the requirements of senior managers and purchasers), nor able to determine the working practices of the other teams working in the same area. Yet if the consultancy day were opened out to include others, I was warned, the team was likely to feel 'their' time had been hijacked by a superordinate agenda, which was likely to fuel resentment rather than being helpful. In the end, the service director was invited to one of the four sessions to provide information about the Trust's and purchasers' priorities, and to clarify the team's scope of discretion in relation to these. Representatives from two other local teams were invited to another of the sessions to contribute to a mapping exercise, identifying what services were available to the local population and where the gaps and overlaps were. This proved very fruitful and seemed to free up the team to tackle some of their internal interdisciplinary issues in the afternoon, as well as to consider what further interagency planning they needed to set up.

Here again we see a powerful wish to maintain an illusion of autonomy, this time by denying the team's dependence on purchasers and managers, and their interdependence with other local service providers. However, the cost of such denial is very high, in terms not only of effectiveness but also of morale, as the conflict is driven 'downwards' to be acted out in the team. In this case, as in many others, the denial of some of the more painful realities of the purchaser–provider split and the new market-place orientation of the public sector had led to the scapegoating of individuals and subgroups in the team who were blamed for the lack of progress.

It is not just the dynamics of the market-place and the consequent overt competition for clients and resources which foster this denial of interdependence. The illusion of autonomy also defends against the anxieties inherent in the work of human service organizations, not least by providing an endless supply of 'bad objects' in the shape of other teams and services which can be blamed for any failure to produce the desired outcomes.

Furthermore, where there is no formal boundary around multiple interrelated agencies providing different components of services to the population of a designated geographical locality, it is particularly difficult to arrive at any shared 'organization-in-the-mind'. Attempts to do this are sometimes made by external bodies set up, for example, to 'reconfigure' (rationalize) such services. A different approach was used by staff at the Tavistock Clinic (Foster and Grespi

1994) who set up a workshop to which they invited representatives from a range of statutory and voluntary sector agencies involved in community care of the mentally ill. The workshop was designed to provide a safe, contained setting where the anxieties generated by community care of the mentally ill could be identified and thought about. Subsequently, the design was modified for a similar workshop with a membership recruited from a single locality (Foster and Grespi 1998). Although the focus of these later workshops remained the same, the fact that all participants worked in the same locality and therefore actually or potentially encountered one another 'in real life' made for a first step towards a boundary in the mind around a cluster of ostensibly separate but interdependent agencies involved in a shared task.

LEADERSHIP, FOLLOWERSHIP, AND MEMBERSHIP IN A CHANGING SOCIETY

Hutton (1997) notes that an important question in thinking about the primary task of any organization is what that organization is being asked to do by society. Thus, for example, she suggests that the police force is required to be more than a criminal justice agency: it has the dual task of upholding the law *and* keeping the peace. Similarly, for the different organizations described above, there is a task on behalf of society that each is being asked to perform in addition to its explicitly stated purpose. Their respective primary tasks were formally defined as reducing the harm associated with drug abuse, enabling disturbed adolescents to develop into mature adults, and providing a decent quality of life for mentally ill people. But these organizations can also be regarded as serving to contain societal anxieties about the impulses and vulnerabilities in all of us which could lead to our being extruded and marginalized.

Whilst sustaining the core technology within the institution is one aspect of management on the boundary, the other is the 'reading' of the context and alertness to the meaning and demands, conscious and unconscious, on the institution . . . the distinctiveness of a human service institution is that the human beings they are serving are seen not simply as people with personal specific needs and requirement, but they are also signs and symbols of the society they are in. (Hutton 1997: 79.)

As society changes, so too the covert and unconscious demands on human service organizations change. For example, whereas Victorian insane asylums could be thought of as having the societal task of keeping mad people out of sight and out of mind, contemporary society requires simultaneously to be protected from the impact of having mentally ill people living in the community, *and* to sleep easily in the belief that these people's rights to a 'normal' life are being met.

Moreover, people working in organizations—being themselves at the same time also members of society—import into their organizations their own relatedness to it. This includes not only their interpretations of the purpose of their work, but also their assumptions and beliefs about managing and being managed, leadership and followership, and belonging.

For some years, I consulted to study groups convened at the Tavistock Institute of Human Relations. These groups of eight to twelve strangers met weekly over ten weeks to learn about the dynamics of small social groupings by studying the group's behaviour in the here and now. There was no agenda. My role was not to guide the group as to how to start or proceed, but only to offer hypotheses about what was happening, based on my own experiences and observations in the group.

In the early years, the beginnings of groups like these were almost invariably around competition for leadership. Someone would suggest a way to start, 'since our consultant here obviously isn't any help'. There would be alternative bids for leadership and some jockeying for position. By the early 1990s, there was a noticeable change. When someone would suggest a way to start, one or two others might agree; others would object—sometimes loudly, often silently—but without putting forward any alternative suggestion, that is, without trying to grasp the leadership roles for themselves. As before, the group might divide into subgroups: those who wanted the group to be cosy and friendly, maybe go to the pub after the meeting, and others who defended their anonymity and refused to participate in the *bonhomie*. But whereas before, forming a pub group represented a rebellion against the Tavistock, a bit naughty but fun, now the idea tended just to fade away, as no one committed themselves either to going or to opposing the proposal. Both fight and fun waned. Instead, members felt increasingly oppressed by unstated rules which were neither challenged nor accepted. Lawrence, Bain, and Gould (1996) describe similar changes, as do others working in group relations conferences run along similar lines to these study groups and explicitly designed to explore issues of authority and leadership. There is, on the whole, less overt rebellion against the conference staff than there used to be and less vying for leadership, more individuals refuse to join groups, preferring to stand alone or to snipe from the back benches, and there is virtually no expectation that managers might be a source of help or that leadership might be a good thing.

However artificial these training events may seem, I believe that they do reflect something of what is going on in society, suggesting changes in prevailing assumptions and fantasies, in the relatedness (or lack of it) of members to each other, and in attitudes towards authority.

Based on his study of groups, Bion (1961) proposed that in every group there is an impulse to work—to mobilize members' competencies in the service of the task in hand, to be self-reviewing, to collaborate effectively—and an impulse against work, based on members' needs to belong and the desire to be led in a way that protects them from anxiety. When anxiety dominates over the impulse to work, the group behave as if there are shared assumptions about the role of the leader. Bion identified three 'basic assumptions': dependency, where the group members look to the leader to take care of them; fight/flight, where they look to the leader to identify an outside enemy and to lead them either into battle or to escape; and pairing, where the group looks to the leader to pair with someone or something to produce future salvation.

Later, Turquet added a fourth basic assumption, 'one-ness', wherein 'members seek to join in a powerful union with an omnipotent force, unobtainably high, to surrender themselves for passive participation and thereby to feel existence, well-being and wholeness' (Turquet 1974: 76). More recently, Lawrence, Bain, and Gould (1996) identified a fifth basic assumption which they called 'basic assumption me-ness'. Here there is withdrawal and dissociation from the group, which is predefined as a bad object *not* to be joined. No one is actively for or against anything, but instead members are preoccupied with getting and preserving their share. The overriding question becomes 'What will be to my advantage?'—a climate in which any compromise may be made, but no real stand taken, in which one must always look out for oneself rather than invest in the enterprise as a whole.

Whereas it can been argued that neither one-ness nor me-ness is really an additional basic assumption, but rather, they are different manifestations of those identified by Bion, they do seem to refer to an essential dilemma of our times. On the one hand, there is the desire to submerge the self in the group and its leader, without any personal boundaries; and on the other there is the counter-impulse which produces the stand-alone organization, the holding back from joining with others, and the denial of our interdependence illustrated in the various case studies in this chapter. Perhaps we are becoming more afraid of our impulse to give ourselves over to others, more distrustful of others' motives, more fearful of losing what we have, as deprivation comes ever closer to our doorsteps; and also more anxious about anger and hostility, our own as well as others', as the level of aggression all around us mounts, so that we barricade ourselves psychologically just as we barricade our doors.

Regardless of whether we are in designated management roles, we all have to manage ourselves. We must manage the boundary between our inner world and the external environment, between our individual self and the group, in order to be the author of our own actions—that is, to take our own authority. It is not only leadership which has become more difficult, but also authoritative followership, the exercise of one's authority in relation to the task in hand. As a result, it is harder to allow oneself to be managed or led to the benefit of the system in which one has a role and, when necessary, to challenge others' decisions but not their right to make them. There seems at present to be evidence of greater anxiety both in organizations and in society generally about taking initiative, perhaps greater fear of being blamed, of raising one's head above the parapet. But there is also less consensus about the leader's 'inalienable right to executive action' (Turquet 1974), including within managers themselves.

Instead there appears to be only an inalienable right to dispute authority, without offering alternative leadership.

Obholzer has identified the importance of 'sanction from within' the individual who seeks to exercise appropriate authority. This sanction from within depends on the nature of one's relationship with one's inner objects, introjects based on past authority figures in the mind. The attitude of these inner world authority figures 'is crucial in affecting how, and to what extent, and with what competence, external institutional roles are taken up' (Obholzer 1994: 41). To the extent that we lack a good authority within, as described by Pitt-Aitkens and Ellis (1989), our capacity both for authoritative leadership and for authoritative followership and membership will be impaired, to our own cost as individuals and to the cost of our organizations.

A SHIFT IN PERSPECTIVE

In each of the examples above, a change in perspective proved useful in tackling previously unmanageable problems. Thus, the problem individual or pair (Examples 1 and 2) required a shift to a group-as-a-whole perspective, the problem team (Example 3) to an organization-as-a-whole perspective, and poor intergroup/interagency relations to a system-as-a-whole perspective (Example 4). Many apparently localized difficulties, such as pilfering, rebelliousness, or bullying can be more effectively managed when they are seen not merely as localized difficulties to be 'solved' locally (for example by removing the troublesome individual, or by restructuring the organization), but as manifestations of deeper dilemmas that need to be faced across the system. Unconscious collusion to avoid these dilemmas can make the presenting problem intractable, create casualties through scapegoating, or lead to expensive solutions which prove unsatisfactory in the long term.

This shift of perspective requires a capacity for a particular kind of reflectiveness in managers, in the first instance through being aware of their own experience and how to use their own emotional responses as valuable data about what is going on. For example, the manager concerned about pilfering—say, false information on time sheets, or staff taking office supplies home—might wonder whether the pilfering could be an unconscious request for more support or, on the other hand, for more control. He or she might then look for evidence to support one or other hypothesis before taking action, since the different possible unconscious meanings of the behaviour require different interventions.

One of the most valuable sources of evidence is managers' own emotional experience, but to attend to this requires that they be willing to acknowledge, say, their own impulse to pilfer, rather than locating the impulse in 'bad' staff who need to be punished. In Example 3 above, it was Sarah's availability to attend to her own feelings that enabled the group to reflect on what had happened in a new and more related way.

Personal therapy is perhaps the best-known route to gaining insight into denied and repressed aspects of one's emotional life. However, by itself it will not necessarily lead to becoming a more effective manager. What managers need is not just self-awareness, but an understanding of how to use their emotional experience as data. Consultancy can provide this through repeatedly bringing to light evidence of the interrelatedness of individual and group emotional life, and providing repeated experiences of how insight can inform decision making. Finally, group relations training can be invaluable—such as the kind of study groups described above or the more extended learning opportunities provided by group relations conferences lasting several days. The connections between apparently random behaviours and the underlying issues participants are dealing with, and the relatedness of the parts—whether individuals or small groupings—to the whole, are brought into focus in a way that makes them very difficult to continue to ignore (E. J. Miller 1990*a*).

TOWARDS RECOVERING MEANING AND RELATEDNESS

As we have seen, there are powerful forces mitigating against acknowledging relatedness. As Bion pointed out, we all struggle between our impulse to belong to groups and even to submerge ourselves in group life, and our impulse to remain individual and separate: 'The individual is a group animal at war not simply with the group, but with himself for being a group animal and with those aspects of his personality that constitute his "groupishness".' (Bion 1961: 131.)

Belonging brings certain satisfactions, both conscious and unconscious, and exclusion (including self-exclusion) from the group can be to 'fraternize with death' (Turquet 1974). But group membership also threatens our sense of identity and our need to experience ourselves as the authors of our actions. Theoretically, it is in seeking satisfaction of basic assumption needs that the individual gives up his or her individuality, while in a work-mentality group this exchange is not required. However, it is doubtful whether total work mentality is ever achieved. Some abdication of individual identity is probably the inevitable price of group membership or, indeed, any interpersonal relationship.

The question which concerns us here is why the withdrawal from membership—in groups, in organizations, and in society—seems to be increasing. As suggested in the introduction to this chapter, the most obvious reason would seem to be that what we hope to get in return for membership is decreasing. We get less of the security and sense of belonging that used to accompany employment, that is, less satisfaction of our dependency needs. But more fundamental, it seems to me, is the decrease in opportunities for fulfilment or 'work satisfaction'. There are a number of reasons for this, two of which are prevalent in the 'caring' sector.

The first is that workers increasingly rarely have the basic satisfaction of doing what they regard as a good job. This satisfaction has always been subject to great vicissitudes. For example, to work with mentally ill people, or with people with severe learning or physical disabilities, or even to teach 'normal' children, is to come constantly up against the limits of one's capacity to bring about the desired degree of change. Now, with ever-diminishing resources, these limits draw more and more tightly. Staff–client ratios continue to worsen significantly in classrooms and clinics, in hospitals and prisons.

But this is only part of the story. There is also a growing sense of alienation in staff between their professional values and what they perceive to be the values of their employing organizations. The perception of front-line workers across these organizations is that 'They [the people "at the top"] care only about the bottom line'. Meanwhile, these decried senior managers are struggling to make it possible for these services to survive at all. In many cases, they are only too well aware of the plight of both clients and staff, but their jobs are difficult enough without their allowing too much of this pain to reach and 'get inside' them. As a result, feeling emotionally connected diminishes, while denigration and alienation increase.

In every organization, there are dilemmas which cannot be resolved in a way that satisfies everyone and which therefore remain a source of internal tension and conflict. For example, a core dilemma in the second case study in this chapter is between permissiveness and limit setting (or care and control). In a school, it might be between fostering social and personal development on the one hand, and imparting formal knowledge on the other. Now, increasingly, it is between needs and resources—the rationing dilemma. The traditional dilemmas were often split up between different disciplines: say, between nurses and therapists in a mental health clinic, or between wardens and social workers in a prison. However, when the dominant dilemma is framed in terms of 'values' (meaning professional values, but often used as if referring to human values) and 'value for money' (implicitly meaning anti-humanitarian preoccupations), the emotional split profoundly affects the professional staff's sense of affiliation with the organization. In this situation, it is as if the organization *is* the senior managers, 'them', from whom the rest need to disassociate themselves.

How, then, can we recover some sense of meaning in these organizations? Merely to drive business anxiety 'downwards' is not a solution. This often leads only to a 'doubling up of anxiety' (McCaffery 1998), which can cause intolerable degrees of stress in middle managers and an increase in anti-task defences, rather than to the intended widening of 'ownership' of responsibility for organizational survival and development.

According to Reed and Armstrong (Grubb Institute 1991: 4), to take up a role in an organization involves an individual's identifying the aim of the system they belong to, taking ownership of that aim, and choosing the actions which best contribute to achieving the aim. However, in considering the function of management, they point out some of the limitations of attending only to questions of effective service or product delivery. They suggest that effective management requires two different kinds of thinking:

1. *Purposive systems thinking*: this focuses on what the organization's stakeholders seek to achieve (that is, the organization here is regarded as a piece of sophisticated social engineering designed to use resources to achieve a specific purpose).
2. *Containing systems thinking*: this focuses on the patterns of rules, customs, behaviours (and, I would add, meanings) which characterize what actually happens, irrespective of defined aims and intentions. (ibid.: 10–11.)

It is not enough to treat unexpected and undesired behaviours as unfortunate impediments to the 'real' task in hand. Rather, it is crucial to attend to and try to understand these. Taking this one step further, the effective manager needs to get back in touch with those aspects of his or her own beliefs and longings which may have been split off and located in others now regarded as troublesome, and perhaps also to enable staff to get back in touch (at times and only to some extent) with what they have projected 'upwards'. As regards the core dilemmas in organizations, a crucial function of managers is to help those they manage to be aware of these, rather than to divide them into right and wrong. This is not to say that managers should necessarily try to achieve consensus, but rather that they need to make space for recognizing that both horns of the dilemma, so to speak, are part of the life of the organization. Heifetz puts it even more strongly when he points to the core task of leadership as adaptive work:

Adaptive work consists of the learning required to address conflict in the values people hold, or to diminish the gap between the values people stand for and the reality they face … The exposure and orchestration of conflict—internal contradictions—within individuals and constituencies provides the leverage for mobilizing people to learn new ways. (Heifetz 1995: 22.)

He also emphasizes the need to attend to the meaning and relatedness of the enterprise to the wider community as stakeholders. This requires that leaders of organizations stay in touch with their roles as citizens as well as with their roles as managers.

CONCLUSION

It has always been the task of each member of an enterprise—whether a family, a team, or an organization—to manage the tension between individuality and 'groupishness'. Managers, in their position at the boundary between their own particular system and what surrounds it, have always had to manage corresponding tensions at higher levels: between group and group, department and department, organization and environment. This task is becoming ever more difficult as the environment becomes more turbulent and complex. There is a widespread perception that we are living and also operating our businesses in an increasingly hostile and competitive world, without the old pay-offs which used to come from collaboration and self-denial. This contributes to our instinctive retreat into focusing on our own needs and goals, as if we can or should be entirely self-determining. The breaking up of old structures and patterns of relationships can easily foster this state of mind.

As this chapter has sought to demonstrate, however, we can never be simply a loose network of individuals or units. We are interdependent both as regards our conscious strivings, in that we cannot work to achieve our goals without affecting and being affected by the strivings of others, and also because of the unconscious group and intergroup processes in which we get caught up. As Hinshelwood (1998) puts it, we are 'creatures of each other' and we ignore our interdependence at our peril. To recognize it, on the other hand, can bring new rewards as well as new demands, as we rediscover that our feelings and experiences have meaning in a larger—both broader and deeper—context of mutual influences. New patterns of relationship and relatedness become available, helping to counteract the isolation and alienation which can so easily spoil our quality of living.

NOTE

1 This example was first published in Obholzer and Roberts 1994: 132–3.

16

The Team as a Sponge: How the nature of the task affects the behaviour and mental life of a team

Francesca Cardona

INTRODUCTION

In my capacity as organizational consultant to a number of teams in the help-ing professions, I am constantly struck by the fact that similar individuals or groups can behave in extremely diverse ways when working with different client groups.

I describe in this chapter four teams working respectively with chronically mentally ill patients, young people who take drugs, abused children, and ado-lescents. Their contexts, organizational frameworks, and structures are differ-ent, but in each case the flavour of what it is like to work with their client groups comes straight to the centre of the consultancy relationship. There are no screens that can hide the team's experience, if one is prepared to see it. The core of their task is laid bare in front of the consultant.

'The team as a sponge' is a crucial, fascinating, but dangerous area of work and research for the consultant. The term sponge describes the striking way in which the team absorbs and soaks up the central dynamics which operate within its client group, often without realizing that this is happening. This process can also be described as 'mirroring' or 'a reflection process', as in casework supervision, when the relationship between client and worker is reflected in the relationship between worker and supervisor (Mattinson 1992): 'The core idea is that dynamic interactions that belong and originate in one area of relationship are acted out in an adjacent area as though they belong there, being carried from one area to the other by a "player" common to both' (Hughes and Pengelly 1997: 83).

This chapter explores the complexities of dealing with the core issues of an organization in a group setting and of unfolding the team's dilemmas and difficulties in a way that allows them to be worked on. Understanding the 'sponge effect' can be translated into meaningful actions and changes within the team and can help the staff to reach a more mature approach to its task. But the consultant has to be prepared to be a sponge her/himself, to soak up the group's projections, in order to help the staff to identify the main processes affecting them.

Fundamental to this approach is being open to the experience and to the projections of the people to whom you are consulting. This often implies experiencing very uncomfortable feelings. Only through a constant review of the consultant's own feelings and emotions and holding on to the uncertainty of the experience, resisting the pressure of giving immediate answers and advice to the client organization, bearing the anxiety of 'getting nowhere', is it possible to reach some understanding of the underlying dynamics which affect the whole organizational process and uncover the core issues with which organizational members are struggling (Cardona 1995).

When I cross the boundary of an organization that I am consulting to, I am usually full of my own concerns and thoughts which are often completely unrelated to the life of that particular organization or group. I sometimes feel quite unprepared and reluctant to be open to the team's projections, to listen to and tune into what is going on. I know it is going to be difficult, harder than I would like it to be. And then I am suddenly 'hit' by the mood of the group, by their undercurrent. The four examples which follow illustrate what I mean. (In the interests of confidentiality, all names have been changed.)

CASE STUDY A: CHERRY HOUSE

Team A sit with their backs to the wall, waiting for my interventions. They say very little and look at me in a sleepy, absent way, while I struggle to get their attention and to encourage them to reflect on their work and their difficulties.

Team A work in a hostel for chronically mentally ill people. Most of its residents have come directly from the street. Cherry House is often these clients' first permanent home after years of neglect and wandering in and out of psychiatric hospitals. Team A is a 'nice' team: people are kind to each other, to me, and to their manager. Their 'niceness' has a quality of lifelessness, however. People seem unable to present issues and thoughts about their work. I feel the pressure of having to cajole them into engaging with me. I find myself constantly asking questions about their practice and trying to make the situation livelier.

The only time the team come alive is when accidents or crises have occurred. It is as if this gives them an immediate task to deal with rather than having to wait for the inexorable passing of time. Hospitalization of residents is both hoped for and dreaded by the staff. It brings failure as well as respite: failure for having been unable to keep the residents in the community; respite from the boredom and repetitiveness of their tasks and from the exposure to profound disturbance.

A new regime has created a different ethos from the previous one: the emphasis is now on rehabilitating patients, making them more responsible for their lives, encouraging initiatives and collaboration on house tasks with a view to moving most of the residents on to semi-independent accommodation. Dependency is discouraged and a considerable autonomy is seen as the ultimate goal of the team's interventions. Rationally, the staff have accepted and embraced the new approach: they have engaged in the plans and expressed cooperation and interest in the new developments. But in reality they find it incredibly difficult to implement any real change. For example, the plan for residents to organize their meals and participate in the cooking, falls by the wayside. Most of the time, the staff are the ones who do all the work. The dependent relationship at the core of their work does not seem to alter.

> Mary, the deputy manager, wants to talk about rehabilitation. She thinks the staff are not clear about this concept. People do not respond to her request: they want to talk about Karl, a resident who keeps causing problems. 'Karl was almost going to blow up at lunch,' a care worker says. Others do not seem worried: 'He is all right now.' Someone else complains about the hand-over which is not working; relevant information is exchanged informally.
>
> Mary suggests that there were signs of Karl's distress. He talked to himself a lot, put on funny voices, and wet himself. Nobody seemed to notice.
>
> I comment on their wish to keep the situation quiet, to reassure themselves that, on the whole, everything is fine. Having to acknowledge that what happened is not all right would force them to face a number of dilemmas. They have to think of creating a tighter structure around Karl and considering the possibility of discharging him, which they feel quite guilty about.
>
> I pick up an enormous reluctance to make any plan or commitment to change anything: the hand-over, the way the meals are organized, etc. It is as if engaging more with the structures and with the running of the hostel they will lose their 'immunity' to the awfulness of working with such a difficult and disturbing client group.

My experience of the team's passivity and their inability to engage in a dialogue with me mirrors their experience with their static and dependent residents. The staff, too, keep trying to enliven and motivate the residents and to make their lives fuller through rehabilitation plans, activities, and ideas for discharge. Like their residents, they use a passive resistance to my various attempts to review their work practice and to reflect on how the work might be done differently.

Staff talk about the residents as if they were little children who need constant help, guidance, and supervision—if only one could forget their age, their disturbance, and their odd behaviour. It is difficult for them to acknowledge to me and to each other the unpleasantness of working with people who have dropped out of society, who cannot develop proper relationships, and who show so little will to change or to improve. Despite the apparent shift towards active rehabilitation, the staff continue to put most of their effort into maintaining positive relationships with the residents and also with me. This serves to shield them from the full power of the negative and from the fear of a violent eruption, which can jeopardize years of work and put the staff's reputation, as well as their achievements, at risk. The emphasis in Cherry House is on maintaining a good dependent relationship which provides an invisible armour for the staff against the ambivalent feelings about their task.

Winnicott in his seminal (1947) paper, 'Hate in the counter-transference', describes the importance of acknowledging the feelings of hate in the relationship between mother and baby and between therapist and patient. Only when the hate is recognized can the treatment really progress and have an impact. Cherry House staff cannot let their hatred emerge, but denying their negative feelings makes them unable to engage in a more dynamic therapeutic relationship. The team is trapped between two contrasting models of care that E. J. Miller and Gwynne (1972) have vividly described as a 'warehouse' and a 'horticultural' model. Both models can be used to repress hate.

CASE STUDY B: ORCHARD LODGE

Team B are mute. The temporary manager who has represented the team's first experience of good management for a long time is leaving. The group's usually lively meeting is now dead. There are no words to express their feelings of abandonment and worthlessness. There is only emptiness. I seem to be talking to myself.

Orchard Lodge is a therapeutic community for abused children. The unit has a troubled history. It was created twelve years ago with an ambitious brief: to care for and treat young children who have been traumatized in early life by long-term physical and emotional abuse. Its founders 'abandoned' the project early on and left it under the umbrella of an organization with little experience in this field. Orchard Lodge had to struggle for many years to survive in a context of many management changes and constant financial difficulties.

Like children from a 'dysfunctional family', the staff often feel abandoned and unworthy of proper attention, leadership, and care. At the root of their difficulties in creating and maintaining a healthy organization is the unbearable element at the heart of their task: having to deal with the breaking of the ultimate taboo between adults and children, namely child abuse. Often, when faced with an internal crisis, the team react as if they are incapable of exercising control or authority, or as if they are unworthy of proper leadership and guidance.

> The session starts with Mark, a team leader, explaining how difficult it has been during the weekend. The children were restless and it was difficult to contain them. The previous week a manager from headquarters had a meeting at Orchard House to explain the financial difficulties the organization is facing and the need to make savings on all fronts. People report this back in a remarkably calm and thoughtful way. Then there is a short silence and I ask them what are they thinking.
>
> Jane says she feels guilty: she forgot to take the children to therapy twice last week. Other care workers comment that Stephen, the psychotherapist, should remind them and there should be a different system. In Orchard Lodge there are 'the thinkers and the doers', someone says. I suggest that in this case the doers are the care staff who assume their 'role' as parents, and who feel ambivalent about therapy. They often have to convince or drag the children to therapy, maybe having to interrupt something they enjoy doing together. On the other hand, people did not dare to ask the therapist to change some sessions during half-term, which conflicted with an interesting outing, as if there were no possibility of negotiating a different time. The perception and the ambivalence about authority is, in this case, located in the relationship with the therapist, in his role as a senior staff member. The therapist is sabotaged, left waiting and forgotten, while, at the same time, he is experienced as rigid and inflexible. The discussion leads to some awareness of this relationship and the implications for other relations with authority figures within the system; awareness of their constant struggle between sabotage and fear of negotiation.

As Walker points out, 'Adult abuse survivors easily get caught into a generalised feeling that everything is beyond their control, as it was in their childhood, whereas in adulthood some things are not' (Walker 1997: 101). In a similar fashion, Orchard Lodge staff often behave as if they did not have any choice or say in what was happening to the unit. In situations of stress the staff behaviour seems to move between a 'blaming' model—like an abuser 'in search of a victim'—and a hopeless and paralysed model—being the victim—with no sense of worth or of potential effectiveness.

Hughes and Pengelly (1997) use the Karpman (1968) drama triangle, comprising the roles of persecutor, rescuer, and victim, to illustrate the shift of roles between care worker and client and between supervisor and the one who is supervised. In Orchard Lodge this triangular dynamic is emphasized by the nature of the task. Different members of staff and management move constantly between these three positions. I also shift between these three roles, both in terms of my own experience and in the way I am perceived by Orchard Lodge's staff. I find it difficult to stay with these three dimensions and to accept that they are part of my own experience of my role and function, as well as their experience of me.

As I feel deeply committed to the staff's development and growth it is hard not to feel a victim when they describe my sessions as not being effective or if they claim that our work together does not help their practice on the ground. At the same time, it is also easy to be carried away when there are signs of progress in their work and good results with the children. It is hard to resist feeling that my input was the essential ingredient for their development and success.

The aggressive or 'perpetrator' feelings are often a reaction to some of their failings or to the repetitiveness of their dynamics. I then experience a deep wish to dump them or I fantasize that they should close down and end their abortive attempts to make the project work. All these feelings and fantasies are deeply connected with the pain and struggle of their task, with the constant adjustments that have to be made between the possible and the impossible, in relation to the children and to themselves.

The chief motivation for staff to work with this client group is their wish to make an impact, to promote meaningful shifts, to repair some of the damage inflicted on the lives of the children in their care. Some damage is beyond repair but some can be healed. It is the notion that things are still possible that generates hope and creates opportunities for a deeper understanding that can result in some real changes. Sometimes my task is to help the team to move from the area of the possible to the area of the impossible in order to realize that some children in their care cannot be healed, that some irreparable damage has taken place, and that both children and staff must learn to live with it.

CASE STUDY C: HARBOUR CENTRE

Team C eye each other with hostility. Once again, someone is under the spotlight for having done something wrong. People look uncomfortable and angry. There is an atmosphere of blame and a sense of contempt for the hypotheses I put forward.

Harbour Centre provides initial support and information for drug users. It is a relatively new unit which has brought together staff who are used to working autonomously in the community. The team has been 'motherless and homeless' for some time. The original manager left, and for a couple of years there were internal staff difficulties and there was no acting figure of authority either outside or within the system. Rose has recently been appointed as the new team manager. She is experienced in the field and interested in developing the new post but finds it difficult to assert her authority over the team. After a brief honeymoon the team have started to sabotage her initiatives and do not engage with her proposals.

Harbour Centre's core task is to try to introduce users to a network of services which provide treatment and detoxification programmes. The staff come from a 'community culture' where individual staff have learned to rely mainly on their own skills in dealing with very disturbing and complex situations, without the protection of a clearly identifiable organization or of a respected professional status. Being able to work on your own means that you do not have to rely very much on others. It can create the illusion that you do not need others. Like their clients, the staff of Harbour Centre often function in 'survival mode', a sort of street ethos where you can only feel safe if you rely on yourself, since nobody else can really be trusted. This is connected with an anti-authoritarian stance, a strong sense of advocacy in relation to the drug users seen as victims of very difficult circumstances, and a sense of wanting to repair some of the damage inflicted by family and society. And, finally, working independently creates a sense of freedom, of fewer organizational ties, and of less control from the overall system.

When working with drug addiction, staff constantly face issues of trust, dependency, and disruptive behaviour. These issues have been very much at the core of the consultancy process. It has been almost impossible to create an atmosphere of trust in which staff could examine the way they function as a team and accept help in understanding and working through some of their difficulties. Their negative feelings towards each other, their self-centred perspective, and their contempt for my contribution parallel their own experience of working with clients who do not value others and who do not have any sense of worth in themselves.

> Rose, Harbour Centre's team manager, starts the session by expressing her anxiety about Charles, a staff member who, while working with some clients in a council estate, was involved in a confrontation between drug dealers and the police. He was hurt, but not seriously. People ask for details about what happened. Rose knows very little. We discover that she has not managed to ask Charles to report back to her. The need for debriefing in order to understand what happened has been overlooked. Rose's authority and responsibility have not been recognized by the staff or by herself. I point out the need to reclaim responsibility and accountability within the team, together with the need to give Charles support and guidance.
>
> Behind Rose's inability to negotiate with Charles is also her anger with a worker who absconds and behaves in an anarchic and unorthodox way. It is the same worker who sits, session after session, always with his coat and hat on, regarding my efforts to consult to the team with scorn and contempt. He is the one who often ends the sessions for me and who laughs and giggles with his pal or adopts quite threatening behaviour. At the end of this session Rose and the other staff are more aware of the part they play in avoiding control and of the risks of relinquishing their authority and responsibility.

Although staff are often at the receiving end of abusive and aggressive behaviour, feelings of hatred towards their clients never come up in the sessions. The staff's hatred is often displaced in their relationships with each other, with management, and with myself. I often feel unheard, unappreciated, and not worthy of their trust, which I relate to their experience with the drug users, in a context where there is no sense of a benign authority nor of positive dependency. We see here a situation of fear of dependency in an environment where dependency is associated with something bad (the drugs), which makes you unable to lead an independent and full life.

'There is a vast difference between those patients who have had satisfactory early experiences which can be discovered in the transference and those whose very early experiences have been so deficient and distorted that the analyst has to be the first in the patient's life to supply certain environmental essentials' (Winnicott 1947: 198). What Winnicott describes has strong similarities with my work with Harbour Centre's team. Their primary experience has been of 'organizational deprivation' where there has been no 'good experience' of management or of organizational life.

Reflecting, looking critically and constructively at their practice, is a virtually impossible task. Occasionally people do make a small shift: the blame on one member of staff is defused, someone shares some difficult feelings about a client, the manager plans a Friday meeting for hand-over of the most difficult cases. However, the fundamental inability to think does not change and I struggle to maintain my clarity of thought.

The pervasive effect of their attacks on the setting and on myself stays with me during the week, and I often dread going back. It is the hopelessness and the self-disruptiveness of the drug addiction which contaminate any attempt to develop a relationship. My attempt to provide the 'environmental essentials' does not get very far. I can only survive their attacks and feed back to them what I think is going on.

My attempts to help the Harbour team to see the 'sponge effect' in the dynamic of their relationships were not successful. Maybe that mirrored too their working situation where the success rate is very low.

CASE STUDY D: IVY STREET

Team D are arguing about who has the vision of the organization and who is entitled to decide their approach and working methods. The positions are rigid and dogmatic: everyone knows best; there is no space for differences.

Ivy Street is a day centre which provides counselling for adolescents. The manager, Lucy, has been in her post for many years and has developed a distinctive approach to intervention with adolescents. This specific approach is not officially acknowledged: staff are implicitly expected to work in a particular way without any clear recognition of what it is. Lucy and her deputy have great faith in this approach, which they regard as unique and the best available. They think it provides containment and support through its setting of tight boundaries and well-thought-out principles. The manager is the main source of supervision and expertise in the centre. The use of different methods or external interventions is not only discouraged, but almost forbidden. Differences of opinion are not taken on board because their method is seen as the only effective way of engaging young people in treatment and counselling. Inevitably, staff are resentful about not having a voice and not being able to influence the development of their practice.

The development of a centralized approach seemed necessary because many staff were either part-time or very inexperienced and because Ivy Street workers were spread throughout a large geographical area. However, the centralization of expertise in one person has created a dependency culture, with very little sense that staff can grow or develop. Internal negotiations are very difficult: there is tension and conflict between the manager and the staff. Each side is unable to see the other's point of view. This dynamic mirrors perfectly the ambivalence of parents who cannot trust adolescents to find their own way, and the core dilemma for parents of how to balance necessary limit-setting and guidance with space for individual discovery. There is an atmosphere in Ivy Street of a closed system, with no nourishment coming from outside.

From the beginning, I felt that I was walking in a minefield, and that I had to guard myself from the traps of a 'family dispute'. I had to be very careful to keep my distance and my boundary position. At the same time, I felt the pain that this family dispute was creating among staff members, particularly in the 'parental' pair, Lucy and her deputy. I have been constantly struck by the fundamentalist tone of the debate within the Ivy Street team and by the deep antagonism between the 'faithful' and the 'unfaithful': the 'faithful' being those who consider their approach unique and irreplaceable (mainly the manager and her deputy); the 'unfaithful' those who want change, different input, and even a new leadership.

This unique culture reflects one of the central dynamics of adolescence: the need for dogma and absolute certainty in a context of profound psychological and physical changes. The impulses of adolescence and emergent sexuality are rigidly controlled by a dogmatic culture. Adolescents' uncertainties and conflicting needs about life and the future are channelled in a rigid container. Differences are too complex to be tolerated. Diversity of opinion is experienced and practised as 'delinquency' or rebellion by staff and management. There is a sense of claustrophobia when there does not seem to be space for different views. I feel compelled both to take sides and to observe in a neutral capacity, as if making connections and being able to see different points of views is a very dangerous business. Dogmatism and rigidity become defences which seem to make the uncertainties and responsibilities of moving into adulthood more bearable.

The way the manager and her deputy perceive criticism and requests for change from the staff, and the way the need for change is put forward by the staff, have the dramatic tones of a Greek tragedy, of an impending catastrophe, as if only by 'killing the parents' will the young person develop a separate identity. In discussing Bion's ideas on 'catastrophic change' (Bion 1970), Copley describes 'how change that is necessary for growth can be dreaded and disruptive to the group . . . the idea necessary for change needs to be made available for use without implementation of the accompanying sense of catastrophe arising from the dynamic disruptive impact of the new alongside the old' (Copley 1993: 27–8). There is little room for negotiation where parents and children—managers and staff—can collaborate. My task as a consultant is to enable the team to separate the ideas for change from the associated idea of catastrophe: that is, to be the guardian of a potential space (Winnicott 1971) where some negotiation and mutual understanding can take place.

HOW THIS APPROACH CAN BE USED BY MANAGERS TO RUN HEALTHIER AND MORE EFFECTIVE ORGANIZATIONS

The organizations I have been describing are very different, as are my relationships with them. Their circumstances vary enormously as regards their structures and resources, the therapeutic potential of their interventions, and the quantity and quality of disturbance of their client groups. An understanding of the sponge effect, of the projections coming from the client group, can only work and be effective in a context where the majority of people involved have a sense of structure, roles, and accountability. This is not easy in a world where organizations are no longer able any more to provide enough containment for negative projections and do not provide a dependable environment (E. J. Miller 1993c; Stokes 1994). It is the managers who increasingly have to provide that containment and support while being able to tolerate negative projections from staff as well as clients.

Managers of Cherry House, Orchard Lodge, Harbour Centre, and Ivy Street have a great deal of responsibility and not much authority to go with it. In other words, they are answerable for their units but do not have the right to make the ultimate decision or to make decisions which are binding on others (Obholzer 1994). They have to juggle scarce resources, regulate pressures and requests from the client group, and respond to demands from staff in order to provide better support and provision for them. The manager's role requires being inside the system, having an in-depth understanding of the clients' and staff's needs, and being sufficiently outside to get an overall view of the organization in its environment. In other words the manager has to hold what E. J. Miller described as a 'boundary position'. It is a difficult role to perform competently. It requires both paternal and maternal skills, an ability to move constantly between inside and outside the system, great resilience to pressure and demand, self-containment, and some capacity to be alone.

Consultancy can enhance these skills and can be an essential key to understanding what is required for holding this inside/outside position. It requires an ability to bear people's negative feelings to help staff to stay in touch with the essence of their job. In a similar way, managers should be able to develop an ability to tolerate their staff's projections while maintaining a boundary position.

To facilitate this process, my consultancy to teams in the helping professions always includes separate sessions with the team manager. The individual session provides the manager with an opportunity to look at the team's issues in a more systemic way, to look more directly at his or her role and function, and to address problems that it might not be possible to raise in the group session. The intention of this session is to support and model the manager's inside/outside position and to offer a specific place for looking at the sponge effect within the organization as a whole.

The new manager of Orchard Lodge, the therapeutic community for abused children, is now in place. He has to face a number of problems. For instance, three staff members have resigned and seem very reluctant to engage in a formal leaving process. All three are off sick and do not seem able to return. The team are furious with them but seem powerless and unable to take any action. We explore in the group sessions what happened and the possible reasons behind the three staff members' difficulties in saying goodbye properly.

The same theme is explored with the manager, who appears very eager to negotiate with the three staff but finds it difficult to adopt a firmer position towards them. I realize how strong my wish is to force the 'absconders' to come back. I fantasize about retaliating against them, whereas the manager seems much more in touch with understanding and forgiving feelings. The children have been calmer since his arrival. There has not been any serious acting out or disruptive behaviour.

The staff express anger and resistance to yet another change of management through absconding and being disruptive. In the individual sessions, we look at the manager's own difficulties in taking a firmer stance, at his need to be perceived as a good and caring manager. He begins to see how difficult it is for anyone openly to assume a more clearly authoritative role for fear of being perceived as a potential negative figure or 'perpetrator'. I manage to see from my own feelings how strong the wish is to punish, to retaliate, which is the dynamic the manager tries to keep at bay with his soft approach. Eventually all three staff members come back, however briefly, to say goodbye to staff and children.

The session with the manager is a role consultancy firmly linked to the organization in which both the role and the organization are in focus. Staff who are struggling to recognize differences and diversities between themselves do not find it easy to accept this model of intervention. There is often a fear of an unhealthy and collusive alliance between consultant and manager. In reality, the model strengthens the alliance between consultant and manager in relation to the organization's task and can provide a better holding of the consultancy process. This model should help the managers to make use of what Keats has described as 'negative capability', a particular ability to 'be' in the middle of uncertainty without pressing for certainties, facts, and answers (Keats 1817; Lanzara 1993).

CONCLUSIONS

The approach to consultancy described in this chapter is based on the concept that the experience projected on to and into the consultant is a fundamental tool that can be used to understand some of the central issues which affect the life of an organization: the capacity to listen to one's own experience, to hear the message coming from the client, is central to such consultancy work. This is also true for staff and managers of organizations: if they are able to identify some of the projections coming from clients, they are much more likely to be in touch with the core issues of the task they are trying to perform.

These organizations work with client groups that society tends to forget and to exclude, or who are mainly remembered when a major crisis or violent episode occurs. In simplistic terms it could be said that society wants to lock away the mad, punish the abusers, clean up the drug addicts, be tough with difficult adolescents. The organizations I have described have to soak up the powerful dynamic of their clients' systems: the passivity and disengagement of the chronically mentally ill; the sense of worthlessness and betrayal of abused children; the desperate anger and self-destructiveness of drug addicts; the arrogance and dogmatism of adolescents. In addition, these organizations have to deal with the projections and expectations that society puts into them: they are expected to contain, to treat, to detoxify, to support. In essence, they are expected to protect and purify society from the negative and disruptive dynamics that these client groups inevitably bring with them.

When teams and managers are able to identify some of these dynamics and disentangle themselves from the web and the power of their effect, they can leave their 'psychic prisons' (Morgan 1986), they can free some energy to engage with the task in a more effective and creative way. They can also recognize that understanding what is happening to them is the key to the treatment of their client groups.

17

After the Conference is Over

Sheila Ramsay

INTRODUCTION

I have a vivid memory from the first time I was a member of the Leicester conference on 'Leadership, Authority and Organization' sponsored by the Group
Relations Training Programme of the Tavistock Institute of Human Relations.
Sitting in my room at the end of a long day I had the sudden realization that 'I
can't unlearn this', although at that point I could not articulate exactly what
'this' was. I realized however that my understanding of how organizations
worked, and how I related to them and to the roles I held within them, was irrev-
ocably changed. This realization was both exciting and frightening because it
meant that my way of working and being in those organizations would also
change, with unknowable consequences. Sixteen years on from that conference, with considerably more experience both of group relations work and of
being in different roles in organizations, including senior management roles, I
am aware of how that learning is integral to how I go about my daily business
and take up my role in my work situation. And yet, trying to relate exactly how I
have used the learning from my conference experiences feels like an elusive and
complex task. Nevertheless it is important, when thinking about the development of group relations work, to try to describe how conference members
might be able to take their learning back into their organizational worlds after
the conference is over.

The membership of group relations conferences is varied, with members
coming from business, social services, education, psychiatry and psychotherapy, the church, and the police, to name just some of the professional backgrounds. There is also a growing number of people who are independent or
self-employed consultants. In their organizations members may have the roles
of consultants, therapists, teachers, advisers, policy makers, or managers. For
the purposes of this chapter I am particularly interested in looking at the experiences of those who are managers. My examples are taken from my experience

in social welfare agencies, though I believe that the processes and issues referred to have parallels in most organizations.

THE CONFERENCE AND AUTHORITY

Group relations conferences have now been taking place for approximately forty years, the first Leicester Conference having taken place in 1957. There is now a wide network of organizations, both in the UK and internationally, which sponsor and run conferences based on the 'Leicester Model'. Although there are some variations in design, they share the same theoretical foundations and focus, which is the application of psychoanalytic thought and an open systems approach to understanding organizations. Eric Miller, in his account of the history and development of group relations conferences, describes the Leicester Conference as having 'a specific focus on learning about the nature of authority and the problems encountered in its exercise' (Miller 1989: 8). It is this focus on the nature of authority that will be explored in this chapter.

What all the conferences share is an emphasis on the study of unconscious processes which take place at individual, group, and organizational levels, often also linking this to the societal context within which the conference is taking place. The methodology is to use the conference itself as a temporary educational institution for the object of study. Thus members are given the task of studying their own participation in creating, maintaining, and changing the institution's culture and of understanding their responsibility for what happens within it. Members need therefore to demonstrate a willingness to try to understand their own and others' behaviour at an unconscious as well as a conscious and concrete level. Thus the emotional life of the institution becomes available for examination in such a way that its integral contribution to the concrete behaviour of individuals and groups within their organizational roles can be directly and powerfully experienced. Staff in the conferences take on consultant roles within the various events, but also act as collective management. Management in this case means being responsible for creating the conditions in which members can engage with the task. Members are expected to use their own authority for deciding how to do this. The model of management which is experienced is one of managing boundary conditions rather than people and their behaviour.

The way in which staff members carry out their management responsibility is to create the boundary structures within which members can learn, if they choose to do so, and to stay within and work from the roles they have taken up. This requires staff to be alert to their own experiences within the different events. The feelings which are generated are not seen as a distraction from the task but, to the contrary, provide invaluable data for understanding the unconscious aspects of the organizational behaviour which is emerging. When the staff member is then able to offer an interpretation of this behaviour, as revealing the unconscious systemic process taking place, members have the opportunity to build on this in furthering their own understanding. This may itself effect a change in the process. In this way staff and membership work together to create a temporary educational institution, where understanding the process of this creation is itself the main task of the conference. A crucial aspect of management by the staff is therefore to maintain the boundaries of the events—that is, of time, territory, and task—and to stay within and work from the staff role. This role is likely to come under various forms of attack, which can be angry and overt, or more subtle through idealization or attempts to seduce into membership. The model of management which is experienced is one of reflection, interpretation, and containment.

Within this context, leadership is exercised when members speak to their here-and-now experience of being in the member role. Others can then link that to their own experiences, building the learning that becomes available. Doing this carries a risk of rejection or envious attack or, on the other hand, of a mindless followership who dependently cling on to an idea—from which they can then dissociate themselves if it does not work. The possibility is that members may use their authority to exercise both positive and authoritative leadership and followership.

In the beginning stages of conferences, the way of working can seem alien and the level of attention paid to unconscious processes can generate anxiety. The conference is seen as a risky place. This often leads to some members (on behalf of the whole membership) questioning the validity of the method, with consultants being experienced as manipulative or speaking a strange psychological language. There are frequently angry statements that this is not the 'real world'. At some point during the conference, however, some members will begin to connect their conference experience with their lives in their outside institutions, even though it might at this stage be difficult to articulate or make rational sense of the connection. There comes a realization that what they are experiencing within the conference are exactly the same processes that take place in the 'real world'.

Towards the end of the conference 'Application' events are held which allow members to think about the connections between their conference experience and their home institutions. It might be expected that being back on familiar territory would make these sessions easier and less anxiety provoking than the here-and-now events. However, they are often very difficult. Members will offer one another highly competent consultations on the work problems which have been raised, but without making direct links with their experiences within the conference. They can equally begin to reflect on and understand some of their conference experiences. However, the link with the outside seems to be felt but hard to articulate or examine. It is not unusual to find in the closing plenaries that members are expressing considerable anxiety about returning to their outside institutions. The conference, which had been so risky, is now seen as home, and the 'real world' to which members are returning is perceived as threatening and unsafe. Within the final plenary there is often an element of idealization of the conference experience, which is evidence of a need to keep that experience as an idealized object so that it can be kept safe from attack. This might itself be an expression of the anxiety felt about the difficulty of holding on to the learning from the conference back in one's own organization and its fragility in an uncomprehending or hostile environment.

A manager who returns from a group relations conference is therefore returning from a culture where, unlike most work contexts, success in undertaking the task of the organization is seen to depend crucially on understanding the unconscious meaning of behaviour and the exercise of authority in the various roles one takes up.

THE ORGANIZATION AND AUTHORITY

Like most organizations, social welfare agencies in the UK have experienced enormous structural and cultural change over the past ten years. Indeed a process of continuous change within a turbulent environment is now the norm. One of the most profound changes has been the move towards a contractual relationship between purchasers and providers of services. This contract culture is all pervasive. It applies whether the provider is a voluntary charitable or private agency, whose services are purchased by local or central government, or the provider section of a local authority or health board in an internal market. The growing emphasis on value for money and performance measurement, along with the import of concepts like total quality management from business and manufacturing, have produced fundamental changes in the culture of such organizations. In addition, the reduction and tighter control of resources, both in the public and voluntary sectors, has resulted in a much less secure environment for employees. This in turn has required a shift in the ways that management and leadership are understood.

I have suggested elsewhere (Feuchtwang and Ramsay 1995) that social welfare organizations are unconsciously needed to offer total containment of the ambivalent and confused feelings held by wider society about the groups of people with whom they work. In other words, the guilt, rage, and impotence felt towards abused children (or groups such as the mentally ill, demented elderly, or offenders) are projected into the institutions which work with them. At an unconscious level, they are expected to keep these feelings within the organizational system, as securely as the people themselves were once kept in the total institutions which used to be located behind high walls and locked doors.

To be able to do this work on behalf of society, the organization then needs to construct its own internal defence system. We hypothesized that the constructs of the contract culture itself provide this. Thus a fantasy is created, which we describe as the omnipotent deification of conscious activity where all there is is behaviour which can be changed to the required specifications. The contract or service level agreement which specifies objective outcomes and performance indicators linked to targets can provide the reassurance that something can be done. A quality assurance scheme linked to this provides the containing ritual in specifying activities which involve staff, and often service users, in maintaining a culture of measurable achievement. (Feuchtwang and Ramsay 1995: 15.)

The effect on managers in this kind of culture is an instrumental retreat into technique, where conscious motivation and intent are all. 'Irrational' behaviour or resistance becomes located in individuals who are then seen as problematic or in need of help themselves (possibly through a staff counselling scheme), or as technical problems with a mechanistic solution. This process is not unique to one type of organization. An example is the experience, common in organizations, where persistent and recurring difficulties in implementing a change are seen as being due to poor and inadequate communication.

However, often all attempts by management to improve communication through new ways of distributing information or structural changes, involving people in consultative forums, still fail to achieve commitment to the desired change. A more productive way forward might be for the manager to try to understand and form a hypothesis about what unconscious purpose might be being served by poor communication. This could be a difficult and painful process as it would necessitate owning one's own resistance and fears about change which might be contributing to the sabotage within the system. However, offering this interpretation in a way which acknowledges and legitimizes the anxiety being felt, without either being overwhelmed by it or surrendering one's own management role, could enable unconscious anxiety to be known and therefore addressed. It might then be possible to communicate the real need for change.

In the 1990s there has been an emphasis within organizations and management development training on leadership, as defined in terms of exceptional or charismatic individuals. The management role, on the other hand, is increasingly reduced to a collection of tools and techniques—an off-the-shelf solution for every eventuality. Krantz and Gilmore have written about the resulting split between leadership and management, where one of these aspects is idealized while the other is denigrated. They suggest that this split 'constitutes an attack on the critical function of leadership to link means to ends' and that this is itself a defensive process resulting from the overwhelming anxiety generated by the extent of the changes within both the internal and external environments of organizations (Krantz and Gilmore 1990: 189).

I perceive a similar process underlying how authority is understood within this kind of organizational culture, with the split between personal and organizational authority mirroring that between leadership and management. The concept of personal authority is subsumed into the idealization of the inspirational and motivational leader, whereas organizational authority is associated with outdated notions of hierarchy and status. This devalues the strength and effectiveness that result when someone operates at a high level of personal competence, in a clear and confident understanding of their role within their work system. Larry Gould offers a useful examination of organizational and personal authority. He defines organizational authority as 'the authority that is delegated to roles, and therefore gives the role occupant the right to work', whereas personal authority is 'a central aspect of one's enduring sense of self no matter what role one may occupy. It is therefore defined as the "right to be"—that is, the right to exist fully and to be oneself in the role' (L. J. Gould 1993: 51).

If someone is confident in the exercise of his or her personal authority but is unclear about his or her role in relation to the total system, then that person will find it difficult to work in a fully competent way. This does not mean that the person will be totally ineffective, but he or she will be vulnerable as an individual and his or her ideas and actions can be marginalized. Ideas, decisions, and actions have to be connected to and in furtherance of the primary task of the organization, and it is the role that links the individual to that task and legitimizes his or her actions (Larry Gould's 'right to work').

If those in leadership or management roles are clear about their organizational authority but lack confidence in their personal authority, or exercise it inappropriately, they are unlikely to offer leadership in the organization, or may do so in the authoritarian manner which is often confused with real authority. This splitting of personal and organizational authority tends to be accompanied by an idealization of the first and denigration of the latter and so contributes to the split between leadership and management. Leadership becomes a characteristic of charismatic individuals and management a collection of pragmatic problem-solving tools and techniques.

The defensive wish to see processes only in their concrete manifestations, which can be manipulated and changed, is also demonstrated in an increasing trend in organizations to try to improve team functioning by using one of the many exercises which help to identify personality types or styles of working (for example, the Myers–Briggs Inventory, the Belbin Team Roles Inventory, or the Margerison–McCann Team Management System). Although these may be useful in looking at the range of skills and preferences available in a team and in identifying gaps, they rarely offer insight into the unconscious processes which are hindering the effective performance of the task. 'Differences in style' can provide an explanation congruent with the prevalent cognitive culture, in the hope that difficulties can be dealt with through some kind of behaviour modification. Painful and threatening feelings of dependency, rivalry, and envy can continue to be denied and remain unavailable for examination and reflection. The exercise of both the personal and organizational role authority of team members is undermined as the complexity of managing the boundary between one's internal world and one's work role is unrecognized.

FROM CONFERENCE TO ORGANIZATION: MAKING THE LINK

Group relations conferences offer the opportunity both to experience and to reflect on our unconscious anxieties and how these influence our behaviour. However, it is possible for members to move beyond just a better understanding of group and institutional behaviour, valuable though this may be, to developing their competence in taking responsibility for their individual part in that process and using it to enhance the performance of the task. At its most useful the learning becomes integrated into how one perceives, understands, and acts at both a personal and a systemic level.

The risk when returning from a conference to one's own organization, especially as a manager, is that a culture of measurable performance, predetermined outcomes, and management by technique will not provide the necessary containing environment for the continuation of the individual's learning and its subsequent import into the system within which he or she works. On one level the sharing of learning in an organization is currently a widely promoted concept (see Senge 1990). This could be seen as indicative of a willingness in organizations to welcome new ideas, thoughts, and behaviour. However, Long and Newton have taken a psychoanalytic perspective of learning in organizations which sees Senge's ideas as located within that same concrete and rational world to which I have referred above. They describe Senge's idea of a 'learning organization' as one which takes 'a cognitive approach which denies the strength of the unconscious hatred of learning. It is as if we could change any situation if only we could see the broader picture like a map. It is made without exploring or even acknowledging the feelings people have about their dependence before creating new inter-dependencies . . . Managing uncertainty becomes a question of systems control' (Long and Newton 1995: 7). There is a wish to learn in a way which reframes or manipulates meaning without experiencing one's own dependency, envy, aggression, and so on, and having to take responsibility for how one deals with such feelings.

In these circumstances the risk is that the learning brought back from a group relations conference is used defensively, or becomes locked in the conference experience. In this case, conference learning becomes just another (but still useful) tool to add to the management tool kit, thereby colluding with the split between management and leadership. One might gain a clearer perception and understanding of the unconscious processes being enacted but then use this in a defensive way or in an attempt to protect one's own position, rather than in pursuit of the task. Alternatively, the memory of a similar process from a conference might simply be transferred into the workplace and interpreted in the same way. This might offer an alternative and possibly helpful view but it will remain at a theoretical level and therefore encourage a technical response. By contrast, an interpretation that comes out of one's own direct here-and-now experience is more likely to authentically address the uniquely immediate process taking place in the system. In this case, the learning from a conference has become integrated into how one understands what is happening at both an instrumental and emotional level.

One fundamental aspect of the conference that managers might bring back into their own workplaces therefore is that of paying constant attention to one's here-and-now experience and using that to contribute to building an understanding of the state of the system one is in and its relationship across the boundary with its external environment. The importance of conceptualizing management as a role on the boundary of a system might seem obvious. However, when management has become a problem-solving and performance-measurement function, the meaning of being a manager on the boundary of a particular system at a particular time remains unexplored. How one is being used in one's role is a significant piece of information which could give important clues about the unconscious dynamics within the organization and between the organization and its external environment. Often, this dynamic process is predominantly about avoiding anxiety by setting up various defence mechanisms. Offering an interpretation of one's experience in the management role can help identify these processes, bring them into conscious awareness, and allow them to be addressed. Once people can acknowledge the anxiety, they can then begin to understand it and find ways of managing it, rather than deny it. Thus, taking a consultative stance from within the management role can enable a shift to take place which could not have been achieved through a technical approach which only addressed the concrete manifestation of an unconscious process. Sharing one's emotional experience is risky, and to do so in a reflective way is to exercise one's personal authority. Moving this from the realm of the personal to the systemic can link it to the authority of the role in a way which furthers the task.

During a conference, members are likely to gain insight into their own personal unconscious anxieties and motivations and how these influence their behaviour, but this is for private reflection. The focus is not on the individual's personality, and consultants will only interpret individual behaviour within the context of how it might be representing an aspect of the unconscious emotional life of the group. It is therefore not possible to explain away difficulties in group functioning by blaming them on personality clashes or incompatibility. It might well be that two members have very different personalities, or a different approach to forming relationships, or opposing views on controversial issues. The interventions of the consultant will attempt to look beyond (or below) this, in order to understand how the conflict or clash is serving the unconscious need of the group.

This is in contrast to the trend referred to above to improve team functioning by identifying personality types and styles of working. Self-knowledge is not the same as taking responsibility for one's own personal psyche which includes, of course, how one is contributing to the group process through managing one's internal world. This is an essential element in the exercise of authority. Self-awareness and personal insight are inextricably linked to being confident in our personal authority; self-awareness in our role underpins our competence in exercising our organizational authority.

CASE EXAMPLES

The following two case examples are taken from my own experience as manager and as consultant. The first shows how reaching an understanding of the unconscious meaning of an organizational issue enabled significant movement to take place in a process that appeared to be stuck. The second demonstrates how a focus on personality variables and styles of working became a defence against confronting real differences and rivalries in a team.

Example 1: Forms, lists, and tick boxes

In my role as a regional manager within a large childcare organization, I was delighted when there was a significant decentralization of corporate services from national headquarters to the regions. This was accompanied by a downward shift of authority with much wider decision-making responsibility being passed from national to regional managers. Initially, this seemed to be accomplished relatively easily and was a change welcomed by most people in all parts of the organization. After a while, however, my colleagues and I began to notice the increasing number of requests for information which were landing on our desks from headquarters. The purpose of these requests was never very clear and soon they began to expand into checklists and monitoring forms. This was accompanied by a growth in the number of areas where formal policies were requested. For a while, I dealt with this growth in bureaucracy either by providing the information in a perfunctory and minimalist way, accompanied by much complaining, or by ignoring the requests. The level of irritation in the regional management team grew and we started to make angry protests to the national management team. There was an acknowledgement that some of the requests were unreasonable and we were assured that the demands would be reduced. They were for a short while but then built up again.

One day a very large and, to my mind, unnecessary monitoring form arrived at a time when I was particularly busy. My first reaction was to tear it up in irritation. However, I suddenly found myself thinking about the number of phone calls I had made that week to a team which was currently working with a family where there were serious concerns about possible child abuse. I had confidence in the competence of the staff and knew the team manager would contact me if she needed to consult me, and yet I had still not successfully resisted making all those phone calls. Providing services to vulnerable and troublesome children is by its nature a risky business. Most of the time I was not consciously over-anxious, believing that we had highly competent staff, good supervision systems, and helpful procedures. I was not preoccupied with the knowledge that, despite all this, tragedies can still happen; but at that moment I was suddenly feeling almost overwhelming anxiety and my mind became full of all the things that could possibly go wrong, resulting in disaster.

Eventually these feelings abated and the nagging anxiety, which had been building up for a while and of which I had not been conscious until that point, lessened considerably. I realized that it was the receipt of the 'trivial' and 'unnecessary' monitoring form that had brought these feelings to my conscious awareness. I had successfully projected on to headquarters my deep anxiety about our work, and with it the fantasy that, if I knew more, there was less chance of anything going wrong. I decided that, rather than tear up the form or begrudgingly fill it in, I would describe my experience to the person from whom it had originated. I phoned him and told him about my feelings and consequent reflection when I had received the form. I suggested that, being even further removed from direct service delivery than we were in the regional management team, he must experience anxiety about what could go wrong which must sometimes be very difficult to deal with, to the extent that most of the time it was unconscious. I asked him whether he thought the bureaucratic demands were part of a fantasy that it was possible to know enough to ensure that tragedies did not happen. Clearly the changes that had been made in the devolving of authority might have increased the level of anxiety, as it involved a lessening of control. His response was thoughtful and he acknowledged that he was finding it difficult to adapt to the changes, even though he knew they were necessary and had been active in making them happen. The conversation felt helpful to us both. (We enjoyed a good working relationship and I knew that my comments would not be dismissed out of hand.)

At the next regional management team meeting I asked if we could talk about the risk and danger of some of the work that we did, and how we found the balance between supporting project staff and interfering in their work. How did we contain the anxiety generated without its becoming overwhelming? We realized that we had never overtly talked about that before and it felt tremendously liberating.

The issue of how to manage the anxiety which was inherent in the work that we do became the topic of extensive discussion within the region, between the management team and the different services and between the service teams themselves. It was an energizing process that helped us to acknowledge the excellent work that was done while accepting that the possibility of disaster would always be there. We also made several changes in our reporting and monitoring procedures which resulted in less bureaucracy at the regional level. (In the mirroring process that pervades organizations, our service managers experienced the same irritating bureaucratic demands from us that we complained about from headquarters.) It became possible to have a dialogue with the national managers about the demands made on us and this began to involve the other regions. The bureaucracy did not disappear (there will always be anxiety in the system) but it certainly dramatically reduced, and concerns and worries could be more openly addressed, with beneficial effects on the quality of work done with children and families.

We had all been caught in an unconscious defensive system and only by recognizing this and consciously addressing the anxiety could anything change. Being reflective about experience and sharing a possible interpretation enabled a significant change in a system.

Example 2: It's all a matter of style

I was acting as a consultant to a senior management team in a local authority social work department whose responsibility was for the residential units and children and family teams within the authority. I knew from other work I had done in the department that there was increasing unhappiness among the heads of the units and teams about the overall management of childcare services. The unit heads felt that the ways in which they were managed varied greatly between the different members of the management team. Some managers were experienced at enabling and allowing the unit and team heads the authority to manage their teams, others were felt to be intrusive and interfering, leaving the unit heads unsure of what authority they had. There was a general unspecified sense of dissatisfaction with the director for not being clear enough about how she felt the section should be managed.

The management team had a clear vision for how they wanted the section to develop and had demonstrable skills in strategic planning. I was struck by the absence of conflict in their meetings. Disagreements were aired in a very rational and adult manner with sensible decisions being reached. The meetings were very task-centred, competently chaired by the director, but there was a sense of flatness about them. I found myself with little to say in the first few meetings and was aware of only having quite bland feelings. After one meeting I found myself thinking, 'It's as if there was no unconscious life in this group'. At the same time, I was aware of the dissatisfaction among the unit and team heads.

In a meeting with the director prior to starting the consultancy, she told me that the team had done quite a lot of work identifying their different styles of working and the roles they tended to take on in the team. They had spent an away-day doing the Myers–Briggs Inventory and had found this very helpful in understanding the differences that sometimes emerged between team members. They were also able to look at the best combinations of people to work together on different kinds of tasks. At another away-day a year later, they had worked with the Margerison–McCann Team Management System which had also helped them to look at the different skills which lay in the team and to identify their particularly strong and weak areas. Both of these days had clearly been helpful and positive experiences and had enabled them to think quite creatively about how they worked together and how they allocated tasks. However, I began to realize that, having identified and talked abut their different styles, they had now accepted 'style' as the reason for all differences between them. Also, as a 'style' was largely seen as a personal attribute, it became impossible to criticize or comment on how someone carried out their management role as this could be seen as a personal attack. Thus, all styles were seen as equally valid and appropriate, and differences remained at a conscious cognitive level. In this way unconscious feelings such as dependency, rivalry, and envy remained unavailable and therefore unexplored.

At the next meeting, there was a discussion about a difficulty in one of the units. Some of the unit staff had complained about the unit head, saying he was not demonstrating clear leadership, which left them unsure of what was expected of them. Consequently there was no consistency in the way the children who were resident in the unit experienced the expectations of staff. The member of the management team responsible for the unit described how he intended to respond to this and a fairly low-key discussion ensued. The director was silent during this discussion and I began to feel a desperate wish for her to speak.

The discussion was beginning to feel strained, repetitive, and anxious and I was now feeling angry with the director for her silence. I suggested to the group that the anxiety which had crept into the discussion might be because they recognized that the lack of consistency experienced by the children in the unit was mirroring the lack of consistency experienced by the unit and team heads from them as a management team. I said that there might be anger with the director for not telling them which particular management style she thought was best, in the same way that the unit staff were angry with their head. One of the team members agreed with this and said he sometimes felt uneasy about the differences within the team but felt that how colleagues managed their units was not really his business. If the director was happy with it then that was okay. The director became angry at this and said that she felt the team had a collective responsibility for managing the services but that they never expressed disagreement between themselves about how the units should be managed. I suggested that if they moved away from thinking about 'style' and looked at how they saw the management task, differences might not be so threatening, as they became less personal. They were then able to begin to talk about their relationships with their unit heads and how they viewed their respective roles.

In future meetings, competition and rivalries began to emerge and, although this caused anxiety, it was manageable. This, in turn, led to emerging differentiation in their relationships with one another, including with the director. These became available for examination and therefore less frightening than they had been as unconscious fantasies. In a strangely topsy-turvy way, the identification of differing styles of working had allowed the existence of an unconscious myth that there were no differences between them. All styles were equal and therefore they were all the same. Differences in experience and competence could not be acknowledged and therefore a major area of possible learning was closed off.

Shortly after this, I was no longer able to offer consultancy to this group. This occurred at a time when they were beginning to be able to look at their relationships with their unit heads and to involve the unit heads in this process.

In both of these examples, the real anxieties underlying behaviour were being denied and a great deal of energy was going into maintaining the defensive system allowing this denial. When the real anxieties were identified and the defensive process understood, it was possible to return to authentic engagement with the primary task and for managers to regain their authority and competence.

CONCLUSION

The shape and structure of organizations is changing. Downsizing and delayering may have been the euphemisms of the 1980s and 1990s to deny the sometimes devastating effect of the changes, but there is now hardly an organization in existence which is untouched by them. Rapid advances in information technology have accelerated the pace of our work while changing the framework of social relations in the workplace. Hierarchies still exist, but more fluid networks across more permeable boundaries are as significant as vertical lines of accountability. The anxiety generated by these changes can threaten to overwhelm us, and the defences we then create, while offering an illusion of control, can in themselves undermine our competence, as energy is diverted into the maintenance of the defensive system, rather than engagement with the task of the organization.

Within this context a skilled manager is one who enables others to be confident in the exercise of both their personal and organizational authority. This requires a well-developed capacity to tolerate anxiety, a constant alertness to one's own feelings, reactions, and experiences and to those of others, and the ability to think systemically. Where there are no longer rigid or fixed hierarchies and vertical structures, a reflective, interpretative, and containing management is essential. Leadership can then emerge from the integration of both personal and organizational authority and survive the envious attacks which it will inevitable attract.

Group relations conferences offer important opportunities to learn about these processes and develop these skills. However, their real value comes after the conference is over and members continue the learning back in their organizational roles.

BIBLIOGRAPHY

AGAZARIAN, Y. M. (1994). 'The phases of group development and the systems-centred group', in V. L. Schermer and M. Pines (eds.), *Ring of Fire: Primitive Affects and Object Relations in Group Psychotherapy*. London/New York: Routledge, 36–85.

ARGYRIS, C. (1982). *Reasoning, Learning and Action*. San Francisco: Jossey-Bass.

—— (1994). 'Good communication that blocks learning', *Harvard Business Review*, 72/4: 77–85.

ARMSTRONG, D. (1991). *The 'Institution in the Mind': Reflections on the Relation of Psycho-Analysis to Work Institutions*. London: Grubb Institute.

—— (1995). 'The analytic object in organizational work'. Paper presented to the Symposium of the International Society for the Psychoanalytic Study of Organizations, London.

—— (1998). 'Thinking aloud: Contributions to three dialogues', in W. G. Lawrence (1998), 91–106.

ASHBACH, C., and SCHERMER, V. L. (1987). *Object Relations, the Self and the Group*. London: Routledge.

BAIN, A. (1982). *The Baric Experiment—The Design of Jobs and Organization for the Expression and Growth of Human Capacity*. London: Tavistock Institute of Human Relations, Occasional Papers 4: 2–4.

—— (1997). 'A "College of socio-analysis", an idea', *AISA News—a Newsletter of the Australian Institute of Social Analysis*, 5: 3–5.

—— (1998a). 'On socio-analysis'. Paper presented at the Inaugural Scientific Conference of the Australian Institute of Socio-Analysis, Canberra. Unpublished.

—— (1998b). 'Social defenses against organizational learning', *Human Relations*, 51/3: 413–29.

BALMARY, M. (1986). *Le sacrifice interdit. Freud et la Bible*. Paris: Grasset.

BARBER, W. (1987). 'Role analysis group: Integrating and applying workshop learning', in W. B. Reddy and C. C. Henderson, *Training Theory and Practice*. Arlington, VA: NTL Institute and University Associates, 179–84.

BATESON, G. (1973). *Steps to an Ecology of Mind*. St Albans: Paladin.

BEM, S. L. (1993). *The Lenses of Gender: Transforming the Debate on Sexual Inequality*. New Haven: Yale University Press.

BENNIS, W. G., and SHEPARD, H. A. (1956). 'A theory of group development', *Human Relations*, 9/4: 415–37.

BICK, E. (1987). *Collected Papers of Martha Harris and Esther Bick*. Strath Tay, Perthshire: Clunie Press.

BION, W. R. (1946). 'The leaderless group project', *Bulletin of the Menninger Clinic*, 10: 77–81.

BION, W. R. (1959). 'Attacks on linking', in W. R. Bion (1984). *Second Thoughts. Selected Papers in Psychoanalysis*. London: Karnac, 93–109.

—— (1961). *Experiences in Groups*. London: Tavistock Publications. (1976, *Recherches sur les petits groupes*. Paris: PUF).

—— (1962). *Learning from Experience*. London: William Heinemann.

—— (1970). *Attention and Interpretation*. London: Tavistock Publications.

—— (1978). *Bion in New York and Sao Paulo*. Strath Tay, Perthshire: Clunie Press.

—— (1985). 'Container and contained', in A. D. Colman and M. H. Geller, 127-33.

—— (1992). *Cogitations*. London: Karnac Books.

BION TALAMO, P., BORGOGNO, F., and MERCIAI, S. A. (eds.) (1998). *Bion's Legacy to Groups*. London: Karnac.

BIRAN, H., and CHATTOPADHYAY, GOURANGA P. (1998).'The burden of the barbarian within', *Free Associations*, 7/42: 151–70.

BOALT BOËTHIUS, S. (1983). *Autonomy, Coping and Defense in Small Work Groups*. Stockholm: Almquist & Wiksell International.

—— (1987). 'The view from the middle', *International Journal of Small Group Research*, 3/1: 1–15.

—— (1989). 'Forskning om grupper och organisationer' [Research on groups and organizations], in C. Crafoord (ed.), *Psykoanalytiker utan soffa*. [*Psychoanalysts without a Couch*]. Stockholm: Natur och Kultur, 72–106.

—— (1992). 'What can consultants gain by sharing experiences?'. Paper presented at the 10th Scientific Meeting of the A. K. Rice Institute, St. Louis, USA.

—— (1996). 'Den nödvändiga diferentieringens pris' [The price of unavoidable differentiation in an organization], in S. Boalt Boëthius and S. Jern, 241–67.

—— and JERN, S. (eds.) (1996). *Den svårfångade organisationen* [*The Difficult-to-Catch Organization*]. Stockholm: Natur och Kultur.

BOHM, D., and EDWARDS, M. (1991). *Changing Consciousness*. San Francisco: Harper & Row.

BOLLAS, C. (1987). *The Shadow of the Object: Psychoanalysis of the Unthought Known*. London: Free Association Books.

BOWLBY, J. (1969). *Attachment and Loss*, Vol. 1, *Attachment*. London: Hogarth.

BOXER, P. (1994). 'The future of identity', in R. Boot, J. Lawrence, and J. Morris (eds.), *Managing the Unknown*. London: McGraw-Hill, 207–29.

—— and PALMER, B. (1994). 'Meeting the challenge of the case', in R. Casemore, G. Dyos, A. Eden, K. Kellner, J. McCauley, and S. Moss (eds.), *What Makes Consultancy Work—Understanding the Dynamics*. London: South Bank University Press, 358–71.

BRIDGER, H. (1990). 'Courses and working conferences as transitional learning institutions', in E. L. Trist and H. Murray (1990), 221–45.

BROWN, L. D. (1983). *Managing Conflict at Organizational Interfaces*. Reading, Mass.: Addison-Wesley.

BROWN, R. (1988). *Group Processes: Dynamics Within and Between Groups*. Oxford: Blackwell.

BUBER, M. (1965). *The Knowledge of Man*. London: George Allen & Unwin Ltd.

BUNKER, B. B., and ALBAN, B .T. (1996). *Large Group Interventions: Engaging the Whole System for Rapid Change*. San Francisco: Jossey-Bass.

BURGOYNE, J. G. (1994). 'Managing by learning', *Management Learning*, 25/1: 35–55.

BUSHE, G. R., and SHANI, A. B. (1991). *Parallel Learning Structures: Increasing Innovation in Bureaucracies*. Reading, Mass.: Addison-Wesley.

CALVIN, W. H. (1996). *How Brains Think*. London: Weidenfeld & Nicolson.

CARDONA, F. (1995). 'Vulnerable leadership—Consultancy to management in transition'. Paper presented at the Symposium of the International Society for the Psychoanalytic Study of Organizations, London, 7–9 July.

CARR, W. (1996). 'Learning for leadership', *The Leadership & Organization Development Journal*, 17/6, 46–52.

CECCHIN, G. (1987). 'Hypothesizing, circularity and neutrality revisited: An invitation to curiosity', *Family Process*, 26: 405–13.

CHAPMAN, J. (1996). 'Hatred and corruption of task'. Presentation to Australian Institute of Social Analysis Scientific Meeting, Melbourne, 16 September.

CHATTOPADHYAY, GOURANGA P. (1994). 'The battle for boundaries', *Indian Society for Applied Behavioural Science*, Newsletter, 8/3–4: 4–6.

—— (1995). 'Hierarchy and modern organization', in S. Long (ed.), *International Perspectives on Organizations in Times of Turbulence*. Hawthorn, Victoria: Swinburne University of Technology & AISA, 13–22.

—— (1997*a*). *Bhagavat Geeta: A Treatise on Managing Critical Decisions—In Work Organizations, in Society, in Family*. Calcutta: Eureka Publishers.

—— (1997*b*). 'Institution in the mind', *Here and Now*, 10/3: 9–12.

—— (1999, forthcoming). 'The burden of the internalized aggressor', in Gouranga P. Chattopadhyay, *Managing Organizational Processes*. Calcutta: Eureka Publishers.

—— (1999, forthcoming). 'Managing illusion', *Free Associations*.

—— and LAWRENCE, W. G. (1991). 'The private nature of public sector enterprises in India', in Gouranga P. Chattopadhyay (ed.), *Organizational Culture*. New Delhi: Discovery Publishing House, 306–44.

—— and MALHOTRA, A. (1991). 'Hierarchy and modern organization : A paradox leading to human wastage', *The Indian Journal of Social Work*, 52/4: 561–84.

CHURCH, S. (1978). *Oliver Cromwell*. New York: Simon and Schuster.

COLMAN, A. D., and GELLER, M. H.(eds.) (1985). *Group Relations Reader 2*. Washington DC: A. K. Rice Institute.

COPLEY, B. (1993). *The World of Adolescence*. London: Free Association Books.

CZANDER, W. M. (1993). *The Psychodynamics of Work and Organizations*. New York: Guilford Press.

DE ĐUVE, C. (1995). *Vital Dust*. New York: Basic Books.

DE MARÉ, P., PIPER, R., and THOMPSON, S. (1991). *Koinonia: From Hate, through Dialogue to Culture in the Large Group*. London: Karnac.

DURKHEIM, E. (1930). *Le Suicide*. Paris: Libraire Felix Alcan.

EISOLD, K. (1997). 'Freud as leader: The early years of the Viennese Society', *International Journal of Psycho-Analysis*, 78/1: 87–104.

ELIOT, T. S. (1962). *The Complete Poems and Plays 1909–1950*. New York: Harcourt, Brace and World Inc.

EMERY, F. E., and TRIST, E. L. (1965). 'The causal texture of organizational environments', *Human Relations*, 18: 21–32.

—— —— (1972). *Towards a Social Ecology: Contextual Appreciations of the Future in the Present*. London: Plenum Press.

ERIKSON, E. H. (1950). *Childhood and Society*. New York: Norton Press.

—— (1959). 'Identity and the life cycle', *Psychological Issues*, 1/1: 1–171.

—— (1968). *Youth: Identity and Crisis*. London: Faber & Faber.

—— (1985). *The Life Cycle Completed*. New York: W. W. Norton and Company.

EVANS, D. (1996). *An Introductory Dictionary of Lacanian Psychoanalysis*. London: Routledge.

FEUCHTWANG, M., and RAMSAY, S. (1995). 'In Fagin's kitchen: Social defences against children in the post modern world'. Paper presented at the Annual Symposium of the International Society for the Psychoanalytic Study of Organizations, London, July.

FINEMAN, S. (ed.) (1993). *Emotion in Organisations*. London: Sage.

FINK, B. (1997). *A Clinical Introduction to Lacanian Psychoanalysis: Theory and Technique*. Cambridge Mass./London: Harvard University Press.

FOSTER, A., and GRESPI, L. (1994). 'Managing care in the community: Analysis of a training workshop', *Journal of Social Work Practice*, 8/2: 169–83.

—— —— (1998). 'Learning to keep one's head', in A. Foster and V. Zagier Roberts, 188–202.

—— and ROBERTS, V. ZAGIER (eds.) (1998). *Managing Mental Health in the Community: Chaos and Containment*. London: Routledge.

FOUCAULT, M. (1972). *The Archaeology of Knowledge*. London: Tavistock (original French publication 1969).

FOULKES, S. H. (1990). *Selected Papers: Psychoanalysis and Group Analysis*. London: Karnac.

—— and ANTHONY, E. T. (1975). *Group Psychotherapy: The Psychoanalytic Approach*. London: Penguin.

FRANKL, V. E. (1959). *From Death-Camp to Existentialism*. Boston, Mass.: Beacon Press.

FRENCH, R., and GREY, C. (1996). *Rethinking Management Education*. London: Sage.

FREUD, S. (1900). *The Interpretation of Dreams*. Standard Edition of the Complete Psychological Works of Sigmund Freud, Vols. 5 and 6. London: Hogarth Press.

—— (1913). *Totem and Taboo*. Standard Edition of the Complete Psychological Works of Sigmund Freud, Vol. 13. London: Hogarth Press.

—— (1917). *Mourning and Melancholia*. Standard Edition of the Complete Psychological Works of Sigmund Freud, Vol. 14. London: Hogarth Press, 237–58.

—— (1921). *Group Psychology and the Analysis of the Ego*. Standard Edition of the Complete Psychological Works of Sigmund Freud, Vol. 18. London: Hogarth Press. Penguin Freud Library 12, 1991.

FROMM, E. (1991). *You Shall Be As God: A Radical Interpretation of the Old Testament and Its Traditions*. New York: An Owl Book.

GAMBHIRANANDA, S. (1989). *Eight Upanishads, 1 and 2*. Calcutta: Advaita Ashrama.

GIBBARD, G. (1975). *Bion's Group Psychology: A Reconsideration*. West Haven, Conn.: Veterans Hospital.

GIDDENS, A. (1984). *The Constitution of Society*. Cambridge: Polity Press.

GILLETTE, J., and McCOLLOM, M. (1990). *Groups in Context: A New Perspective on Group Dynamics*. Reading, Mass.: Addison-Wesley.

GILLIGAN, C. (1982). *In a Different Voice*. Cambridge, Mass.: Harvard University Press.

GLASER, B. B., and STRAUSS, A. L. (1979). *The Discovery of Grounded Theory: Strategies for Qualitative Research*. New York: Aldine Publishing Company.

GOFFMAN, E. (1959). *The Presentation of Self in Everyday Life*. Garden City, NJ: Doubleday.

—— (1961). *Asylums: Essays on the Social Situation of Mental Patients and Other Inmates*. New York: Doubleday Anchor.

GOULD, L. J. (1979). 'Political vision and political action: A developmental perspective'. Paper presented at the American Political Science Association Meetings, Washington, DC.

—— (1982). 'Adulthood comes of age'. Book review of C. A. Colarusso and R. A. Nemiroff (1981). *Adult Development: A New Dimension in Psychodynamic Theory and Practice.* New York: Plenum Press, in *Contemporary Psychology*, 27/8: 649–50.

—— (1991). 'Using psychoanalytic frameworks for organizational analysis', in M. F. R. Kets de Vries, 25–44.

—— (1993). 'Contemporary perspectives on personal and organizational authority: The self in a system of work relationships', in L. Hirschhorn and C. K. Barnett, 49–63.

—— (1997). 'Correspondences between Bion's basic assumption theory and Klein's developmental positions: An outline', *Free Associations*, 7/1 (No. 41): 15–30.

GOULD, R. (1978). *Transformations.* New York: Simon and Schuster.

GRANSTRÖM, K. (1996). 'Vårt behov av ledare' [Our need of leaders], in S. Boalt Boëthius and S. Jern, 43–68.

GROTSTEIN, J., and KINSLEY, D. (1994). *Fairbairn and the Origins of Object Relations.* London: Free Association Press.

Grubb Institute (1991). *Professional Management: Notes Prepared by the Grubb Institute on Concepts Relating to Professional Management.* London: Grubb Institute.

—— (1997). *Leadership and Authority in Systems.* Conference Brochure. London: Grubb Institute.

GUTMANN, D. (1989). 'The decline of traditional defences against anxiety'. Proceedings of the First International Symposium on Group Relations, Keble College, Oxford, A. K. Rice Institute. (1990, 'Le déclin des défenses traditionnelles contre l'anxiété', *Notes de Conjonctures Sociales*, 342: 18–30, Paris.)

—— PIERRE, R., TERNIER-DAVID, J., and VERRIER, C. (1997). 'The paths of authority: From the unconscious to the transcendental. Intervention at the Arab University of Jerusalem', *Feelings Work in Europe.* Milan: Guerini Studio, 172–82. (1997, 'Los caminos de la autoridad: del más acá al más allá. Intervencón en la Universidad Arabe de Jerusalém', *Perspectivas de Gestion*, 2: 4–13. 1998, 'Die Wege der Autorität: vom Unbewußten zum Transzendentalen', *Organisationsentwicklung*, 1/98: 4–13.)

—— TERNIER-DAVID, J., and VERRIER, C. (1995). *Gruppe og transformation—en beskrivelse af en ledergruppes udviklingsproces* [*Groups and transformation*]. Ubevidste Processer, Dansk Industri (ed.). Copenhagen, 171–81.

—— —— —— (1996a). 'Paradoxer och förvandling i konsultrollen: Från reparation till uppenbarelse' [Paradox and transformation in the role of consultant: From reparation to revelation], in S. Boalt Boëthius and S. Jern, 133–60.

—— —— —— (1996b). 'Transformation et collusion. De la conformation à l'alliance', *Insight*, 3: 47–85. (1997, *Management et Conjoncture Sociale*, 507: 9–23.)

HADLEY, R., and YOUNG, K. (1990). *Creating a Responsive Public Service.* London: Harvester Wheatsheaf.

HANDY, C. B. (1981). *Understanding Organizations.* Harmondsworth: Penguin.

HARDING, W. (1996). 'Hierarchy as a social defense', Masters Thesis in Business, Organization Behaviour. Melbourne: Swinburne University of Technology.

HEIFETZ, R. (1995). *Leadership Without Easy Answers.* Cambridge, Mass., and London: The Belknap Press of the Harvard University Press.

HEILBRUN, C. G. (1988). *Writing a Woman's Life.* New York: Ballantine Books.

HEISENBERG, W. (1974). *Across the New Frontier.* New York: Harper & Row.

HINSHELWOOD, R. D. (1998). 'Creatures of each other', in A. Foster and V. Zagier Roberts, 15–26.

HIRSCHHORN, L. (1985). 'The psychodynamics of taking a role', in A. D. Colman and M. H. Geller, 335–51.

HIRSCHHORN, L., and BARNETT, C. K. (eds.) (1993). *The Psychodynamics of Organizations*. Philadelphia: Temple University Press.

HOCHSCHILD, A. R. (1983). *The Managed Heart: The Commercialization of Human Feeling*. Berkeley: University of California Press.

HOGGETT, P. (1992). *Partisans in an Uncertain World: The Psychoanalysis of Engagement*. London: Free Association Books.

—— (1998). 'The internal establishment', in P. Bion Talamo, F. Borgogno, and S. A. Merciai, 9–24.

HOPPER, E. (1997). 'Traumatic experience in the unconscious life of groups: A fourth basic assumption', *Group Analysis*, 30: 439–70.

HORWITZ, L. (1985). 'Projective identification in dyads and groups', in A. D. Colman and M. H. Geller, 21–36.

HUGHES, L., and PENGELLY, P. (1997). *Staff Supervision in a Turbulent Environment*. London: Jessica Kingsley.

HUTTON, J. (1997). 'Re-imagining the organization of an institution: Management in human service institutions', in E. Smith, 66–82.

—— BAZALGETTE, J., and REED, B. (1997). 'Organization-in-the-mind', in J. E. Neumann, K. Kellner, and A. Dawson-Shepherd (eds.) *Developing Organizational Consultancy*. London: Routledge, 113–26.

ISAACS, W. N. (1993). 'Taking flight: Dialogue, collective thinking, and organisational learning', *Organisational Dynamics*, 22/2: 24–39.

JANIS, I. L. (1972). *Victims of Groupthink: A Psychological Study of Foreign Policy Decisions and Fiascoes*. Boston, Mass.: Houghton-Mifflin.

JAQUES, E. (1955). 'Social systems as a defence against persecutory and depressive anxiety', in M. Klein, P. Heimann, and R. E. Money-Kyrle (eds.), *New Directions in Psychoanalysis*. London: Tavistock Publications, 478–98.

—— (1965). 'Death and the mid-life crisis', *International Journal of Psycho-Analysis*, 46: 502–14.

—— (1989). *Requisite Organizations*. Arlington, Va.: Cason Hall and Co.

—— (1995). 'Why the psychoanalytical approach to understanding organizations is dysfunctional', *Human Relations*, 48/4: 343–9 (response by G. Amado, ibid.: 351–7; further response by Jaques, ibid.: 359–65.)

JAY, A. (1976). *How to Run a Meeting*. London: Video Arts.

JOYCE, J. (1992 edn.). *Finnegans Wake*. Harmondsworth: Penguin Books.

JUNG, C. G. (1971). 'The stages of life', in J. Campbell (ed.), *The Portable Jung*. New York: Viking Portable Library, 3–22.

KAHN, W. A. (1990). 'The psychological conditions of personal engagement and disengagement at work', *Academy of Management Journal*, 33/4: 692–724.

—— (1992). 'To be fully there: Psychological presence at work', *Human Relations*, 45: 321–50.

KANTOR, R. M. (1977). *Men and Women of the Corporation*. New York: Basic Books.

KARPMAN, S. (1968). 'Fairy tales and script drama analysis', *Transactional Analysis Bulletin*, 7/26: 39–44.

KEATS, J. (1817). *The Letters of John Keats*. Oxford: Oxford University Press, 1952.

KERNBERG, O. F. (1980). 'Regressive effects of pathology in leaders', in O. F. Kernberg, *Internal World and External Reality*. New York: Jason Aronson, 253–73.

KETCHUM, L. D., and TRIST, E. (1992). *All Teams Are Not Created Equal: How Employee Empowerment Really Works*. Newbury Park, Cal./London: Sage.

KETS DE VRIES, M. F. R. (ed.) (1991). *Organizations on the Couch: Clinical Perspectives on Organizational Behaviour and Changes*. San Francisco: Jossey-Bass.

KHALEELEE, O., and MILLER, E. J. (1984). *The Future of Work: A Report of the West Yorkshire Talkabout, July–November 1983*. London: Work and Society.

—— —— (1985). 'Beyond the small group: Society as an intelligible field of study,' in M. Pines, 353–83.

KLEIN, M. (1928). 'Early stages of the Oedipus conflict', *International Journal of Psycho-Analysis*, 7: 167–80.

—— (1935). 'A contribution to the psychogenesis of manic depressive states', *International Journal of Psycho-Analysis*, 16: 145–174.

—— (1940). 'Mourning and its relation to manic depressive states'. *International Journal of Psycho-Analysis*, 21: 125–53.

—— (1945). 'The Oedipus complex in the light of early anxieties', *International Journal of Psycho-Analysis*, 26: 11–33.

—— (1952). 'Some theoretical conclusions regarding the emotional life of the infant', in M. Klein (1975a), 61–93.

—— (1959). 'Our adult world and its roots in infancy', in M. Klein (1975a), 247–63.

—— (1975a). *Envy and Gratitude and Other Essays 1946–1963*. London: Hogarth Press. (1968, *Envie et gratitude, et autres essais*. Paris: Ed. Gallimard.)

—— (1975b). *Love, Guilt and Reparation and Other Works*. New York: Dell Publishing.

KRAM, K. E. (1985). *Mentoring at Work*. Glenview, Ill.: Scott, Foresman and Co.

KRANTZ, J. (1993). 'On the future of group relations work', in *Changing Group Relations*, Proceedings of the 9th Scientific Meeting of the A. K. Rice Institute. Washington, DC: A. K. Rice Institute.

—— and GILMORE, T. N. (1990). 'The splitting of leadership and management as a social defense', *Human Relations*, 43/2: 183–204.

KREEGER, L. (1975). *The Large Group: Dynamics and Therapy*. London: Constable and Co. Ltd.

KRISHNAMURTI, J., and BOHM, D. (1986). *Ending of Time: Thirteen Dialogues*. London: Victor Gollancz Ltd.

KUNDERA, M. (1985). *The Unbearable Lightness of Being*. Tr. M. H. Heim. London: Faber & Faber.

LACAN, J. (1979). *The Four Fundamental Concepts of Psychoanalysis*. Harmondsworth: Penguin.

—— (1991). *Le Seminaire XVII: L'Envers de la Psychanalyse*. Paris: Seuil.

LAING, R. D., and COOPER, D. G. (1964). *Reason and Violence*. London: Tavistock.

LANGS, R. (1976). *The Bipersonal Field*. New York: Jason Aronson.

LANZARA, G. (1993). *Capacita Negativa*. Bologna: Il Mulino.

LAPLANCHE, J., and PONTALIS, J.-B. (1988). *The Language of Psychoanalysis*. London: Karnac.

LAWRENCE, W. G. (1985a). 'A psychoanalytic perspective for understanding organizational life', in G. Chattopadhyay, Z. H. Gangjee, M. L. Hunt, and W. G. Lawrence, *When the Twain Meet: Western Theory & Eastern Insights in Exploring Indian Organizations*. Allahabad: A. H. Wheeler, 47–66.

—— (1985b). 'Beyond the frames', in M. Pines, 306–29.

—— (1995a). 'Totalitaere i sindstilstande i institutioner', *Agrippa*, 16/1–2: 53–72.

—— (1995b). 'The seductiveness of totalitarian states of mind', *Journal of Health Care Chaplaincy*, 11–22.

—— (1998). *Social Dreaming at Work*. London: Karnac.

LAWRENCE, W. G. (ed.) (1979). *Exploring Individual and Organizational Boundaries: A Tavistock Open Systems Approach.* New York: John Wiley and Sons.

—— and ARMSTRONG, D. (1998). 'Destructiveness and creativity in organizational life: Experiencing the psychotic edge', in P. Bion Talamo, F. Borgogno, and S. A. Merciai, 53–68.

—— BAIN, A., and GOULD, L. (1996). 'The fifth basic assumption', *Free Associations*, 6/1, No. 37: 28–55.

LEVINSON, D. J. (1977). 'The mid-life transition: A period in adult psychosocial development', *Psychiatry*, May: 99–112.

—— (1996). *Seasons of a Woman's Life.* New York: Alfred A. Knopf.

—— DARROW, C. N., KLEIN, E. B., LEVINSON, M. H., and MCKEE, B. (1978). *Seasons of a Man's Life.* New York: Alfred A. Knopf.

LEVINSON, H. (1991). 'Diagnosing organizations systematically', in M. F. R. Kets de Vries, 45–58.

LONG, S., and NEWTON, J. (1995). 'Educating the gut: An application of psychoanalytic understanding to learning in organizations'. Paper presented at the Annual Symposium of the International Society for the Psychoanalytic Study of Organizations, London, July.

MARCH, J. G. (1962). 'The business firm as a political coalition', *Journal of Politics*, 24: 62–78.

MATTINSON, J. (1992). *The Reflection Process in Casework Supervision*, 2nd edn. London: Tavistock Institute of Marital Studies (first published, 1975).

McCAFFERY, T. (1998). 'The pain of managing: Some dynamics of the purchaser/provider split', in A. Foster and V. Zagier Roberts, 96–105.

MENZIES, I. E. P. (1960). 'A case study in the functioning of social systems as a defence against anxiety', *Human Relations*, 13: 95–121. Reprinted in I. Menzies Lyth (1988), 43–85.

MENZIES ⅝YTH, I. (1988). *Containing Anxiety in Institutions. Selected Essays, Volume 1.* London: Free Association Books.

—— (1990). *The Dynamics of the Social. Selected Essays, Volume 2.* London: Free Association Books.

MILES, M. B., and HUBERMAN, A. M. (1984). *Qualitative Data Analysis.* London: Sage.

MILES, R. H. (1980). *Macro Organizational Behavior.* Glenview, Ill.: Scott, Foresman, and Co.

MILLER, D. (1990). 'Organizational configurations: Cohesion, change and prediction', *Human Relations*, 43/8: 771–89.

MILLER, E. J. (1959). 'Technology, territory and time: The internal differentiation of complex production systems', *Human Relations*, 12: 243–72.

—— (1975). 'Socio-technical systems in weaving, 1953–1970: A follow-up study', *Human Relations*, 28: 349–86.

—— (1977). 'Organizational development and industrial democracy: A current case-study', in C. Cooper (ed.), *Organizational Development in the UK and USA: A Joint Evaluation.* London: Macmillan, 31–63.

—— (1983). *Work and Creativity.* London: Tavistock Institute of Human Relations, Occasional Papers 6.

—— (1985). 'The politics of involvement', in A. D. Colman and M. H. Geller, 383–98.

—— (1986). 'Making room for individual autonomy', in M. Srivastva and Associates, *Executive Power.* San Francisco: Jossey-Bass, 257–88.

—— (1987). 'The female entrepreneur and the organization: A tentative hypothesis'. Unpublished paper.

—— (1989). *The 'Leicester' Model: Experiential Study of Group and Organisational Processes*. London: Tavistock Institute of Human Relations, Occasional Papers 10.

—— (1990*a*). 'Experiential learning in groups I: The development of the Leicester Model', in E.L. Trist and H. Murray, 165–85.

—— (1990b). 'Experiential Learning in Groups II: Recent developments in dissemination and application', in E. L. Trist and H. Murray (1990), 186–98.

—— (1993*a*). 'The human dynamic', in R. Stacey (ed.), *Strategic Thinking and the Management of Change: International Perspectives on Organizational Dynamics*. London: Kogan Page, 98–116.

—— (1993*b*). 'The vicissitudes of identity'. Opening address, international group relations and scientific conference: exploring global social dynamics, Victoria, Australia, Document No. 2T670. London: Tavistock Institute of Human Relations.

—— (1993*c*). *From Dependency to Autonomy: Studies in Organization and Change*. London: Free Association Books.

—— (1993*d*). 'Some reflections on the role of the diplomatic wife', in E. J. Miller (1993*c*), 132–45.

—— (1998). 'Are basic assumptions instinctive?', in P. Bion Talamo, F. Borgogno, and S. A. Merciai, 39–51.

—— (ed.) (1976). *Task and Organization*. New York: John Wiley and Sons.

—— and GWYNNE, G. (1972). *A Life Apart*. London: Tavistock Publications.

—— and RICE, A. K. (1967). *Systems of Organization: Task and Sentient Systems and Their Boundary Control*. London: Tavistock Publications.

—— and STEIN, M. (1993). 'Individual and organization in the 1990s: Time for a rethink?', *Review*, 1992/93: 35–37. Tavistock Institute.

MILLER, W. B. (1955). 'Two concepts of authority', *American Anthropologist*, 57: 271–89.

MILLS, T. (1990). 'Emotional dynamics and higher-order feedback', *Advances in Group Processes*, 7: 203–34.

MITCHELL, V., and HELSON, R. (1990). 'Women's prime of life: Is it the fifties?', *Psychology of Women Quarterly*, 14: 451–70.

MOHRMAN, S. A., and CUMMINGS, T. G. (1989). *Self-Designing Organisations: Learning How to Create High Performance*. Reading, Mass.: Addison-Wesley.

MORGAN, G. (1986). *Images of Organizations*. London: Sage.

MULLER, J. P. (1996). *Beyond the Psychoanalytic Dyad: Developmental Semiotics in Freud, Peirce and Lacan*. London: Routledge.

NEGROPONTE, N. (1996 edn.). *Being Digital*. London: Hodder & Stoughton.

NEUMANN, J. E., HOLTI, R., and STANDING, H. (1995). *Change Everything At Once! The Tavistock Institute's Guide to Teamwork in Manufacturing*. Didcot, Oxfordshire: Management Books 2000.

NIKHILANANDA, SWAMI (1987). *The Mandukya Upanishad* (5th edn.). Calcutta: Advaita Ashrama.

NUTMAN, P. N. S. (1995). 'The UK group in the Global Event: Church, family, business or what?' (Unpublished.)

OBHOLZER, A. (1994). 'Authority, power and leadership: Contributions from group relations training', in A. Obholzer and V. Zagier Roberts, 39–47.

—— (1996). 'Psychoanalytic contributions to authority and leadership issues', *Leadership & Organization Development Journal*, 17/6: 53–6.

—— and ROBERTS, V. ZAGIER (1994). 'The troublesome individual in the troubled institution', in A. Obholzer and V. Zagier Roberts, 129–38.

OBHOLZER, A. and ROBERTS, V. ZAGIER (eds.) (1994). *The Unconscious at Work: Individual and Organizational Stress in the Human Services.* London: Routledge.

OGDEN, T. (1985). 'On potential space', *International Journal of Psycho-Analysis*, 66: 129–40.

—— (1986). *The Matrix of the Mind: Object Relations and the Psychoanalytic Dialogue.* London: Jason Aronson.

—— (1992). *Projective Identification and Psychotherapeutic Technique.* London: Karnac, Maresfield Library.

PALMER, B. (1979). 'Learning and the group experience', in W. G. Lawrence (ed.), *Exploring Individual and Organisational Boundaries.* Chichester: John Wiley, 169–92.

—— (1998). 'The Tavistock paradigm: Inside, outside and beyond'. Unpublished.

PEDERSON-KRAG, G. (1951). 'A psycho-analytic approach to mass production', *Psycho-Analytic Quarterly*, 20: 434–51.

PFEFFER, J. (1977). 'Power and resource allocation in organizations', in B. M. Staw and G. R. Salancik (eds.), *New Directions in Organizational Behavior.* Chicago: St. Clair Press, 235–66.

PHILLIPS, A. (1988). *Winnicott.* New York: Fontana/Collins.

PINES, M. (ed.) (1985). *Bion and Group Psychotherapy.* London: Routledge & Kegan Paul.

—— (1994). 'The group-as-a-whole', in D. Brown and L. Zinkin (eds.), *The Psyche and the Social World: Development in Group-Analytic Theory.* London/New York: Routledge, 47–59.

PITT-AITKENS, T., and ELLIS, A. T. (1989). *Loss of the Good Authority: The Causes of Delinquency.* London: Viking/Penguin.

POPPER, K. R. (1934). 'Scientific method', in D. Miller (ed.) (1983), *A Pocket Popper.* Glasgow: Fontana, 133–42.

RAYNER, E. (1995). *Unconscious Logic.* London: Routledge.

REED, B. D. (1976). 'Organisational role analysis', in C. L. Cooper (ed.), *Developing Social Skills in Managers.* London: Macmillan, 89–102.

—— (1978). *The Dynamics of Religion: Process and Movement in Christian Churches.* London: Darton, Longman & Todd.

REICHARD, B. D., SIEWERS, C. M. F., and RODENHAUSER, P. (1992). *The Small Group Trainer's Survival Guide.* Newbury Park, Calif.: Sage.

RICE, A. K. (1958). *Productivity and Social Organization: The Ahmedabad Experiment.* London: Tavistock Publications.

—— (1963). *The Enterprise and its Environment.* London: Tavistock Publications.

—— (1965). *Learning for Leadership: Interpersonal and Intergroup Relations.* London: Tavistock Publications.

—— (1969). 'Individual, group and inter-group processes', *Human Relations*, 22/6: 565–84.

ROBERTS, P., and NEWTON, P. (1987). 'Levinsonian studies of women's adult development', *Psychology and Aging*, 2, 154–63.

ROSENFELD, D. (1988). *Psychoanalysis and Groups: History and Dialectics.* London: Karnac.

ROSSI, A. S. (1985). *Gender and the Life Course.* New York: Aldine.

RUFFIN, J. E. (1989). 'Stages of adult development in black, professional women', in R. L. Jones (ed.), *Black Adult Development and Aging.* Berkeley, Cal.: Cobb and Henry Publishers, 31–62.

SARASWATI, SWAMI SATSANGANANDA, and SARASWATI, SWAMI SATYANANDA (1984). *Karma Sanyasa* (1st edn.). Munger: Bihar School of Yoga, 1–2.

SARASWATI, SWAMI SATYANANDA (1984). *Tattwa Shuddhi—The Tantric Practice of Inner Purification*. Munger: Bihar School of Yoga.

—— (1989). *Four Chapters on Freedom: Commentary on Yoga Sutras of Patanjali* (3rd edn.). Munger: Bihar School of Yoga.

SARAVAY, M. S. (1975). 'Group psychology and the structural theory: A revised psychoanalytic model of group psychology', *Journal of American Psychoanalytic Association*, 23: 69–89.

SARTRE, J.-P. (1960). *Critique de la Raison Dialectique*. Paris: Librairie Gallimard.

SCHEIN, E. H. (1993). 'How can organizations learn faster?: The challenge of entering the green room', *Sloan Management Review*, 34/2: 85–92.

SCHUTZ, W. C. (1958). *FIRO: A Three-Dimensional Theory of Interpersonal Relations*. New York: Holt.

SCHWARTZ, J. (1992). *The Creative Moment*. London: Jonathan Cape.

SENGE, P. M. (1990). *The Fifth Discipline: The Art and Practice of the Learning Organization*. London: Century Business.

SETTLAGE, C. F. (1992). 'Psychoanalytic observations on adult development in life and the therapeutic relationship', *Psychoanalysis and Contemporary Thought*, 15/3: 349–74.

SHERIF, M., and SHERIF, C. W. (1956). *An Outline of Social Psychology*. New York: Harper.

SIMMEL, G. (1950). *The Sociology of Georg Simmel*, trans. K. H. Wolff. New York: Free Press.

SMITH, E. (ed.) (1997). *Integrity and Change: Mental Health in the Marketplace*. London: Routledge.

SMITH, K. K., and BERG, D. N. (1987). *Paradoxes of Group Life*. San Francisco: Jossey-Bass.

SPITZ, R. A. (1957). *No and Yes*. New York: International Universities Press.

STACEY, R. D. (1996). *Complexity and Creativity in Organizations*. San Francisco, Cal.: Berrett-Koehler Publishers.

STEINER, J. (1985). 'Turning a blind eye: The cover-up for Oedipus', *International Review of Psychoanalysis*, 12/2: 161–73.

STEWART, W. A. (1976). 'The formation of the early adult life structure in women'. Ph.D. diss., Teachers College, Columbia University.

STOKES, J. (1994). 'Institutional chaos and personal stress', in A. Obholzer and V. Zagier Roberts, 121–28.

TARNAS, R. (1996 edn.). *The Passion of the Western Mind*. London: Random House.

TAYLOR, D. (1996). 'Some of Bion's ideas on meaning and understanding'. London: Tavistock Clinic. Unpublished.

TAYLOR, S. (1981). 'Seven lives: Women's life structure evolution in early adulthood'. Ph.D. diss., City University of New York.

THOMPSON, E. P. (1963). *The Making of the English Working Class*. Harmondsworth: Penguin Books.

TRIST, E. L., and BAMFORTH, K. W. (1951). 'Some social and psychological consequences of the longwall method of coal-getting', *Human Relations*, 4: 3–38.

—— HIGGIN, G. W., MURRAY, H., and POLLOCK, A. (1963). *Organizational Choice: Capabilities of Groups at the Coal Face Under Changing Technologies*. London: Tavistock Publications.

—— and MURRAY, H. (eds.) (1990). *The Social Engagement of Social Science: A Tavistock Anthology, Vol. I, The Socio-Psychological Perspective*. London: Free Association Books,

—— —— (eds.) (1993). *The Social Engagement of Social Science: A Tavistock Anthology, Vol. 2, The Socio-Technical Perspective*. Philadelphia, Pa.: University of Pennsylvania Press/London: Free Association Books.

TUCKMAN, B. (1965). 'Developmental sequence in small groups', *Psychological Bulletin*, 63/6: 384–99.

TURQUET, P. M. (1974). 'Leadership: The individual and the group', in A. D. Colman and M. H. Geller, 71–88.

—— (1975). 'Threats to identity in the large group', in L. Kreeger, 87–144.

VALLIANT, G. (1977). *Adaptation to Life*. Boston: Little Brown.

VINCE, R. (1996). *Managing Change: Reflections on Equality and Management Learning*. Bristol: Policy Press.

—— (1998). 'Questions of responsibility: The psychodynamics of "managing" equalities in local government'. Paper presented at 'Gender, Work and Organization' Conference, Manchester Metropolitan University, 9–10 January.

—— and MARTIN, L. (1993). 'Inside action learning: The psychology and the politics of the action learning model', *Management Education and Development*, 24/3: 205–15.

VON BERTALANFFY, L. (1950). 'The theory of open systems in physics and biology', *Science*, 3: 23–9.

WALKER, M. (1997). 'Working with abused clients in an institutional setting: Holding hope amidst despair', in E. Smith, 99–113.

WEDGWOOD, C. V. (1966). *The Life of Cromwell*. New York: Collier Books.

WELLS, L. (1985). 'The group-as-a-whole perspective and its theoretical roots', in A. D. Colman and M. H. Geller, 109–26.

WHITAKER, G. (1995). 'Win–lose and win–win interactions and organisational responses to scarcity', *Kunskapsabonnemanget*, Rapport 50. Vänersborg: Samarbetsdynamik AB.

WHITE, T. H. (1962). *The Once and Future King*. London: Collins/Fontana.

WHITMAN, R., and STOCK, D. (1958). 'The group focal conflict', *Psychiatry*, 21: 269–76.

WINNICOTT, D. W. (1947). 'Hate in the counter-transference', in D. W. Winnicott (1958), 194–203.

—— (1958). *Collected Papers: Through Paediatrics to Psychoanalysis*. London: Tavistock Publications.

—— (1971). *Playing and Reality*. London: Tavistock Publications.

YOGANANDA, P. (1991). *The Autobiography of a Yogi* (2nd Indian edn., 9th impression). Bombay: Jaico Publishing House.

YOUNG, R. M. (1994). *Mental Space*. London: Process Press.

ZUKAV, G. (1982). *The Dancing Wu Li Masters*. London: Fontana/Collins.

INDEX